ORIGINS OF THE SECOND ARAB–ISRAEL WAR

Origins of the
Second Arab–Israel War

EGYPT, ISRAEL AND THE
GREAT POWERS
1952–56

Michael B. Oren

Ben-Gurion Research Center
Ben-Gurion University
of the Negev

FRANK CASS

First published in 1992 in Great Britain by
FRANK CASS & CO. LTD.
Gainsborough House, Gainsborough Road,
London E11 1RS, England

and in the United States of America by
FRANK CASS
c/o International Specialized Book Services, Inc.
5602 N.E. Hassalo Street
Portland, Oregon 97213

British Library Cataloguing in Publication Data
Oren, Michael B.
    Origins of the second Arab–Israel war : Egypt,
    Israel and the great powers, 1952–56.
    I. Title
    956.046

ISBN 0-7146-3430-1

Library of Congress Cataloging-in-Publication Data
Oren, Michael.
    Origins of the second Arab–Israel war : Egypt, Israel, and the
    great powers, 1952–56 / Michael B. Oren.
        p.   cm.
    Includes bibliographical references and index.
    ISBN 0-7146-3430-1
    1. Sinai Campaign, 1956—Causes. 2. Middle East—Politics and
    government—1945–79. I. Title
    DS110.5.074 1992
        956.04'4—dc20   91-22477
                                                                 CIP

Typeset by Regent Typesetting, London
Printed and bound in Great Britain by
BPCC Wheatons Ltd, Exeter

For my parents, Lester and Marilyn Bornstein,
who taught me to appreciate the deepest
and most enduring of all relations

Contents

Acknowledgments

This work would not have been possible without the assistance – financial, physical and emotional – of many people and institutions.

My research in Britain, the United States, Israel and Egypt was facilitated through the generosity of Princeton University, the Lady Davis Fellowship Trust and the Truman Institute of Hebrew University, the British Council, and the Ben Gurion Research Center of Ben Gurion University. I am particularly grateful to the librarians and staff of the Eisenhower Archives, the John Foster Dulles Papers, the Truman Institute, the Israel National Archives, and the Israel Academic Center in Cairo. Special thanks are reserved for Lili Adar and her assistants at the Ben Gurion Archives in Sde Boker.

Throughout the course of my research and writing I enjoyed the advice and support of a great many people. The concept behind the study, which resulted in my doctoral dissertation, 'From Revolution to Crisis: Egypt–Israel Relations, 1952–1956' (Princeton, 1986), was developed in consultation with Professors Norman Itzkowitz and Charles Issawi of Princeton. I am also indebted to Professors Bernard Lewis and Sasson Somekh, of Princeton and Tel Aviv Universities, respectively, who served as readers for the dissertation. The adaptation of the thesis into book form was accomplished with the help of Professor Itamar Rabinowitz of Tel Aviv University and Dr Raymond Cohen and Dr Yakov Bar Siman-Tov of Hebrew University. Invaluable assistance in locating sources was rendered by Professor Shimon Shamir and Mr Eli Podeh of Tel Aviv University, and by Lieutenant Colonel Zev Lachish of the Historical Research Branch of the Israeli Air Force.

For their contribution to my understanding of the Suez period, I wish to thank the Honourable Chaim Herzog, the President of the State of Israel, and Teddy Kollek, the mayor of Jerusalem, Mordechai Gazit of the Truman Institute and Dr Muhammad al-Wahbi, Assistant Secretary of State for Information of Egypt, for their time and insights.

Acknowledgements are due to three Princeton undergraduates, Jonathan Karp, Paula Russo, and Fredrick Frank, who donated their energies toward the formidable tasks of checking sources, collating and map-making, and to Mrs Judy Gross and Mrs Mary Craporotta, administrative assistants at Princeton's Department of Near Eastern Studies, who provided an 8,000-mile lifeline between me and the Department.

My deepest gratitude is reserved for Professor L. Carl Brown, my

ORIGINS OF THE SECOND ARAB–ISRAEL WAR

former adviser at Princeton, and for Professor Ilan Troen, Director of the Ben Gurion Research Center, whose wisdom and encouragement guided me throughout the course of this undertaking. And finally, and most warmly, to my wife Sally and my children, Yoav and Lia, to whom I owe this book and so much more, thank you.

x

Abbreviations

Note on Transliteration

Personal and place names in this study appear in their generally accepted forms, e.g., Gamal Abdul Nasser, and not Jamal Abd al-Nasir. Titles of sources, if not transliterated by the publisher, follow the Arabic transliteration system of the *International Journal of Middle East Studies*, and the Hebrew transliteration system of the *Jerusalem Post*. Authors' names, if they do not appear in English or are not known to the reading public by a specific spelling, have also been transliterated.

Maps

Chronology

Date	Egyptian–Israeli Affairs	Regional Affairs	International Affairs
1949			
Feb.	Egypt–Israel Armistice Agreement.		
1950			
April		Arab Collective Security Pact founded.	
May		Tripartite Declaration issued.	
Oct.	First IDF raid. Gaza.		
1951			
Feb.		Britain's Gen. Robertson visits Middle East; explores possibilities MEDO.	
Sept.	Security Council condemnation blockade.		
Oct.		Egypt abrogates Anglo-Egyptian treaty.	
1952			
Jan.	US–Egypt arms offer.		
July	Free Officers' revolution. US renews arms offer, Egypt.		
Aug.	Ben Gurion invites Free Officers to peace talks; Divon approaches Shawqi in Paris.		
Sept.	Gohar, Egyptian delegate to EIMAC, agrees to co-operate on tension-reducing measures.		
Oct.	Egypt leads Arab League protest against Israel–German reparations treaty.		
Nov.	Egypt seizes *Rimfrost* in the Suez Canal; withdraws from border		Republican victory US presidential elections.

	tension-reducing measures.	
1953		
Jan.	IDF raid into Gaza. Egypt sends arms mission, Washington; US expands arms offer to Egypt. Richard Crossman mediation. Israel sends peace proposals to Nasser.	
Feb.	Herzog–Ghalib talks in Washington.	Egyptian irregulars clash with British troops along Suez Canal.
	Zafrullah Khan mediation.	
		Anglo-Egyptian agreement on Sudan. USSR suspends ties with Israel.
March		Death of Stalin.
May	Nasser replies Israeli peace proposals.	Dulles visits Middle East.
June	Distress Vessels Agreement. Israel sends second list peace proposals to Nasser.	
July	Israel transfers capital to Jerusalem; announces Jordan diversion project.	Iraqi efforts for Fertile Crescent Unity.
		Breakdown Anglo-Egyptian talks on evacuation.
	Egypt founds Voice of the Arabs radio.	Arab Chiefs-of-Staff Meeting, Cairo.
Aug.	IDF attack, al-Burayj.	
Sept.	Israel begins Jordan diversion project; builds Kibbutz Ketziot in DZ. Egypt seizes the *Parnon* in the Canal.	
Oct.	Ben Gurion retires to Sde Boker. IDF raid, Qibyah Egypt expands contraband laws.	Johnston Mission.
Nov.	Ali Mahir presents plan for refugee resettlement	

in the Negev.
Ralph Bunche
mediation.

Dec.   Egypt seizes *Franca
Maria* in the Canal.
Egyptian Foreign
Minister Fawzi sends
peace plan to Nahum
Goldmann.

1954

Jan.   Egypt releases the
Franca Maria.

Feb.   Security Council debate
on blockade.

March   Scorpion Pass massacre.
Egypt creates National
Guard in Gaza.
IDF attacks Nahhalin.

April   Nasser ousts Naguib.   US–Iraq arms deal.
Proposed Riad–Tekoah
meeting.
Intense fighting, Gaza
border.

July   IDF raid, Deir al-
                                Big Four Conference,
Balah.   Geneva.
First Israel–French arms
deal.

                                Heads of Agreement
                                signed on evacuation.
Israel activates sabotage
ring, Cairo.

Aug.   Egypt rejects second   Egypt–Iraq talks,
US arms offer.   Sarsank.

Sept.   Israel launches *Bat
Galim* test case.

Oct.   Muslim Brotherhood   Evacuation treaty
tries to assassinate   signed.
Nasser.

Nov.   Blaustein mission,   Anglo-American
Tunisia.   planning begins on
                                Alpha.
Border friction   CIA peace initiative,
escalates; Burns' Four Camelot.
Points.

Dec.   Divon–Sadiq talks,
Paris;
Nasser note to Sharett.

1955

Jan.   Execution of two

xvi

	suspects in Cairo spy trials.	
	Egypt frees *Bat Galim* crew.	
	Rafael–Sadiq talks, Paris.	
Feb.	Troops massing on Egypt–Israel border.	Baghdad Pact signed.
		al-Khuri government falls, Syria.
		Egypt announces joint military command with Syria.
	Ben Gurion returns to Defence Ministry.	
	IDF launches Gaza raid.	
March	Fida'iyun attack Patish, Kfar Vitkin.	Alpha presented to Nasser.
	Security Council condemns Israel for Gaza raid.	
	Ben Gurion asks Dayan to formulate plan for the conquest of Gaza.	
April			Anthony Eden, Prime Minister.
		Britain joins Baghdad Pact.	
	Burns second shuttle mission.		Bandung Conference.
	Clash at Nahal Oz.	
May		Dulles devises 'kissing triangles'.
June	Nasser rejects Camelot.	
July	Israeli elections.	
	Elmore Jackson mediation.	
Sept.	Egypt tightens Straits blockade.	
Oct.	Dayan plans invasion Sinai.	
	Egyptian soldiers attack Israeli police post, Bir Ayn.	
	IDF raid, Kuntilla.	Arab League rejects Johnston plan.
Nov.	Battle at al-Sabhah, DZ.	Eden's speech,

	Ben Gurion returns to premiership.	Guildhall.	
Dec.		US peace initiative, Gamma. Britain's abortive attempt to enlist Jordan in the Baghdad Pact.	
	Foreign Minister Sharett requests arms from Tripartite Foreign Ministers, Geneva. IDF attack on Golan Heights (Tiberias raid) Egypt signs second Czech deal.		
1956 Jan.	Hammarskjöld mediation begins.		
Feb.		Anglo-US talks on Middle East defence.	Guy Mollet, French Prime Minister.
March		Sir John Glubb ousted as commander of Arab Legion.	
April		Planning ceases on Alpha; Gamma failed.	
	Fighting Gaza border; IDF shells Gaza market.		
	Egypt launches Fida'iyun attacks. Hammarskjöld achieves ceasefire.	Soviet peace initiative.	
May	Ibrahim Izzat, Egyptian reporter, visits Israel.		
June	Second Hammarskjöld mediation.	US withdraws Aswan dam project.	
July	Fawzi presents peace plan to Hammarskjöld. Mustapha Hafiz, Salah Mustapha assassinated by Israel. Operations Tide and Dove; massive French arms shipments to Israel.		Egypt nationalizes Suez Canal.
Sept.	Fighting on Jordan border. Ramzi–Ariel talks;		

	second Egyptian approach to Goldmann.	
Oct.	Sèvres Agreement signed.	Egypt–Syria–Jordan Defensive Alliance signed.
	Fida'iyun attacks, Gaza border.	
	IDF launches Kadesh.	

Preface

The second Arab–Israel war was neither exclusively Israeli nor comprehensively Arab. Rather than pitting Israel alone against a configuration of Arab forces, as was the norm in other Arab–Israel confrontations, the 1956 war set a single Arab state, Egypt, against an alliance of Israel and two Western Powers. The war was further distinguished by its significance as a major turning-point in Great Power diplomacy and in Middle East history. For these reasons, the war has always been a subject of fascination for both scholarly and popular audiences. In recent years, such interest has risen considerably due to the declassification of official British, American and Israeli documents from the 1950s, and the publication of several Egyptian works on the war. These materials, by providing new insight into the events and personalities of the period, have facilitated a thorough re-examination of the war, from its origins to its impact.

The present study comes, first, as a contribution to the growing corpus of scholarship on the early years of the Arab–Israel conflict. It is a work of history, whose primary task is to reconstruct events and portray them accurately in their proper regional and international contexts. My purpose is not to explain the reasons for the belligerency between Jews and Arabs – such an explanation, lying deep within the culture and history of those peoples, is surely beyond the capacity of any researcher – but to describe the process of escalating tensions which culminated in the second Arab–Israel war. The study focuses on the relations between Egypt and Israel – the core of that process – and their interaction with Great Power diplomacy. It traces the course of those relations from the Egyptian Revolution of 23 July 1952, an occasion which many regarded as opening opportunities for Arab–Israel peace, to 29 October 1956, the date of Israel's invasion of Sinai. In doing so, I aim to broaden our understanding not only of the origins of the 1956 war, but of the nature of the Arab–Israel conflict in general.

My methodology is thematic, rather than strictly chronological. The primary origins of the second Arab–Israel war – for example, the border, the blockade, the arms race – are examined individually, with emphasis on their legal and technical characteristics and their roles in the formulation of Egyptian, Israeli, and Great Power policies. The aim is to demonstrate the great complexity of these issues – a factor often underestimated in histories of the conflict – and to generate an appreciation of the dynamics of Egypt–Israel relations. A final chapter follows the process through which these issues combined to ignite the second Arab–Israel war.

Any researcher dealing with the early stages of the Arab–Israel conflict must grapple with the fundamental imbalance of source material. Though the Egyptian government has recently relaxed restrictions on works dealing with the early Nasser period, Egypt's archives – as well as those of other Arab states – remain inaccessible. Accounts of internal Egyptian discussions can be culled from Western and Israeli documents, but these tend to be superficial if not speculative. The inevitable result is a study not of Egypt–Israel relations but of British or Israeli policy towards Egypt. In the face of this discrepancy, I have attempted to maintain, to the greatest degree possible, a uniform depth in the reconstruction of decision-making processes, with the Egyptian side setting the standard. There is a price for this, of course, a sacrifice of intimacy for accuracy, as emphasis is placed less on the influence of personalities than on the actions of states. The end result, I am nevertheless convinced, will better serve the purpose of expanding our knowledge of the Arab–Israel conflict.

A final word must be said about the phrase 'Egypt–Israel relations', which appears often in the text. The term *relations*, when used to describe the totality of interaction between two states, usually implies a mutuality of goodwill. Generally it would not apply to states actively at war; one does not speak, for example, of US–Japanese relations during the Second World War. For this reason, perhaps, historians have hesitated to speak of *Arab–Israel relations*, preferring the more peremptory *Arab–Israel conflict*. In doing so, they overlook the fact that *relations* might also pertain to situations of mutual hostility – say, US–Soviet relations in the Cold War – which allow for other, less belligerent types of encounters. It is in this sense that we may refer to Egypt–Israel relations, for though the two countries were locked in a technical state of war, they rarely clashed on a large scale, while they did engage in numerous non-violent contacts. Thus, within the context of the Arab–Israel conflict, relations existed between Egypt and Israel. Hostile relations, for the most part, but relations nevertheless.

Introduction

For the Middle East, the 1950s was a period of profound changes: the emergence of new ideas and identities, the introduction of modern technology, the discovery of untapped sources of political and economic power. Such changes transformed the Middle East, altering the traditional relationship between the individual and the state, between states themselves, and between the region and the rest of the world. Invariably, changes of this magnitude generate instability and, in the Middle East, produced an almost unbroken series of revolutions, inter-state tensions and, ultimately, war. This was the dynamic context in which Egypt and Israel conducted their relations between 1952 and 1956.

To a large extent, the source of these transformations and the instability they wrought, can be traced to Western imperialism. The 1950s are perhaps best remembered as a transitional phase between imperialist control and national liberation. During the decade, most Middle Eastern states, if not actively engaged in combating foreign rule, were still suffering the indignity of qualified independence or the trauma of decolonization. Such dislocations were compounded by the persistence of political systems previously imposed by the Europeans and now viewed by their own constituents as collaborationist and corrupt. For a growing segment of local populations, resistance to imperialism meant active opposition to these regimes, resulting in domestic unrest and, in many cases, revolt.

Even as the imperialist era drew to a close, its vestiges were already causing considerable instability in the Middle East. The crystallization of an Arab state system, arguably the West's most enduring legacy, gave rise to conflicting irredentist claims, dynastic rivalries, and struggles between local leaders for regional pre-eminence. The pan-Arabist movement, itself an offshoot of Western nationalist thought, sought to settle these disputes by replacing the system with a united Arab state. The effect, however, was more often one of exacerbation as pan-Arabism served to justify the intervention of states in the internal affairs of others and, by expanding the borders of the Arab world, to increase the number of states competing in the system. A more practical venue for resolving these differences was the Arab League, in part a product of the imperialist past, which in principle aimed at eradicating the system but in practice

1

worked to preserve it. But again, rather than reducing friction, the League often intensified it by providing an arena for the waging of inter-Arab contests. The contradiction between the Arab unity ideal and the reality of Arab pluralism would prove to be a perennial source of Middle East instability throughout the 1950s.

Pan-Arabism was only part of the ideological imprint made by imperialism on the Middle East. Sweeping the region in the 1950s was a wave of movements – communist, Islamic, particularist-nationalist – which, though all antagonistic to colonialism, were either heavily influenced by, or directly imported from, the West. They also constituted a reservoir of instability, for while they occasionally allied with one another towards the realization of short-term goals, their platforms remained mutually irreconcilable and fundamentally inimical to the state system. Neutralism, after pan-Arabism the most potent idea to emerge from the ideological effervescence of 1950s, was also of foreign origin and also opposed to imperialism. Like pan-Arabism, it too sought strength in unity, in this case between the newly-independent nations of the world, and often created discord by serving as a weapon in the struggle for regional domination.

Advanced technology, one of imperialism's most tangible legacies in the Middle East, was another wellspring of change and instability. It facilitated the spread of ideas from the West and the export of oil to the West; it fomented unrest and created great disparities in wealth. Furthermore, for all its political freedom, the Middle East remained technologically dependent on its former masters. Arab leaders, in establishing their legitimacy as enemies of imperialism, were totally reliant on modern media and, in maintaining their security, on Western defence and intelligence systems. Such dependence remained a source of friction between the Middle East and the West, as well as between Middle East states themselves.

The 1950s also saw basic transformations in the relations between the Middle East and the Great Powers. The dawn of the imperialist era would spur the Powers, both Western and Eastern, to redefine their historical roles in the region and to seek new strategic deployments. Over the course of that period, American and Soviet ascendancy would replace Anglo-French hegemony and move the Middle East from a multi- to a bi-polar configuration in the Cold War. Such shifts, tectonic as they were, had an inevitably destabilizing effect on the region.

At the outset of the decade, the Western Powers – the United States, Britain and France – together claimed the Middle East as their exclusive purview, both politically and economically. That attitude found expression in the May 1950 Tripartite Declaration, which affirmed the Powers' sole responsibility for containing the Arab–Israel dispute and for directing Middle East defence. Behind this façade of consensus, however, lay deep-seated differences between the Powers and their policies towards the region.

Despite the independence of India and the advent of the nuclear age, Britain remained convinced of its vital commercial and military interests in the Middle East. Beset by economic crisis at home, and by nationalist opposition within the region, Britain sought to perpetuate its Middle East primacy indirectly through treaties with local governments. Throughout this endeavour, Britain maintained its traditional policy of resisting the spread of French influence in the Middle East, and similarly wished to block US encroachments. Fiscal and political constraints, however, gradually forced Britain to solicit America's intervention in the region.

To all observers, the United States was clearly the rising Power in the Middle East in the 1950s. Having entered the region in response to Britain's inability to safeguard it from Communism and to reach a *modus vivendi* with native nationalism, and having itself become increasingly dependent on Arab oil, the US soon discovered that it, too, had vital interests in the Middle East. Ideally preferring a Middle East free of the remnants of imperialism, the US cultivated the goodwill of moderate nationalist forces and worked to exclude France from Middle East arrangements. At the same time, though, it could not ignore Britain's crucial strategic role in the region. Thus, the US agreed to co-ordinate Middle East defence policies with Britain, but in order to avoid Britain's imperialist taint, refrained from openly associating with them.

France was generally regarded as an ex-Power in the Middle East by the 1950s, its position there having been greatly weakened by the events of the Second World War. Nevertheless, Paris continued to point to its colonial possessions in North Africa and its avowed primacy in the Levant as proof of its continuing status as a Middle East Power. However, the US and Britain were reluctant to recognize this claim – a fact which caused deep resentment among the French. Faced with opposition both inside and outside the region, France pursued a *faute de mieux* policy of clinging to its colonies in North Africa and to its traditional ties with Lebanon and Syria, and of resisting, whenever possible, the perceived Anglo-American conspiracy against its Middle East interests.

As the decade progressed, various domestic and external pressures would widen the contradictions between the Powers' Middle East policies and steadily erode the superficial consensus. Britain, exasperated with America's appeasement of the nationalists, would embark on a course independent of the US. In similar fashion, France would finally reject Anglo-American restrictions on its Middle East activities and act to fulfil

3

its own regional interests. These trends would eventually result in an anomalous Anglo-French alliance in the Middle East. The US, meanwhile, having failed to reconcile the demands of its European allies with those of the nationalists, would ultimately favour the latter and, in the process, join with its arch-enemy in the Middle East – as elsewhere – the Soviet Union.

The USSR was only marginally involved in the Middle East in the early 1950s. Preoccupied with strategic priorities in Europe and Asia, and bound by ideology to disdain so-called bourgeois nationalist movements, Moscow presented no serious challenge to the West's Middle East monopoly. But again, major domestic and international developments effected a fundamental change in the Soviets' policy towards the region. The Cold War's focus shifted eastward from Europe, while Soviet doctrines were revised to prescribe, rather than prohibit, aid to liberation movements. Through such support, the Soviet Union would become, by mid-decade, a Middle East Power and, after the Suez crisis, emerge together with the US as a dominant force in the region.

At the centre of this milieu of change lay Egypt and Israel, two countries which, though vastly different in terms of territory and culture, would experience similar transformations – and instability – throughout the 1950s.

Though claiming to be the direct descendants of ancient kingdoms, both Egypt and Israel were in reality new states which exhibited many of the characteristics of emergent nations. Eager to assert their newly-won independence, yet still largely dependent on the Powers, they combined temerity with timorousness in their attitudes towards the world. Their populations, while openly confident in their military prowess, had been traumatized by years of occupation, oppression and war, and were thus highly sensitive to threats – real or imaginary – to their security. Egyptian and Israeli leaders, in formulating their policies, had to respond to these contrasting images of invincibility and vulnerability. Not surprisingly, both chose to stress the army's role as the symbol of the nation's élan and its protector from annihilation.

Egypt and Israel were fully exposed to the reverberations of the political awakening of the 1950s. Their governments defined themselves as revolutionary, dedicated to enacting radical change, whether by altering the traditional structure of society or the course of major rivers, the Jordan and the Nile. Furthermore, their revolution was not restricted to the domestic arena, but aimed at larger constituencies – the Arab world and Diaspora Jewry. Such actions, though not without positive effect, created marked instability at home and in the region. No less revolutionary were other groups within the Egyptian and the Israeli

4

political spectra – communists, ultra-nationalists, religious purists – who, in their campaigns for comprehensive social change, also precipitated instability.

Egypt and Israel were afflicted with a number of maladies endemic to post-colonial societies: large-scale population growth, rapid urbanization, polarization of the modern and traditional sectors. Similarly, they suffered from chronic inflation, trade deficits and unemployment. Intensified by the paroxysms of change which shook the Middle East in the 1950s, these factors assured that the course of Egypt–Israel relations never ran smoothly.

Given this dynamic environment, it is not surprising that Egypt and Israel produced extraordinary leaders – the greatest, in fact, in their histories to date. Like the countries they led, David Ben Gurion and Gamal Abdul Nasser were vastly different in many respects, above all in age and professional experience, yet it is possible to identify many similarities between them. Both came from middle-class backgrounds, lost beloved mothers in their childhood, and left home under the shadow of detested stepmothers. Both attended law school; neither finished. Early in their youth, they became involved in politics, protesting, writing anonymous editorials, experimenting with radical ideologies but ultimately rejecting extremism. Endowed with powerful charismas, they quickly rose to dominate their respective liberation movements, eventually depicting themselves as the embodiment of the national ideal. Socialists, neutralists, they were above all nationalists with a strong sense of history and their own, pivotal, place in it. They considered themselves leaders on a world scale and had a common penchant for viewing that world in terms of concentric spheres, with Egypt or Israel at their centres, and at the centre of those, Nasser and Ben Gurion.

The crucible of the 1950s would produce other Egyptian and Israeli leaders of high calibre – Anwar Sadat and Moshe Sharett. The influence of these individuals, together with the impact of change and instability throughout the Middle East, would constitute a key element in the making of the second Arab–Israel war.

THE ARAB–ISRAEL CONFLICT

The Arab–Israel conflict was certainly the most destabilizing of imperialism's consequences, the Zionist enterprise in Palestine having been recognized and, at least initially, facilitated by the British Mandate. According to the November 1947 United Nations resolution, Palestine was to be partitioned into independent Jewish and Arab states. Following termination of the Mandate in May 1948, however, the Arab states invaded Israel in an attempt to block the partition. The 1948 war ended in defeat for the Arab armies and exile for over 700,000 Palestinians, whose proposed state was divided between Israel, Egypt and Jordan. The City of Jerusalem, destined for internationalization under the partition plan, was also divided between Israel and Jordan.

The parameters of the Arab–Israel conflict were already delineated by the beginning of the 1950s. The dispute centred on three main issues: Jerusalem, the refugees, and borders. The Arab states in general insisted that each of these problems be solved according to UN resolutions on Palestine, i.e., that Israel return to its partition borders, permit the refugees' repatriation, and agree to the internationalization of Jerusalem. Israel, for its part, held that the Arabs had rendered void the UN resolutions through their invasion. It called for recognition of its current borders, including West Jerusalem, and for the refugees' resettlement on Arab land. Israel also demanded that the Arabs sign a full peace agreement, while the Arabs refrained from committing themselves to peace, even in return for implementation of the UN resolutions.

Israel's policy, apart from minor points, was essentially inflexible. Many Arab leaders, however, were secretly open to compromise, especially if it brought them territorial gains. But Israeli leaders were highly resistant to the notion of territorial concessions and the repatriation of refugees. The irreconcilability of the Israeli and Arab positions was repeatedly demonstrated at the 1949 Lausanne Conference and in numerous covert contacts conducted between the two sides. Ultimately, however, the failure of efforts to reach a settlement owed less to Israeli intransigence than to the Arabs' fears of violent domestic repercussions to any agreement with Israel. The Arabs' refusal to deal with Israel overtly, and to accept even the symbolic concessions it offered, prevented the Powers from putting pressure on Israel to make the substantive sacrifices necessary for a settlement.

Even more than before the 1948 war, the manoeuvrability of Arab leaders on the Palestine issue in the 1950s was severely limited. Anti-Zionism had become synonymous with Arabism, and the liberation of Palestine a priority goal for Arab governments and ideological movements alike. Far more than a mere reaction to Israeli intransigence on the issues, the Arabs' anti-Zionism reflected profound historical, religious and psychological influences. The very existence of the Jewish State was a gross affront to Arab sensibilities and a perceived threat to Arab security. Israel, moreover, did not simply exist, but consistently aroused the Arabs' animosity with provocative military and political actions. Such an atmosphere effectively precluded Arab leaders from displaying any moderation towards Israel, but on the contrary, compelled them to adopt

6

increasingly assertive positions on Palestine. This was especially true for Arab statesmen who aspired to leadership in the Arab world, and above all for the Egyptians, whose path to regional ascendancy was blocked both politically and physically by Israel. Increasingly over the course of the decade, the military struggle against Israel became enmeshed with the political contest for ascendancy in the Arab world, a basis for establishing the legitimacy of one regime and for impugning that of another.

Arab opposition to Israel did not, however, translate into an immediate mandate for war. Defeated or exhausted in battle, the confrontation states – Egypt, Jordan, Syria and Lebanon – signed Armistice Agreements with Israel in 1949. These prohibited the planning, execution or threat of aggression by the armed forces of either side, but did not, according to the Arabs, end the state of war. Israel insisted that the Armistice amounted to more than a temporary truce, and was, as stated in its preamble, an interim stage towards peace. This fundamental discordance was compounded by conflicting territorial claims as well as by variant interpretations of such terms as 'aggression' and 'armed forces' – all of which had been left purposely ambiguous by the framers of the Armistice.

Thus, in the aftermath of the Armistice, there prevailed a diplomatic and strategic stalemate surrounding the three central issues in the conflict. Arab leaders publicly pledged themselves to alter this status quo by conducting a 'second round' against Israel, while, privately, they sought a negotiated return to the status quo ante of the partition resolution. Lacking, however, the ability to overcome Israel militarily, or the domestic authority and international backing to deal with it diplomatically, the Arabs worked to uphold the status quo. This meant continued refusal to recognize Israel and the affirmation of the *status belli* through such efforts as the economic boycott of Israel and the partial blockade of its shipping. These measures enabled Arab leaders to maintain their legitimacy, and to extend their regional influence, while in effect remaining passive towards the Palestine issue.

Israeli leaders also opposed the status quo – it denied them recognition and security – but preferred it to a solution which impaired Israel's territorial and demographic integrity. This, the Israelis believed, could be preserved through treaties with individual Arab rulers, to be negotiated directly without Great Power interference. While seeking this goal, however, Israel worked to endow its borders with aspects of permanence, to issue peace plans based on the territorial and demographic aspects of the status quo, and to retaliate militarily for Arab attempts to assert the *status belli*.

The status quo was also a prominent consideration in Great Power

7

diplomacy towards the Arab–Israel conflict. Opposed to the Arab insistence on the *status belli*, as they were to Israel's position on the territorial and refugee issues, the Western Powers had attempted to transform the Armistice Agreements into a peace settlement based on a compromise of the central issues. Failing in these efforts, however, the Powers regarded the status quo as essential for safeguarding their strategic and diplomatic monopoly over the Middle East, and for guaranteeing world peace. Consequently, they strove to preserve the status quo until circumstances permitted a viable mediation of the conflict.

The status quo, however, could not be sustained. Factors endogenous to the Arab world – the quest for legitimacy, the struggle for regional leadership – created a steady increase in Arab belligerency towards the Jewish State. Israel, through its assertive military and diplomatic actions, greatly accelerated the rise of Arab hostility, as did the Powers by their interference in Middle East affairs and their removal of constraints on Arab–Israel confrontation. Arab leaders sought to mitigate some of the ramifications of this escalation, and to mollify Israel and the West, by engaging in secret contacts with the Israelis. Such discussions dealt with a wide range of issues including, *inter alia*, the question of peace. But because of political constraints, again compounded by Israeli and Great Power policies, Arab leaders could not translate the contacts into concrete steps towards peace. Instead, Arab–Israel relations drifted ineluctably towards war.

The process of rising Arab belligerency, expedited by Israel and the Powers and unimpeded by secret contacts, was clearly illustrated in the course of Egypt–Israel relations from 1952 to 1956. In those relations, which reflected the principal issues of the period and produced its major events, lay the origins of the second Arab–Israel war.

1

The Border

The Egypt–Israel border extended 250 kilometres from the tip of the Gaza Strip to the Gulf of Aqaba. It was the site of the most intensive interaction between the two countries and the primary source of the second Arab–Israel war. More than a mere line separating hostile armies, the border represented a tangle of legal and political issues which, when exposed to internal and external pressures, produced a steady escalation of tension. This, in turn, greatly influenced other areas of Egypt–Israel relations, resulting, ultimately, in their irreversible drift towards war.

For the most part, the border between Egypt and Israel was determined by ground forces in the 1948 war, with details worked out by Israeli and Egyptian delegates to the Rhodes armistice talks in February 1949. The Egypt–Israel Armistice Agreement (EIAA) of that month, like those signed thereafter between Israel and Jordan, Syria and Lebanon, identified an international boundary 'beyond which the forces of the respective Parties shall not move'. Like the other Agreements, the EIAA established partial or complete demilitarized zones in contested limitrophe areas. It entrusted supervision of the armistice to UN Military Observers (UNMOs) of the UN Truce Supervisory Organization (UNTSO), who monitored compliance with EIAA regulations. Reports of violations were reviewed by an Egypt–Israel Mixed Armistice Commission (EIMAC), composed of three Egyptian and three Israeli officers and a UNMO, invested with the right to publicly condemn the offending party.

Unlike the other Agreements, however, EIAA provided for a Special Committee to facilitate the workings of the MAC. Comprising an Egyptian, an Israeli and a UN officer, the Committee was empowered to hear appeals on questions of principle. In contrast to its authors' intentions, however, the Committee more often obstructed the EIMAC, for, once an issue had been appealed, it remained *sub judice* until resolved. Thus, Egypt and Israel, if dissatisfied with an EIMAC ruling, could appeal it to the Committee where, by raising objections over procedure, they could delay its issuance indefinitely.[1]

The EIAA, though initially successful in imposing a truce, soon proved incapable of sustaining it. Designed as an interim military agreement, the EIAA did not provide for changing conditions along the border, nor did it reconcile conflicting Egyptian and Israeli claims to sovereignty over various border areas. Such omissions would later serve as major sources of border friction.

According to all the Armistice Agreements, the State of Israel had no real borders but only Armistice Demarcation Lines (ADL). These, it was stressed, were 'not to be construed in any sense as a political or territorial boundary', though in fact the Egypt–Israel ADL conformed with the 1947 UN partition lines and, with the exception of Gaza, with the traditional border between Palestine and Egypt. Nor could Egypt and Israel be said to enjoy complete sovereign rights on either side of the ADL, as indicated by the EIAA's stipulations for force limitations and demilitarization. These restrictions did not, however, alter the fact that the ADL separated not only armies but independent states which, by nature, would seek to assert their sovereignty up to, and in some cases beyond, the ADL.

Throughout the period leading up to the 1956 war, Israel worked to erect settlements and barricades along the ADL. These were designed not only to provide security against attack but, insofar as the Armistice did not recognize Israeli sovereignty over the Negev, to bestow upon the ADL some semblance of permanence. Egypt was less concerned with proving its sovereignty over Sinai – such recognition was implicit in the EIAA – than with blocking Israel's attempts to establish the ADL as a legal border. Irredentist claims, Egypt's to the Negev and Israel's to Gaza, further exacerbated this tension, as did certain locations where the ADL had not been clearly delineated.[2]

The contest over sovereignty was particularly bitter in two areas, al-Aujah and the Gaza Strip. Al-Aujah al-Khafirah (Hebrew: Nitzana), a 125-square-mile rectangle situated 70 kilometres south of Beersheva, contained vital axes leading into Sinai and the Negev. In view of the area's strategic importance, the EIAA had designated al-Aujah a Demilitarized Zone (DZ), such as those which existed on the Syrian and Jordanian borders. By contrast, the status of Gaza, a 140-square-mile strip wedged between the Negev and Sinai deserts and the sea, was *sui generis*. Occupied by the Egyptian army in 1948 as a temporary measure pending its inclusion in a Palestinian state, Gaza remained under Egyptian trusteeship, a situation explicitly recognized by the EIAA. The Armistice did, however, establish strict limitations on troop and weapons strength inside the Strip, as well as on the Israeli side of the Gaza ADL.

Israel considered the DZ as part of its territory, a claim rejected by

10

Egypt, which regarded it as a no-man's-land. Egypt disclaimed sovereignty over Gaza – a policy largely directed against Jordan's annexation of the West Bank – and made efforts, such as its support of a local All-Palestine government, to distinguish it from Egyptian territory. In practice, however, Egypt exercised full sovereign rights in Gaza; the All-Palestine government had only symbolic powers. In principle, Israel denied Egypt's right to occupy Gaza but, in signing the EIAA, implicitly recognized it, and held Egypt responsible for maintaining the Armistice along the Strip.

The EIAA also failed to account for demographic changes in key border areas. Again, these were most dramatic in the centres of greatest controversy, in Gaza and al-Aujah. Unlike the other DZs, al-Aujah was uninhabited at the time of the Armistice, with the result that no provision existed for a civilian presence there. This omission invited Egyptian and Israeli attempts to introduce their own personnel into the zone and thus establish control over it.

More destabilizing still were demographic changes in the Gaza Strip, where an estimated 210,000 Palestinian refugees – in addition to 100,000 indigenous inhabitants – were densely crowded.[3] The desire of the Palestinian refugees to regain their former homes deepened with the deterioration of conditions in the Strip, and placed increasing pressure on Egypt to fulfil their aspirations. The situation presented Egypt with a dilemma, for it could maintain neither order in Gaza nor its image in the Arab world without responding to refugees' demands, yet to do so raised the risk of EIMAC censure and, more ominously, Israeli retaliation.

To reconcile these contradictions, Egypt adopted a two-pronged policy of publicly opposing infiltration while secretly harnessing a portion of it for the purposes of sabotage and intelligence-gathering. The policy had many advantages, for not only did it gain Egypt goodwill in Gaza and among the Arab states, but also provided it with information on Israeli forces and a means of retarding Israel's settlement of the border area. The policy also allowed Egypt to escape condemnation in the EIMAC, for though the EIAA proscribed both civilian crossings of the ADL and hostile actions by irregulars, the Commission could find no evidence of direct Egyptian involvement in the infiltration.[4]

The Israelis, however, would not endure even limited infiltration, especially if it resulted in the loss of life and property. In response, they staged armed retaliations across the border, often depicting them as the work of vigilante settlers in an attempt, albeit rarely successful, to avoid the EIMAC's condemnation. The policy's main purpose was to punish the infiltrators, but it had other objectives as well. Insofar as the Israelis believed that the Arab states actively encouraged infiltration as a first

11

step in their campaign to destroy the Jewish State, the retaliations were designed to have a deterrent effect. Hence, the Israel Defence Forces (IDF) reserved the right to retaliate against any Arab target, not necessarily the origin of the infiltration. Retaliations also served to satisfy the demands of the Israeli public for revenge, and of the IDF for action.[5]

Israel's retaliations, even when directed at the West Bank, invariably caused unrest among the Gaza refugees and placed pressure on Cairo to respond in kind. As a result, Egypt had to both bolster its forces in Gaza and upgrade its sponsorship of infiltration. Israel interpreted these moves as further proof of Egypt's commitment to war, and, as such, resolved to launch even larger-scale retaliations. The result of this vicious cycle of provocations and reprisals was an almost continuous escalation of Egypt–Israel tensions along the border.

For all its volatility, however, the Egypt–Israel border remained relatively quiet for nearly two years after the signing of the EIAA. In contrast to their political disagreement over the meaning of that document, Egypt and Israel concurred in its practical provisions for the border. While major fighting erupted on the Syrian and Jordanian borders, violence between Egypt and Israel was limited to chance encounters between infiltrators and Israeli soldiers or settlers. In Gaza, the occupation authorities kept armed infiltration to a minimum, and in the DZ, Egypt sought a *modus vivendi* with Israel through the organization of joint patrols.

Their bellicose rhetoric notwithstanding, the Egyptians had no intention of waging war against Israel. Resistance to the idea was especially strong in the army, whose leaders feared risking another humiliating defeat. Even Faruq, Egypt's corrupt and corpulent monarch, who harboured an abiding ambition for a 'second round' with Israel, was too preoccupied with growing opposition to his rule to contemplate such action.[6] A similar outlook prevailed in Israel. Though antagonized by Egyptian propaganda and infiltration from Gaza, Israeli leaders wanted to avoid the resumption of open hostilities with Egypt. Military commanders shared this opinion, particularly in light of the IDF's poor performance in clashes with the Jordanian and the Syrian armies. Thus, at this juncture, there existed a rare confluence of Israeli and Egyptian interests in maintaining the status quo. Such harmony was evident in the EIMAC which, in 1950, was rated by the UN as the most efficient of the Armistice Commissions.[7]

Beginning in late 1950, however, Egypt–Israel border relations began a process of steady deterioration. Egypt withdrew from the joint patrols in the DZ, while Israel evicted from the area Azazme bedouin allegedly sent by Egypt to establish a foothold in the Zone. Egypt protested the action in the Security Council, which condemned it, but failed to force Israel to reinstate the tribe. Armed infiltration meanwhile increased on the Gaza border and, for the first time since the Palestine war, appeared to be aimed at the IDF. On 21 October, following the shooting of two IDF officers by infiltrators, Israel launched its first reprisal into Gaza, killing an undisclosed number of refugees and causing extensive damage to property.[8] In the EIMAC, co-operation between the delegations ceased as Israel appealed the MAC's ruling on the bedouin expulsions to the Special Committee, and Egypt responded by appealing an Israeli complaint on the Canal blockade (see Chapter 2). A stalemate ensued in which each delegation refused to discuss the other's appeal, resulting in the paralysis of the Special Committee and, to a great extent, of the EIMAC as well.

These tensions were chiefly the result of domestic instability within Egypt. Opposition to Britain's presence in Sudan and in the Suez Canal Zone led to confrontrations between Egyptians and British forces in Egypt. Tension reached a climax in January 1952, with the outbreak of anti-British riots in Cairo. These events sapped Egypt's military strength in Gaza and diminished its ability to control infiltration. Political upheaval further contributed to the escalation – three Egyptian governments fell in the spring of 1952 – as the beleaguered regime sought to rebut its detractors by demonstrating its steadfastness on Palestine. The marked increase in infiltration, accompanied by the intensification of hostile propaganda, deeply provoked the Israelis. In the first months of 1952, the IDF conducted 11 small-scale raids into Gaza and scheduled a major retaliation for July. The operation was postponed, however, with news of the Free Officers' revolution, as Israeli leaders paused to assess the new situation in Egypt.[9]

THE BORDER IN THE AFTERMATH OF THE JULY REVOLUTION

On 23 July 1952, King Faruq was ousted by a military coup conducted by a group calling itself the Free Officers. The event proved to be a turning point in Egypt–Israel relations. Initially, the Officers expressed their intention of concentrating on the country's internal problems and of distancing themselves from the policies of the previous regime. While still bitter over the Palestine defeat, the Officers tended to blame that humiliation on Britain, on other Arab armies and corrupt Egyptian politicians – in that order – and showed little interest in resuming an active role in the fight against Israel. Such a move, in addition to jeopardizing the new government, would serve only to distract the Officers from more pressing issues, such as the economy and relations with Britain, and remove the possibility of attaining US military and economic aid.[10]

The Egyptian coup became the focus of intense interest in Israel. While the Israeli press depicted the event as yet another example of instability and militarism in the Arab world, officials at the Israeli Foreign Ministry kept a close watch on the Officers for any indication of a willingness to negotiate. Though uncertain of the political ideas of General Muhammad Naguib, the regime's figurehead leader, and suspicious of those of other Officers – Anwar Sadat and the Salem brothers, Salah and Gamal – the Israelis were hopeful of a breakthrough. Much of their optimism centred on one man, Gamal Abdul Nasser, a dynamic and charismatic 34-year-old Lieutenant Colonel, whom Israeli intelligence had identified as the real power behind Naguib. Nasser was known to the Israelis; he had participated in ceasefire talks with the IDF in 1949 and had expressed a desire to resolve the conflict.[11] Aiming to appeal to Nasser, Israeli leaders conveyed to Cairo invitations to peace talks (see Chapter 5), and thereafter regarded the border as a barometer of the Officers' receptivity.

The signs were, at first, promising. Lieutenant Colonel Salah Gohar and Lieutenant Colonel Haim Gaon, the Egyptian and Israeli representatives to the EIMAC, agreed to break the deadlock in the Special Committee and to erase the long backlog of complaints. They further arranged a series of two-week periods during which all problems would be handled directly by the representatives outside the EIMAC framework. Gohar also made the extraordinary gesture of volunteering to join with Israel in marking the ADL. In Gaza, the Egyptian authorities curtailed the activities of Palestinian nationalists and reinforced efforts to restrict infiltration.[12]

The period of co-operation in the EIMAC proved, however, short-lived. By November, Gohar refused to renew the fortnightly agreements and retracted his offer to participate in the marking project. These decisions, he explained, were a response to Israel's attempts to exploit Egypt's goodwill gestures by using the EIMAC as a forum for political talks. While Gohar's claim was not without foundation (see Chapter 5), Egypt's altered stance towards the border came within the context of a general hardening of its position on Palestine.[13]

At base, the shift in the Officers' strategy represented the resumption of Egypt's traditional quest for ascendancy in the Fertile Crescent. In the 1950s, this necessitated leadership of the struggle against Zionism, a position hardly consonant with the conciliatory stance initially adopted by the Officers towards Israel. By the autumn of 1952, this moderate position had become the focus of criticism from the regime's domestic

14

opponents – the Muslim Brotherhood and former Wafd party politicians – and from its regional rivals, the Iraqis. The charges were particularly harmful as the Officers were at that time seeking Arab support for their impending talks with Britain over the Suez and Sudan issues. Thus, in an effort to placate their critics, and to fortify their position vis-à-vis Britain, the Officers upgraded their resistance to Israel. Such a démarche, moreover, incurred fewer risks in terms of acquiring US aid. The newly-elected Republican Administration, in contrast to its Democratic predecessor, seemed to be indifferent to Zionist pressures and generally sympathetic to the Arab cause.

Thus, at the same time as Gohar withdrew from co-operation with Israel in the EIMAC, Egypt decided to lead the Arab campaign against West Germany's reparations treaty with Israel, to tighten restrictions against Israel-bound cargoes in the Suez Canal (see Chapter 2), and to rebuff Israeli invitations to peace talks (Chapter 5). On the border, meanwhile, armed infiltration from Gaza rose significantly, causing, by December, a high state of tension along the entire ADL.[14]

As a result of these events, many Israelis revised their first impression of the Free Officers. Most prominent among these was David Ben Gurion, Israel's first and, as yet, only Prime Minister, who also acted as Minister of Defence. A determined and often pugnacious realist, Ben Gurion had conducted secret negotiations with Arab leaders in the 1930s and 1940s in an effort to reconcile various aspects of the Palestine problem. These experiences, all of which failed, left Ben Gurion sceptical of the utility of clandestine contacts and suspicious of the Arabs' motivation in agreeing to them. At a meeting with Foreign Ministry officials in December 1952, Ben Gurion argued against putting any trust in the Egyptian regime. The Free Officers were no different from any other Arab junta. They understood only power and most likely interpreted Israel's peace-feelers as a sign of weakness.[15]

Ben Gurion's understanding of the nature of Arab politics, together with his determination to demonstrate Israel's right to act in self-defence, translated into strong support for the policy of armed retaliation. In terms of Egypt, this meant prompt and forceful response to Palestinian infiltration. In the weeks following Ben Gurion's reassessment of the Free Officers, pressures for such an action mounted in Israel, and not only in reaction to the rise in infiltration. The Republican victory in Washington, as well as the eruption of a fierce anti-Zionist campaign in Eastern Europe, underscored Israel's international isolation, while at home Israel faced economic crisis and clashes on the Syrian and Jordanian borders. Such an atmosphere of frustration and vulnerability reinforced Ben Gurion's inclination to respond militarily to border provocations. The

15

result came on the night of 26 January 1953 when the IDF struck in Gaza. Five suspected infiltrators were killed.[16]

Relations in the EIMAC in the early months of 1953 vacillated between cordial and cool, but on the border itself instances of sniping and mining steadily multiplied.[17] Such friction could, as noted, serve Egyptian interests, but at this juncture the liabilities outweighed the benefits. Throughout the first half of 1953, the Free Officers' regime, now known as the Revolutionary Command Council (RCC), faced a resurgence of domestic opposition and, more seriously, a recrudescence of armed clashes with the British along the Suez Canal. The RCC feared the Israelis would take advantage of the Egyptian army's preoccupation with the Canal Zone to strike over the border – a military defeat which the opposition was sure to exploit politically. Perceptions of such a danger figured prominently in the RCC's decision to enter into covert contacts with Israel (see Chapter 5). Such talks dealt with a wide range of issues, but above all with that of the border.

Through the contacts, the Egyptians expressed their commitment to maintain the status quo on the ADL, but at the same time they explained that a certain level of tension was unavoidable given the exigencies of domestic and regional politics. The Israelis solicited Egypt's co-operation in stopping infiltration and in using the EIMAC as a forum for expanding the EIAA into more permanent political arrangements. In a series of discussions between Colonel Chaim Herzog, then Israel's Military Attaché in Washington, and his Egyptian counterparts, Colonels Ghalib and al-Shaf'i, Egypt specifically requested that Israel should not attack during the period of the Canal Zone clashes. Herzog assured the Egyptians that Israel would show restraint, as it had during previous periods of Anglo-Egyptian fighting.[18]

Though the contacts failed to produce progress towards a settlement, they did result in a relaxation of border tension. It was in this improved atmosphere that the EIMAC registered its most impressive achievement: the Egypt–Israel Distressed Vessels Agreement. Six months earlier, in December 1952, the Egyptian schooner *Samir* strayed into Jaffa port, where it was impounded by the Israeli authorities. Israel offered to return the ship if Egypt signed an agreement providing for the repatriation of all civilian vessels which accidentally entered neighbouring territorial waters. Egypt rejected the proposal, even after Israel released the *Samir*'s cargo and crew. Then, in May, the RCC suddenly reversed its decision.

Egypt's *volte face* reflected not only the slight improvement in its relations with Israel, but also its concern for the impending talks with Britain on the Suez Canal. The RCC feared that the British would evoke the *Samir* seizure to emphasize Egypt's blockade of Israeli shipping through the Canal, thus impugning its ability to assure free passage through the waterway. By accepting Israel's offer, Egypt denied Britain that argument and with seemingly minimal risk to its relations with the Arab world; Syria and Lebanon had similar agreements with Israel. On 25 June, following the *Samir*'s return through UN auspices, Gohar and Gaon met at Kilometre 95 on the Gaza border and signed the Distressed Vessels Agreement (text in Appendix I). It would be the only agreement concluded between Egypt and Israel in the period between the first and second Arab–Israel wars.[19]

The Free Officers may have been naive in discounting the Arab reaction to the agreement. The Arab states, most bitterly Syria, denounced it as the first step towards a separate Israel–Egypt peace. Nor did the agreement contribute to the success of the Anglo-Egyptian talks, which collapsed long before resolving on a plan for evacuating Britain's troops from the Suez Canal Zone. A further setback for the RCC came in July when Iraq renewed its efforts for Fertile Crescent unity under Hashemite leadership. Egypt retorted with the Voice of the Arabs (VOA), a long-distance radio broadcast which had as its major theme the depiction of Iraq as Israel's ally, and of Egypt as the Arabs' protector against Zionism.

The inauguration of VOA generated an increase in Egypt–Israel tensions. Israel also contributed to the escalation by announcing plans to divert the Jordan river at the Syrian border and by transferring its capital to Jerusalem. The situation was clearly reflected on the border. On the night of 30 August, following a spate of infiltration attacks, armed Israelis attacked the al-Burayj refugee camp in Gaza. The raiders killed 13 refugees and wounded 27 others, and made an abortive attempt on the life of Mustafa Hafiz, the chief of Egyptian Intelligence, whom Israel suspected of promoting infiltration. The assault was carried out by 101, a unit of non-uniformed commandos created to improve Israel's retaliatory capability. Captain Ariel Sharon, commander of 101, chose Gaza as the raid's target, despite the fact that evidence suggested the infiltrators had come from Jordan.

The next day, Gaza's refugee camps erupted with demonstrations. Rioters chanting anti-government slogans attacked an Egyptian police headquarters. Bewildered by the attack – Israel's rationale for retaliating against any Arab target consistently eluded the Egyptians – the RCC ordered more troops into the Strip and upgraded its support of infiltration. The following weeks witnessed a sharp rise in the number of sabotage acts against Israeli settlements in the Negev. These developments, in turn, reinforced the demands of those in Israel who advocated a more assertive border policy. Further bolstering their argument was the fact that, though the EIMAC had rejected the vigilante story and condemned Israel for the attack, not a single Israeli casualty had been sustained in the raid. The retaliation policy, it was proved, need not be a costly one.[20]

The al-Burayj raid ended the period of relative stability on the ADL. Thereafter, the focus of tension shifted from Gaza to the DZ. Israeli strategic planners attached great importance to dominating the DZ, as a means not only of establishing their territorial claim over it, but of preventing the Egyptians from using al-Aujah as a springboard for invading the Negev, as they had done in 1948.[21] The Egyptians had long expected Israel to introduce troops into the area. Their suspicion appeared confirmed when, at the beginning of September 1953, Unit 101 entered the DZ to expel another group of Azazme bedouin.

Israel made its move in the final week of September with the establishment of a kibbutz, Ketziot, near a strategic junction in the DZ. Egypt sent several waves of infiltrators to assault the position, but these were easily repulsed. More resolutely, Egypt protested to the EIMAC, charging that Israel had no right to settle the DZ and that it had violated the EIAA by populating the kibbutz with members of *Nahal*, the IDF's agricultural corps. The Commission indeed ordered the removal of the *Nahal* personnel, but could find no legal grounds for ejecting a civilian settlement from the DZ. Israel praised the second decision and nullified the first by appealing it to the Special Committee.[22]

The Free Officers were deeply embarrassed by these events. Compounding their discomfort was the fact that Israel's actions in the DZ coincided with the collapse of Anglo-Egyptian talks and with the opening of show trials designed to attribute the Palestine defeat to politicians of the *ancien régime*. In addition, Israel's Jordan diversion project, begun in September, and its bloody raid the following month on Qibyah village in the West Bank intensified pressures on the Free Officers to respond militarily to border provocations. Unprepared for such a confrontation, however, the RCC could only respond by increasing anti-Israel propaganda, tightening the Canal blockade (see Chapter 2) and, in Gaza, creating a Civil Guard composed of Palestinian volunteers.

Secretly, however, the RCC informed Israeli leaders that these measures were adopted for political purposes, and were not indicative of any belligerent intent on the part of Egypt. Even the Civil Guard, publicly described as 'a practical and decisive stage in the restoration of Palestine from the evils of Israel', was a purely symbolic organization. But Israel, the Officers explained, had to understand Egypt's difficulty in preventing infiltration from Gaza and its sensitivity to the situation in the DZ, and do its best to restrain activist elements in the army.[23]

THE BORDER UNDER SHARETT AND NASSER

In the following months, changes would occur in both the Israeli and the Egyptian governments that would deeply affect all aspects of Egypt–Israel relations, but none so dramatically as the border. In October 1953, Ben Gurion announced that he was retiring from office to become a member of Kibbutz Sde Boker in the Negev. His Prime Minister and Defence Minister portfolios were divided between Moshe Sharett and Pinchas Lavon, respectively. More worldly and polished than Ben Gurion, Sharett also had a greater faith in Israel's ability to reach an accommodation with its neighbours – a belief which reflected his upbringing among Arabs and his knowledge of the Arabic language. Sharett was also less disposed to order armed retaliations against alleged Arab violations of the Armistice. Such displays of force, in his view, not only failed to deter the Arabs, but greatly complicated Israel's relations with the Powers. Though Israel retained a fundamental right to retaliate, it would exercise that right only as last resort, and then only as an auxiliary to, and not a substitute for, a comprehensive diplomatic strategy.[24]

Sharett, however, proved to be a weak leader. His authority was easily circumvented by Lavon who, though once an opponent of retaliations, had now become their fervent advocate. Supporting Lavon's position were several of Ben Gurion's protégés, above all Moshe Dayan, the IDF Chief-of-Staff. If Sharett's views were influenced by a youth spent living among the Arabs, Dayan's were formed by a lifetime of fighting them. Renowned for his daring and dominating personality, and for his eye-patch, Dayan regarded infiltration as a prelude to the 'second round' and retaliations as an integral part of Israel's basic security programme. Thus, isolated within his own government, and confronted with a military willing to act independently of civilian directives, Sharett faced formidable obstacles in the pursuit of his diplomatic strategy.[25]

In Egypt, meanwhile, a bitter rivalry developed between Naguib, the avuncular and titular head of the RCC, and the young Officers under Nasser. The contest came to a head in January 1954, and only after four months and several failed coup attempts did Nasser emerge victorious. Though disturbed by the extent of instability in Egypt, Sharett saw advantages in Nasser's rise to power. Despite pressures from several of his colleagues, in particular Sadat, who were strongly influenced by the Muslim Brotherhood and who demanded a more militant stand against Israel, Nasser insisted on maintaining the status quo and even making contacts with Israeli leaders.

But while Nasser's pre-eminence in the RCC was widely recognized, his powers were far from absolute. Not yet the great leader of the late

19

1950s and early 1960s, Nasser in this period operated under severe constraints not only from within the RCC but from the army in general, and had to confront strong opposition from the Muslim Brotherhood. His latitude on foreign policy was also limited by Britain's presence in the Canal Zone and its influence in the Fertile Crescent, and by Egypt's continued dependence on Western weaponry. These curbs on Nasser's powers were evident on the ADL, where, like Sharett, he proved incapable of controlling the actions of his subordinates.[26]

The effects of these changes were soon felt on the border. In the early months of 1954, there occurred another rise in armed infiltration and for the first time Israeli and Egyptian bunkers exchanged fire. The Israelis attempted to halt the spiral by returning six Egyptian students who had wandered over the border and by proposing the elimination of all appeals then pending in the Special Committee. Another gesture came in March when Israeli declared Jordan responsible for the massacre of 11 Israeli civilians in the Negev's Scorpion Pass (Maaleh Akravim), though evidence pointed to Gaza as the attackers' base. The IDF retaliated – ominously without Sharett's approval – against Nahhalin village in the West Bank.[27]

Although Nasser was indebted to Israel for having been spared retaliation for the Scorpion Pass incident, he could not reciprocate. The raid touched off renewed unrest in Gaza, forcing Egypt to upgrade the Civil Guard to a National Guard and to deploy its troops in border positions. The effects were immediate: 17 major clashes between opposing bunkers were reported in the first two weeks of April. Following a series of condemnations of its actions in the EIMAC, Egypt boycotted the Commission.[28]

Conditions on the ADL in April 1954 were such that an outbreak of large-scale fighting, if not war, seemed imminent. The situation was one which neither Israel nor Egypt could afford. Sharett had just failed in his efforts to achieve direct negotiations with Jordan and to secure Anglo-American approval for the Jordan diversion project; a border war with Egypt would fully discredit his diplomatic strategy. Faced with the need to consolidate his domestic position, Nasser also had to contend with another attempt by Iraq, now fortified with American arms (see Chapter 4), to achieve hegemony over the Fertile Crescent, as well as with the possibility of renewed talks with the British. A major clash with Israel would only reduce Egypt's chances for acquiring Western arms and for expediting the evacuation talks, and, should it result in defeat for Egypt, provide a boost to Iraq's regional prestige. Under pressure from activist elements in their governments to sanction bold military action, Sharett and Nasser sought to defuse the crisis through diplomacy.[29]

THE BORDER IN GREAT POWER DIPLOMACY

The leaders of the US, Britain and France fully shared Sharett and Nasser's interest in maintaining the status quo. In principle, the Tripartite Powers opposed the status quo and sought Arab recognition of Israel on the basis of the partition plan. But given the Arabs' refusal to recognize Israel, and Israel's refusal to concede territory or repatriate refugees, the Powers resolved to maintain the status quo. This, in their view, was essential for preserving traditional Western spheres of influence in the Middle East and for guaranteeing world peace. Realizing the inadequacy of the MAC system to safeguard the status quo, the Powers issued a Declaration in May 1950, which pledged them to intervene militarily to block any attempt to alter the ADL by force.

There did not exist, however, a Tripartite consensus on the form intervention would take, and the Powers were apprehensive over the regional and global implications of such a move. Thus, whenever possible they used diplomacy to stop border violence, as had the US and Britain in mediating several disputes on the Syrian and Jordanian borders. Friction on the Egypt–Israel border, while often causing concern among the Powers, had yet to require their direct involvement. But by the beginning of 1954, with the rapid escalation of fighting in the Gaza area, the US Secretary of State John Foster Dulles quickly interposed with a plan for direct Egypt–Israel talks to restore the status quo.[30]

Cairo welcomed such intervention, for though the Powers in general rejected the claim that the Armistice Agreements had not ended the state of war, their positions vis-à-vis the border issue dovetailed with those of Egypt and the Arab states. These stressed the temporary nature of the ADL, the international status of Jerusalem, and the DZ's nature as a no-man's-land. Furthermore, the Powers viewed infiltration as an understandable consequence of the refugees' plight, and the retaliation policy as morally repugnant and politically counter-productive. 'It is a mystery', one British diplomat wrote, 'that such intelligent people as the Israeli leaders can be so blind of the consequences of their violent acts.'[31] In general, the Powers regarded Israel, and not the Arabs, as the aggressor; almost invariably their intervention came in response to Israeli actions.

The Israeli government, accordingly, objected to the Powers' involvement in border affairs, but fearing economic and political sanctions, could not openly oppose it. Coincidentally, Sharett had also been trying to arrange a direct meeting with the Egyptians, but his efforts had been frustrated by the IDF's actions in Qibyah and the DZ. But while Sharett had in mind discussions on political as well as technical issues, Washington's sole interest was in tension-reducing measures. Its specific goal was

21

to introduce into the Egypt–Israel border an arrangement which already existed in Jerusalem, under which local Jordanian and Israeli commanders met on an ad hoc basis to settle immediate disputes.

Nasser accepted the American proposal, but insisted that the talks be held between officers, not civilians. His candidate was Colonel Mahmud Riad, then an expert on Palestinian Affairs in Egypt's War Ministry. Sharett also approved of the local commanders' concept, but opposed Egypt's demand for purely military representation. He proceeded to name Joseph Tekoah, the Foreign Ministry's observer to the EIMAC, as Israel's representative. Furthermore, in his letter to Nasser formally proposing the talks (Appendix II), Sharett included a veiled warning of retaliatory action should Egypt fail to co-operate in the negotiations. Subsequently, Nasser began to distance himself from the plan, and following an artillery exchange between bunkers on 25 April, officially retracted his offer to send Riad. Thereafter, Egypt would agree only to meetings in the context of an EIMAC police subcommittee – police, Cairo argued, were more familiar with daily events on the border – a position which Israel rejected as a retreat from the EIAA.[32]

Border friction intensified throughout the spring, with Egyptian troops increasingly engaging in provocations. In fact, responsibility for many of these clashes lay with the Palestinian National Guard, which was quick to fire on IDF positions and to provide cover for infiltrators.[33] In May, the EIMAC managed to secure a ceasefire during which Gohar pledged to co-operate in marking the border and in forming joint patrols with the IDF. The Israeli Foreign Ministry, meanwhile, attempted to revive the idea for a local commanders' agreement. The ceasefire broke down the following month, however, and on 10 July the IDF stormed a Palestinian position at Deir al-Balah, killing six and capturing two. Egypt used the confession of an Israeli deserter from Ketziot to resubmit its complaint on the kibbutz to the EIMAC.

The summer of 1954 was a watershed period for Egypt–Israel relations in general and in particular for the border situation. The pivotal event occurred in Cairo on 27 July with the signing of the Heads of Agreement, which outlined a staged British withdrawal from the Suez Canal Zone. Though difficult negotiations over details of the final treaty would continue into the autumn, the evacuation controversy had essentially been solved.

The most immediate effect of the evacuation agreement was to free Nasser to play a more active role in the region. That July, Nasser embarked on an ambitious campaign to establish Egypt's Arabness and its leadership of the struggle for Arab unity. A natural step in the RCC's effort to achieve leadership of the Arab world, the démarche also

22

reflected Nasser's need to counter the Muslim Brotherhood and the Iraqis, both of whom claimed that the evacuation agreement had compromised Egypt's sovereignty. To prove its leadership capacity, and to defend against detractors, the RCC also adopted a more aggressive posture on Palestine. The effect was readily manifest on the border, where the Egyptian army expanded its support for armed infiltration and for the deployment of Palestinians in frontline positions.[34]

These shifts in Egyptian policy greatly disturbed the Israelis, who viewed them as a direct result of the evacuation. That agreement had not only removed a crucial, British, buffer between Egypt and Israel, but did so without securing Israel's right to free passage through the Canal or an Egyptian pledge of non-belligerency. Most distressing to Jerusalem was the possibility that the Egyptians would come into possession of the Canal Zone's massive stores and infrastructure, thus vastly augmenting their offensive capability. For these reasons, the Israeli leadership resolved to prevent, or at least delay, the evacuation.

The Israelis launched two operations: a government-sanctioned attempt to send an Israeli 'test case' ship through the Suez Canal, and an unauthorized plan of IDF intelligence to create chaos in Egypt and cast doubt on the RCC's ability to protect the Canal. These missions, which are examined in greater detail in Chapters 2 and 5, failed in their objectives. They did, however, serve to exacerbate Egypt–Israel tensions, as was again evidenced by events on the border.

Border clashes steadily mounted throughout the summer and autumn, most of them instigated by Egyptian or Palestinian troops. For the first time since 1949, MAC condemnations of an Arab state, Egypt, outnumbered those of Israel. The EIMAC, in an unprecedented decision, found Egypt guilty of supporting armed infiltration. Pressed by Dayan and Lavon to approve a major IDF strike into Gaza, Sharett sanctioned two limited reprisals and sent a personal appeal to Nasser to restrain his troops lest Israel be compelled to retaliate in strength.[35]

The dangerous level of tensions again moved the Powers to intervene diplomatically. In addition to their usual concern for upholding the status quo, the US and Britain now feared that the border situation would threaten project Alpha (see Chapter 5), their secret plan for an Egypt–Israel settlement, and with it the future Middle East defence organization.

The Powers had previously addressed such border issues through the Security Council, but a sudden increase in Soviet diplomatic support for the Arabs made them reluctant to work through the United Nations. Instead, the Powers turned to General E.L.M. Burns, the newly-appointed Chief of the UN Military Observers.

A former commander of Canadian forces in Italy during the Second World War, Burns had a reputation for being at the same time tough and fair and open-minded. Shortly after assuming office in November 1954, Burns put forward four points for decreasing border violence along the ADL: (1) joint UN–Egyptian–Israeli border patrols; (2) the manning of border positions by regular troops only (i.e., not by Palestinians); (3) the fencing of sensitive areas of the ADL; (4) a local commanders' agreement. Presently, he embarked on a shuttle mission between Jerusalem and Cairo to obtain the points' approval by Sharett and Nasser.

Burns's mission met with little success. While eager to reduce border violence, Sharett and Nasser expressed various reservations. Their positions, which continued to characterize those of Israel and Egypt over the next two years, were as follows: Israel accepted points (2), (3) and (4) but rejected (1) on the grounds that it infringed on its sovereignty and limited its manoeuvrability. The Egyptians accepted (1) and (2), but rejected (3) and (4) as conferring an unwarranted degree of recognition on Israel.

In the wake of Burns's failure, armed infiltration from Gaza escalated and reached a peak in December, but a month later, abruptly abated. The immediate reason for the change was the implementation in Gaza of strict regulations to curtail infiltration. Behind these measures, once again, lay Nasser's fear of a large-scale Israeli retaliation. At that juncture, Nasser had moved to suppress the Muslim Brotherhood and to confront Iraq on the regional defence issue (see Chapter 3); an Israeli attack would seriously undermine his ability to eradicate the Brotherhood and to discredit Baghdad. Furthermore, Nasser knew that resentment had been building up in Israel, and not only over border incidents. He had refused to allow Israel's test case ship to pass through the Canal and had tried for treason a number of Egyptian Jews implicated in the sabotage plot. In the hope of dissuading the Israelis from seeking revenge, Nasser agreed to another round of direct contacts (see Chapter 5). On 25 February, the sixth anniversary of the EIAA, he declared: 'Israel's policy is agggressive; however, we do not want to start a conflict. War has no place in the constructive policy we have prepared for our people.'[36]

Nasser, however, proved incapable of stopping the infiltration (which he privately blamed on the Brotherhood) and the bunker firings which, at the end of the month, took the lives of three Israelis and four Egyptians. Furthermore, on 31 January, two of the Egyptian Jews found guilty of treason were executed in Cairo. Though messages were exchanged between Cairo and Jerusalem requesting restraint on the border, Egyptian and Israeli forces began massing on the ADL.

In Israel, at least, retaliation was seen as inevitable. The death

24

sentences dealt a *coup de grâce* to Sharett's diplomatic strategy, which in the preceding months had also failed in such crucial matters as arms acquisitions and regional defence. The momentum towards reprisal was reinforced by the return of Ben Gurion to the Defence Ministry on 17 February, following Lavon's resignation for his alleged involvement in the sabotage operation. 'Sharett', Ben Gurion reportedly told the cabinet secretary, 'is cultivating a generation of cowards ... I won't let him. This will be a fighting generation.'[37]

A week later, Iraq signed a strategic alliance with Turkey – the so-called Baghdad Pact – which, together with the rise of a pro-Egyptian government in Damascus, accentuated Israel's regional isolation. The highly volatile atmosphere in Israel was ignited on 26 February, when a boy was murdered by infiltrators outside Tel Aviv. These developments resulted, on the night of 28 February, in the launching of Operation Black Arrow, known to history as the Gaza raid.

Black Arrow was the IDF's largest retaliation to date and the first against a major Egyptian army facility. Though the attackers had planned to skirt the camp – the objectives were a water tower and railroad station – they stumbled into the centre of the Egyptian bivouac. Sharett, who rather naively had accepted Dayan's assurances that Egyptian casualties would not exceed ten, was shocked by the results: 37 Egyptians killed, 28 wounded, with eight Israeli dead as well. More stunned were the UNMOs who investigated the incident. On the basis of their report, the EIMAC summarily dismissed Israel's claim that the attack had been the spontaneous reaction of an IDF patrol to an Egyptian ambush, and found it guilty of committing 'a brutal and murderous act of aggression'. Nevertheless, Ben Gurion judged the raid a success; it clearly warned the Arab states of the dangers of a 'second round'.

The operation caused shock in Egypt and panic in Gaza; major riots again erupted throughout the Strip. Nasser, though bitter over the violation of what he believed had been Israel's secret assurances against such a retaliation, resisted pressure from his army to order a counter-attack, and limited himself to protesting to the Tripartite Powers and the Security Council.[38] The Powers rapidly responded to these approaches. They rejected Israel's justifications for the raid and sponsored a Security Council resolution, passed unanimously on 29 March, condemning Israel's retaliation policy.

FROM GAZA TO KHAN YUNIS

The Gaza raid inaugurated a new phase in Egypt–Israel relations. Subsequently, efforts to improve those relations, or at least to maintain

25

the status quo, gave way to an ineluctable drift towards war. On the border, the IDF would be restrained so as not to interfere with Ben Gurion's plans for a more comprehensive confrontation with Egypt. By contrast, Egyptian forces would display an even greater tenacity on the border, firing on Israeli positions and violating Israeli territory. The Gaza raid had enhanced Egypt's prestige in the Arab world by thrusting it into the forefront of the Palestine struggle. Nasser was eager to exploit that momentum and, having succeeded in his disputes with the British and the Muslim Brotherhood, he was now free to do so.

On 26 March 1955, Palestinian infiltrators, organized and trained by the Egyptian army, struck two Israeli settlements, Patish and Kfar Vitkin, killing two civilians and wounding 33. The attackers were known as *Fida'iyun* (self-sacrificers) to distinguish them from their predecessors, *mutasallun* (infiltrators). The creation of Fida'iyun units was Nasser's means of conciliating the Palestinians, whose rioting after the Gaza raid had been brutally quelled by the Egyptian army, and of gaining credit in the Arab world during the struggle over the Baghdad Pact. Their purpose was to strike targets deep inside Israeli territory, causing panic and confusion. Officially, however, Egypt denied any involvement with the Fida'iyun, thus avoiding condemnations by the EIMAC.[39]

The Gaza raid also represented a turning point in the Powers' policy towards the border. With their plans for Middle East peace and defence now complicated by Arab demands for sanctions against Israel, the US and Britain still relied on Burns, the UN Chief Military Observer, to mediate an end to the friction. The Powers, however, realized that Burns's chances of success were greatly diminished by the absence of a Security Council mandate. Fortunately, the Gaza raid had given rise to an East–West consensus on Israeli culpability for the situation. Thus, the Soviet Union joined the Western Powers in supporting the 29 March resolution condemning Israel and, in a resolution of 4 April, instructing General Burns to continue his mediation mission. Meanwhile, the US and Britain began pressurizing Israel to abstain from retaliations and Egypt to curb infiltration.[40]

Burns's mission began inauspiciously. Fighting continued on the Gaza ADL where, on 3 April, a clash between an Egyptian bunker and an Israeli patrol near Nahal Oz left two Egyptians and two Israelis dead and 19 Israelis wounded. The UN Chief learned that there had been no change in the antagonists' positions towards the four points. Sharett and Ben Gurion still refused to abjure the retaliation policy while Nasser continued to disclaim responsibility for infiltration.

Having reached an impasse, Burns concentrated on defusing the immediate crisis by proposing the pullback of all forces 500 metres from

26

the border and the erection of additional UN observation posts on both sides of the ADL. The suggestions, based on the assumption that IDF patrols were provoking the Egyptian troops and that the ADL remained, as stated in the EIAA, a temporary military line, were promptly accepted by Nasser. But the Egyptian leader also warned that if Israel attacked again, he would react 'other than through the United Nations'. The Israelis, for the same reason, rejected Burns's plan. The posts, Ben Gurion explained, would infringe on Israel's sovereignty, and the pull-back would impair its ability to react swiftly to Egyptian aggression. Sharett requested a direct meeting with an Egyptian representative and, in virtually the same breath, warned Nasser of a possible IDF retaliation.[41]

Sporadic fighting occurred throughout April in the vicinity of Deir al-Balah/Ein Hashlosha, and in May spread to the Gaza City/Nahal Oz area. Finally, on 17 May, following the deaths of three IDF officers in a mine explosion near Kissufim, Israel retaliated by destroying an Egyptian bunker. Mortar duels erupted along the entire Gaza border, killing six Egyptian and an equal number of Israeli soldiers. Through indirect channels, Israel warned Cairo that it would occupy Gaza if such provocations continued.

Though still convinced of Israel's general responsibility for the border situation, the Powers blamed Egypt for the latest round of violence. Despite Nasser's assurances that strict ceasefire orders had been issued to his border troops, evidence was mounting of Egyptian involvement in mining and sniping. Now it was Israel's turn to demand a Tripartite condemnation of Egypt in the Security Council. But the Powers feared that such a resolution would hamper efforts to interest Nasser in the Alpha peace plan while almost certainly inviting a Soviet veto. To appease Israel while avoiding the Security Council, the Powers increased pressure on Egypt to replace the Palestinian troops deployed on the border and to fence certain areas of the ADL – points (2) and (3) of Burns's formula – and to agree to a direct meeting between high-ranking Egyptian and Israeli officials to discuss further tension-reducing measures.[42]

Having previously clashed with Israel's border policy, the Powers' proposals now conflicted with that of Egypt. Nasser still feared that Ben Gurion would introduce political topics into the high-level discussions, and complained of Israel's 'attempt to shoot its way into such talks'. At a tense meeting on 7 June, Nasser rebuffed Burns's entreaties, averring that he could not trust Ben Gurion nor, after Gaza, could he order his men to hold their fire. He suggested, instead, a one-kilometre pullback and the full demilitarization of the ADL – measures which, while also departures from the EIAA, did not imply such recognition.

27

These proposals proved unacceptable to Ben Gurion, who continued to demand a high-level meeting. The Powers strongly backed this insistence, exerting considerable pressure on Cairo to accept Burns's plan. On 8 June, they sponsored a Security Council resolution, scrupulously devoid of criticism of Egypt, calling for direct discussions on a ceasefire. Nasser relented – he could not easily ignore the resolution – but only after receiving the Powers' tacit assurances that Israel would not be allowed to use the talks as a framework for political negotiations.[43]

The direct talks opened on 28 June at Kilometre 95 on the Gaza border. The atmosphere, already tense from a rash of artillery exchanges at Deir al-Balah and reports of Israeli forces massing on the ADL, was further strained by Egypt's choice of Colonel Gohar as its spokesman. The appointment incensed the Israelis; Jerusalem had envisaged a meeting between heads of state or at least senior ambassadors. 'The whole thing', Sharett remarked to Lawson, the American ambassador, 'has fizzled out.' Nevertheless, Israel again named Tekoah as its representative, which in turn revived Egypt's suspicions of an Israeli attempt to turn the talks into peace negotiations.[44]

Despite these initial impediments, the meeting soon produced acceptance of an Israeli agenda (Appendix III) for the designation of a ten-metre security zone along the border, the organization of parallel patrols, the marking of the DZ, and the drafting of ceasefire orders. Agreement on a local commanders' arrangement, however, proved more elusive. Gohar insisted that a UNMO be present during all the commanders' conversations, even when conducted by telephone, and that the name of the agreement be changed to 'An Arrangement for Maintaining Order' to distinguish it from the Jordan–Israel precedent.

Egypt never fulfilled its offer to co-operate with Israel and the UN in marking the DZ border. On 5 August, two Egyptian bunkers fired on a joint UN–Israeli surveying team which discovered that the posts were actually situated within the zone. The IDF retaliated on 22 August with an assault on the Egyptian position on Hill 79, killing four Palestinians. Citing the attack as well as Israel's attempts to transform the meetings into political negotiations, Nasser withdrew from the Kilometre 95 talks. Exasperated, Burns resubmitted the border issue to the Security Council.[45]

Parallel to these events, the Egyptian army had continued its development of the Fida'iyun, recruiting and training similar units in Jordan and Lebanon. Several of these groups crossed Israel's borders on 25 August, killing nine civilians. The Israelis were perplexed as to the exact motivation behind this action. Some Foreign Ministry officials interpreted it as an attempt to preclude a reconvening of the Kilometre 95 talks; others as

28

a tactic to drive Jordan and Lebanon into Egypt's orbit by provoking Israeli retaliations against those countries.[46]

More plausibly, the Fida'iyun attacks reflected Nasser's continuing need to reconcile Egypt's political and security interests. Egypt's growing assertiveness in foreign policy, soon to be demonstrated in its massive arms deal with the Soviet Union, greatly raised the risks of war with Israel. Compelled to respond to Israeli border actions, but fearing his army incapable of defeating the IDF in war, Nasser again turned to the Fida'iyun. The attacks, reported with great hyberbole in the Egyptian press, served to preserve Egypt's image in the Arab world, but without provoking an Israeli reprisal. To further reduce the danger of an invasion, Nasser continued to deny any connection with the Fida'iyun. Secretly, the RCC assured the Israelis that the guerrillas had exceeded their intelligence-gathering orders and were 'an experiment that would not be repeated'.[47]

The claims of Egyptian propaganda notwithstanding, the raids did not cause mass destruction in Israel – twice as many Fida'iyun were killed as Israelis – but they did succeed in inflaming Israeli public opinion and thus in raising the possibility of a major IDF retaliation. Even before the last of the Fida'iyun had returned to base, Dulles wired Sharett to assure him that the Fida'iyun had not acted on Nasser's orders and urging him to refrain from retaliations. Simultaneously, Burns strove to secure agreement to a total ceasefire. Ben Gurion, however, would only acquiesce if Nasser assumed public responsibility for the Fida'iyun attacks. Though willing to recall the guerrillas to base, Nasser would not take responsibility for their actions.[48]

The IDF scheduled its reprisal for 29 August. At Sharett's insistence, however, the troops were recalled at the last minute in order to give a final opportunity to an American mediator, Elmore Jackson (see Chapter 5), to achieve a ceasefire. That night, however, the Fida'iyun killed two more civilians near Rehovot. The following evening, while Israeli soldiers kept UNMOs from entering the Gaza area, IDF units attacked the Egyptian army headquarters at Khan Yunis, a suspected centre of Fida'iyun activity. Casualties were 25 Fida'iyun, 19 civilians and 10 Egyptian soldiers killed and one Israeli dead.[49] Egypt's humiliation was compounded the next morning when, in the first dogfight between jets in the Middle East, Israel downed two Egyptian planes over the Negev.

Under threats of sanctions from the US, Egypt and Israel accepted a ceasefire on 4 September, thus ending two weeks of intensive fighting in which 70 people died. Five days later, the Security Council, at Burns's request, ordered the erection of barriers along the entire ADL, complete

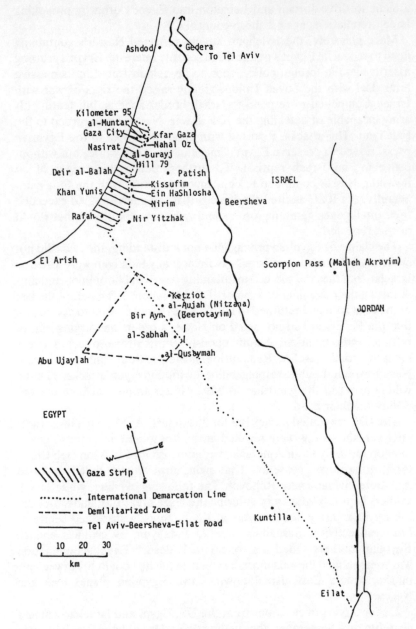

Fighting on the Egypt–Israel border 1952–56

freedom of movement for UNMOs, and the renewal of the Kilometre 95 talks. Burns's subsequent shuttling between Cairo and Jerusalem, however, failed to reveal any change in their basic policies towards the border.

ESCALATION AND INTERVENTION

Ben Gurion's refusal to accept the Security Council's demand for complete freedom of movement for the UNMOs did not prevent him from citing the same resolution to justify unilateral marking of the DZ. On 20 September, with Israel's work almost completed, Egyptian troops tore down the markers and reinforced their two posts inside the DZ.

Egypt's action may have aimed at deterring Israel from launching a pre-emptive strike from the zone. It coincided with Nasser's announcement of the Czech arms deal and the tightening of the blockade against Israeli shipping (Chapter 2) – moves likely to precipitate such an attack. Israel, however, reacted by introducing its own troops into al-Aujah, in the process occupying EIMAC headquarters and wounding its two Egyptian guards. The purpose, as Ben Gurion soon clarified, was to press for a simultaneous withdrawal of all forces from the DZ.

General Burns attempted to bring international pressure on Jerusalem to remove its troops from the DZ. Failing in this, he mediated an agreement by which Israel would replace its troops in the DZ with 30 members of the Israeli Border Guard to be stationed at Bir Ayn (Beerotayim). Egypt would relocate its posts from the zone to three ten-man positions on the DZ's western boundary, the so-called Qusaymah–Abu 'Ujaylah line. Nasser at first appeared amenable to the exchange, but within a week he began to allege that the Border Guard was in fact a paramilitary unit whose presence in the DZ violated the EIAA. Egyptian troops proceeded to mass along the Qusaymah–Abu 'Ujaylah line in numbers far in excess of those stipulated by Burns.

The situation in the DZ again placed the Powers in an awkward position. They believed that the presence of Israel's Border Police violated the EIAA's spirit, but that Egyptian troops had violated its letter by massing along the DZ. Still reeling from Egypt's arms deal with the Eastern bloc, the Powers were reluctant to alienate Egypt further or to grant the USSR an opportunity to veto an anti-Egypt resolution in the Security Council. Yet, the possible outbreak of another Arab–Israel war, and the absence of a Tripartite consensus on intervention, necessitated concerted diplomatic efforts to resolve the crisis. Having rejected a proposal from Canadian Foreign Minister Lester Pearson for the introduction of an international peacekeeping force into the DZ – the Soviets, it was feared, might insist on contributing troops to such a unit – the Powers requested Dag Hammarskjöld, the UN Secretary-General, to mediate in the DZ dispute.[50]

Hammarskjöld's approach was characterized by emphasis on strict interpretation of legal formulae and a profound commitment to protocol. As such, the former Swedish diplomat saw as his only goal the restoration of compliance with the EIAA to the state it had been prior to the DZ imbroglio. Specifically, he sought the evacuation of all troops from al-Aujah, and the marking of its controversial western border. This position conflicted with that of Ben Gurion, who now insisted that compliance with the border provisions of the EIAA be conditional on fulfilment of other articles proscribing war-like acts such as the Suez blockade. Egypt, however, was eager to separate the ceasefire aspects of the EIAA from those dealing with general belligerency. In coversations with his long-time acquaintance, Egyptian Foreign Minister Mahmud Fawzi, in New York, the Secretary-General learned that Egypt would agree to a uni-lateral UN marking of the DZ and a mutual return to the status quo ante in the zone.

Fawzi was an experienced diplomat who rarely failed to impress interlocutors with his moderation and fair-mindedness. But as Western representatives would increasingly discover, the views of Egypt's Foreign Minister were not necessarily those of its Head of State or the comman-ders of its armed forces, who truly determined Egyptian policy. Having received assurances from Fawzi that no action would be taken in the DZ during his absence, Burns flew to New York for consultations with Hammarskjöld. On that day, 25 October, Egyptian forces attacked the Israeli Border Police station at Bir Ayn.

The incident triggered a wave of unprecedented violence. Two days later, Israel destroyed the Egyptian army base at Kuntilla (Operation Egged), 100 miles south of the DZ. Egypt then deployed troops on al-Sabhah, a commanding ridge in the DZ's southern corner. On 3 November, Israel conducted Volcano, its largest operation since the 1948 war, which drove the Egyptians from al-Sabhah. Subsequently, the Egyptians regrouped on the Qusaymah–Abu 'Ujaylah line, while the IDF fortified its position at al-Sabhah. Both armies prevented UNMOs from entering the vicinity of the DZ. In less than a month of fighting, 11 Israelis and 82 Egyptians had been killed.

Hammarksjöld believed he had been close to securing Egypt's ap-proval of his tension-reducing measures at the time of the al-Sabhah battle. For the loss of this opportunity, as well as for border tension in general, he blamed Israel. In the wake of al-Sabhah, Hammarskjöld attempted to focus Tripartite pressure on Jerusalem to comply with his proposals. These were ultimately accepted by Ben Gurion, who had meanwhile replaced Sharett as Prime Minister, but only on the condition that Egypt fully implement the EIAA by withdrawing from the area around the DZ and by lifting the Suez Canal blockade. Nasser demanded the full withdrawal of Israeli units from the DZ, but also insisted on maintaining forces above the permitted levels on the Qusaymah–Abu 'Ujaylah line.

An uneasy stalemate ensued, during which Burns, working in tandem with Colonel Cyril Banks, a Conservative Member of the British Parliament, attempted to mediate a ceasefire. The two had succeeded in persuading Nasser to accept Israel's kibbutz and police station in the DZ in return for a mutual 500-metre pullback from the ADL. Cairo broke off the discussions on 11 December, however, following a massive IDF assault against Syrian positions on the Golan Heights, the so-called Tiberias raid, and threatened to retaliate for the aggression on its own border. In the face of such an explosive situation, Hammarskjöld had little option but to mediate personally between the belligerents.[51]

Hammarskjöld arrived in the Middle East on 21 January 1956. Angered by Ben Gurion's attempt to make acceptance of the tension-reducing measures conditional upon the removal of Egypt's positions west of the DZ, Hammarskjöld concentrated on securing a unilateral Israeli withdrawal from al-Aujah and a freeze on Israeli settlement-building in the zone. Unexpectedly, he found the Israelis now receptive to his ideas, perhaps as a result of the Security Council's blistering condemnation of the Tiberias raid the previous day, or because of the parallel mediation efforts of Robert B. Anderson, President Eisenhower's special peace emissary (see Chapter 5). Though Ben Gurion rebuffed the suggestions of both Hammarskjöld and Anderson for a voluntary Israeli pullback from the border, he accepted the general proposals for tension reduction and further requested the offices of both mediators in arranging a prisoner exchange with Egypt.

The Secretary-General was also received enthusiastically in Cairo, where Nasser evinced an interest in mitigating the DZ dispute while the West finalized its offer to finance the Aswan dam. Though the Egyptians would not agree to the prisoner exchange – it was to include those jailed in the Israeli sabotage plot – they did commit themselves to maintaining a ceasefire. These accomplishments resulted in a general amelioration of Egypt–Israel relations, inaugurating a period of relative calm on the border. In the EIMAC, the Israeli and Egyptian delegates agreed to consider some 130 complaints that had accumulated since September.[52]

The calm, however, proved illusory. While Hammarskjöld returned to New York to seek Security Council approval for more tension-reducing measures – troop pullbacks, a local commanders' agreement and guarantees for UNMO access to all areas of the ADL – friction returned to Egypt–Israel relations. Nasser refused Anderson's secret peace efforts and, on the border, ordered additional troops to the Qusaymah–Abu 'Ujaylah line. These actions, in addition to fighting in Gaza, firing on Israeli patrols, moved Ben Gurion to delay again the IDF's evacuation from the DZ. Nasser, for his part, refused to impose the ceasefire until all Israelis, including the police and the kibbutz members, were withdrawn from the zone and all IDF forces pulled back 500 metres from the border.

The Powers hoped that the Secretary-General would return to the Middle East before the situation could deteriorate further. Having assured Egypt that the mission would deal only with matters pertaining to the EIAA, in particular its ceasefire aspects, they managed to incorporate Hammarskjöld's tension-reducing measures in a Security Council resolution of 4 April. This designated him as the Special Agent for Palestine, charged with preventing the outbreak of war.[53]

Hammarskjöld returned to a veritable maelstrom. A concatenation of events, beginning with an Egyptian ambush of an Israeli patrol on the Gaza border and artillery exchanges between Israeli and Egyptian bunkers, led on 5 April to the IDF shelling of Gaza market; 66 Egyptians were killed and 135 wounded, most of them civilians.

Frustrated by his inability to cause commensurate damage to Israeli settlements, Nasser again responded with the Fida'iyun. Apart from periodic incursions from Lebanon and Jordan, these guerrilla forces had been held in abeyance since the summer. But on 7 April, some 200 Fida'iyun crossed the ADL, their mission to inflict Israeli casualties equal to those suffered by the Palestinians in Gaza. The raids, in fact, caused relatively little damage – four Israelis and 16 Fida'iyun were killed – but they effectively undermined Hammarskjöld's mission.[54]

Arriving in Israel on 8 April, the Secretary-General abandoned his terms of reference and instead focused on achieving Egypt's recall of the Fida'iyun and an Israeli pledge not to retaliate. Ben Gurion charged that the Fida'iyun were only the latest instance of Egypt's persistent violation of the EIAA and gave Nasser only 48 hours to impose a ceasefire. Nasser's position also appeared to have hardened. Convinced that Israel would not respond with a full-scale war (see Chapter 6), and that the raids would generate support for his leadership throughout the Arab world, Nasser did not hasten to order the Fida'iyun back to base.

Confronted with such implacable opposition, Hammarskjöld appealed to President Eisenhower, who sent cables to Ben Gurion and Nasser warning of American military intervention if the two failed to respond to Hammarskjöld's requests. The threat proved ineffective; in addition to

34

expressing resentment over the use of pressure tactics, Ben Gurion refused to commit himself to refraining from retaliation, while Nasser, claiming he had no means of recalling the Fida'iyun, would not issue a ceasefire.

Activist elements in the RCC opposed acceding to Hammarskjöld's proposals, but international pressure, combined with his concern for Western funding of the Aswan dam project, led Nasser to concede. On 11 April, he reaffirmed to the Secretary-General his commitment to uphold Article II, paragraph 2, of the EIAA, which proscribed the perpetration of 'warlike or hostile acts'. But in making the declaration, Nasser also asserted Egypt's right to act militarily in self-defence. Hammarskjöld was willing to accept this in lieu of a ceasefire pledge, but the Israelis were furious. Not only had Nasser's qualification nullified his declaration but, in their view, Hammarskjöld had agreed to separate observance of Article II from compliance with the rest of the EIAA.

Stormy meetings between Hammarskjöld and Ben Gurion, further strained by the downing of another Egyptian jet in the Negev, eventually produced a parallel reaffirmation from Jerusalem, but only after a second letter of warning was sent by Eisenhower to the Prime Minister. On 18 April, the Secretary-General reported to the Security Council on Egypt and Israel's agreement to a complete ceasefire as well as to a 100-metre pullback and the construction of UNMO posts on both sides of the Gaza ADL.[55]

These accomplishments appeared to restore the status quo, but in reality they had contributed to its deterioration. In the view of both Ben Gurion and Nasser, the Powers had demonstrated their willingness to compromise on – if not abandon – aspects of the EIAA. With these checks removed, the two leaders felt fewer restraints in resorting to more general aggression.

Encouraged by his success, Hammarskjöld next undertook to arrange a similar ceasefire between Israel and Syria, and at the same time to seek a solution to the problem of the Demilitarized zone. With regard to the latter, Hammarskjöld devised what he termed the Suez–al-Aujah nexus: the exchange of Israel's withdrawal from the zone for Egypt's lifting of the Canal blockade. The proposal, which evolved in response to Ben Gurion's repeated efforts to link the border and Canal issues under the EIAA, was encouraged by Hammarskjöld in a private capacity, for it fell outside his terms of reference as a mediator. Nasser vigorously denied any connection between the border and the blockade but Fawzi offered 'some relaxation' of the blockade in return for a complete Israeli evacuation of the DZ.[56]

This development revived the Powers' optimism, if not that of Ham-

35

marskjöld – the Secretary-General remained pessimistic about the cease-fire's longevity – with regard to the chance of political agreements between Egypt and Israel.

Hammarskjöld's predictions were substantiated. In the final week of April, while the Secretary-General was mediating in Damascus, the Fida'iyun killed eight Israeli civilians in the Negev. Hammarskjöld personally appealed to Ben Gurion for restraint, though in fact there was little need to do so. While Fida'iyun raids continued throughout May, with Nasser showing increasing willingness to claim credit for their attacks, the IDF did not retaliate. Ben Gurion concluded that such action would hinder Israel's efforts to acquire Western arms and thus its ability to strike Egypt pre-emptively before Nasser could use his new Soviet weaponry.[57]

Thus, for nearly a year before the Sinai Campaign, Israel refrained from any large-scale military action against Egypt. During that period there occurred only two exceptions to this rule, both in the summer of 1956. In mid-July, Israel undertook the letter-bomb assassinations of Mustafa Hafiz, the Gaza intelligence chief, and of Salah Mustafa, Egypt's military attaché in Amman, both of whom it considered responsible for the Fida'iyun attacks. A month later, following the deaths of five civilians by mines on the Beersheva–Eilat road, the IDF killed 13 Egyptian soldiers in ambushes along the DZ. On the border itself, Israel worked to improve its strategic position by building up its forces in and around al-Aujah and by establishing a new kibbutz, Beerotayim, on the site of the former Border Police station.[58]

THE BORDER AS *CASUS BELLI*

The Security Council on 6 June approved a British resolution providing for the resumption of Hammarskjöld mission. In addition to empowering him to achieve compliance with his previous tension-reducing measures, the resolution also charged the Secretary-General with reconciling the fundamental Israeli and Arab disagreements on peace.

From the outset, Hammarskjöld's mission ran into stiff opposition. In their first meeting on 19 July, the Secretary-General discovered that Ben Gurion was again furious over what he claimed was the reduction of the EIAA to a mere ceasefire; Israel still refused to evacuate the DZ or to allow UNMOs unlimited movement in the zone. In Egypt, where he had expected to encounter the same goodwill which had characterized his previous negotiations, Hammarskjöld found the atmosphere equally unaccommodating. Embittered by the recent Anglo-American decision to cancel funding for the Aswan dam, Nasser was in no mood to consider

THE BORDER

a Western peace initiative. Apart from an apparently unauthorized proposal from Fawzi for secret mediation between Egypt and Israel, the Egyptian leadership refused to co-operate on border matters; Nasser specifically rejected the Secretary-General's plan for a three-month unconditional ceasefire.[59]

Hammarskjöld continued his mediation throughout August but with no more success. In a final report to the Council on 12 September, he conceded his failure to convert verbal assurances for ceasefires into binding legal documents. The admission generated little attention, however, for by that time his efforts had been overshadowed by the Suez crisis.

Nasser's nationalization of the Suez Canal on 26 July brought a dramatic improvement in the border situation. In contrast to the previous four years, during which tensions between the two countries had escalated almost uninterruptedly, the summer of 1956 seemingly witnessed the re-establishment of the status quo. In an effort to dissuade Israel from taking advantage of either the immediate political crisis or of the anticipated Anglo-French attack, Nasser greatly moderated his position on Palestine. Hostile propaganda was reduced and the blockade relaxed and, on the border, infiltration and challenges to Israel's presence in the DZ virtually ceased. Nasser issued strict orders removing the Fida'iyun from Gaza and forbidding his regular border forces from provoking Israeli patrols. Following the assassinations of Hafiz and Mustafa, the RCC announced: 'These acts testify to the extent of the confusion in Ben Gurion's policies. Egypt wants peace, and despite its prerogatives, has no intention of attacking anyone.'

A similar restraint characterized the RCC's reactions to Israel's repeated attacks on the West Bank: 'We must know how to restrict and control ourselves. The battle is not with Israel but with those who give her orders.'[60]

Ben Gurion was little impressed by the change in Nasser's attitude, especially as he held Egypt responsible for the Fida'iyun raids which continued to emanate from the West Bank. Persuaded of the Powers' indifference to the EIAA, he remained more than ever committed to the pre-emptive strike. Having secured a reliable source of arms (see Chapter 4), Ben Gurion only hesitated for fear of international sanctions and Egyptian air power. Such concerns, however, were largely removed on 24 October by the signing of the Sèvres Accords (Chapter 6), Israel's secret pact with Britain and France for the invasion of Egypt.

For Egypt, the need to mollify Israel gradually diminished as the Suez crisis neared its apparent resolution in the UN. Domestic and regional elements soon began to compel Nasser to resume his leadership of the

37

Palestine struggle. His decision to return to that role was evident in the redeployment of the Fida'iyun in Gaza. Four groups of Fida'iyun struck in Israel on 26 October, purportedly wounding 24 civilians. Israel had its *casus belli*. Operation Kadesh, the Israeli invasion of Sinai, could be described, at least in its initial communiqués, as a limited strike against guerrilla bases.

2

Boycott and Blockade

The Suez Canal was removed, physically, from the points of direct Egypt–Israel interaction; 150 miles separated it from the ADL at its closest point. Yet, like the border, the Canal lay at the core of Egypt–Israel tensions and, ultimately, of the second Arab–Israel war. Much of this friction could be traced to a single source: the ban on Israeli vessels and contraband cargoes known collectively as the Egyptian blockade.

The Egyptian blockade was an integral part of the Arab economic boycott of Israel. First proclaimed by the Arab League in 1945 with an embargo of Palestinian Jewish products, the boycott was expanded after 1949 to prohibit commerce between Arabs and Israelis and to discourage foreign firms from doing business with the Jewish State. Like support for infiltration, the boycott provided another means for Arab leaders to demonstrate their commitment to the Palestine cause while in effect remaining passive towards it. In this respect, the blockade, defined by international law as an act of war, was the most tangible expression of the Arab interpretation of the Armistice. In addition to its symbolic purposes, however, the boycott also served the more concrete purpose of protecting Arab markets from Israeli competition.[1]

The political and economic benefits of the boycott policy were considerably enhanced by the fact that it incurred few risks. Though an act of war, it could be applied selectively – the blockade did not, for example, extend to Israel's coasts – thus minimizing the danger of Israeli retaliation. Furthermore, conduct of the boycott cost the Arab states little, either financially or politically. Western governments, though opposed to the policy in principle, did nothing to challenge it, while Western corporations, if sometimes begrudgingly, complied with its provisions.[2]

Though Arab leaders often boasted that the boycott was dealing the enemy a major, if not mortal, blow, Israel continued to expand economically. Israeli businessmen succeeded in circumventing many of the boycott restrictions, and routinely camouflaged their products under false labels for export, sometimes even to destinations in the Arab world. Arab countries and corporations were also not above violating the boycott, provided the transactions could be sufficiently dissembled. Incapable of

39

isolating Israel's economy entirely, the Arab states placed added stress on Egypt's blockade of the Suez Canal, Israel's lifeline – or so they believed – to the outside world.

The Canal blockade also served Egypt's political and economic interests. Fearing losses to its own economy, Egypt often ignored the Arab boycott, for example, the embargo on Cyprus, imposed in December 1952 in response to the island's role in re-exporting Israeli goods. The blockade enabled Egypt to compensate for these violations as well as for its inability to confront Israel militarily. When asked by Arab journalists when Egypt would launch a war against Israel, General Naguib replied: 'We are succeeding more without war through the boycott of Israel. Its effect is one of real war.'[3]

More concretely, the blockade impeded Israel's economic penetration of Egypt's traditional East African and Sudanese markets and, by reducing the flow of crude oil through the Haifa refineries, bolstered Egypt's own fledgling oil industry.[4]

Beginning as a ban on Israeli flagships, the blockade was broadened between the years 1949 and 1952 to prohibit third-party vessels from carrying Jewish immigrants or contraband war materials – arms and oil – to Israel. Ships suspected of transporting such cargoes were blacklisted. The tightening of the blockade was not, however, accompanied by greater meticulousness in its application, which remained lax. Nevertheless, the image of the blockade fulfilled Cairo's propaganda needs and hampered Israel's trade by driving up shipping and insurance costs for cargoes carried to and from Haifa via the Canal.

The Canal controversy in certain ways resembled the border dispute. Both arose from the conflicting Israeli and Egyptian interpretations of the EIAA. The Israelis insisted that since the EIAA had ended the *status belli*, it vitiated an act of war such as the blockade. The Egyptians argued that an Armistice, according to international law, did not end a state of war, and therefore, the blockade was legal. To substantiate their positions, Egypt and Israel both referred to the 1888 Constantinople Convention on the Suez Canal. Cairo claimed that Article X of that treaty expressly empowered it to take measures in the Canal to ensure Egypt's defence. Israel refuted this argument by citing Articles I and X. These, respectively, stated that the Canal 'shall always be free and open, in time of war as in time of peace, to every vessel of commerce or war, without distinction of flag', and that measures taken under Article X 'shall not interfere with the free use of the Canal'.[5]

The Canal issue, like that of the border, was exacerbated by conflicting claims of sovereignty. Cairo asserted that the Canal was Egyptian territory; Israel, that it was an international, extra-territorial body. These positions created some curious contradictions within Israeli and Egyptian policy. While holding that the blockade violated the EIAA, Israel also contended that the Canal itself, by virtue of its international status, fell outside the Armistice's territorial scope. Egypt, aware that the West also rejected its claims to the Canal, assigned civilians to implement the blockade. Had Suez indeed belonged to Egypt, the task would have fallen to the army.

For the Israelis, the blockade, no less than the border, was a constant reminder of the Arabs' refusal to make peace and their commitment to a 'second round'. Equally disconcerting, it demonstrated the Powers' indifference to Israel's interests. But in contrast to the border, which afforded ample latitude for diplomatic and military action, Israel had scant recourse against the blockade. Egypt's legal argument, based on international law, the 1888 Convention and Britain's precedent in blockading the Canal during the two World Wars, was virtually unassailable. Nor could Israel act militarily against the blockade – the IDF once proposed dynamiting bridges over the Canal – without incurring international sanctions. Israel's position was further weakened by the fact that the blockade's impact was more symbolic than substantive. Unlike the border situation, which affected the safety of many Israelis, the blockade, which allowed most types of cargoes to reach Israel on foreign ships, caused relatively minor losses to Israel's economy.[6]

The Israelis, thus, had only limited means for combating the blockade. They could make propaganda against it, though by emphasizing their economic losses they risked confirming Egypt's claims of the blockade's efficacy. At the Foreign Ministry, numerous plans were devised: an international Jewish embargo on Egyptian products, a campaign to discourage foreign investment in Egypt, even an Eilat–Mediterranean canal to bypass Suez. None was adopted. In the end, Jerusalem was left with no choice but to challenge the blockade in the UN Security Council, in a case based on moral rather than legal grounds.[7]

The blockade began as an essentially bilateral issue between Israel and Egypt but, like the border conflict, it became increasingly multilateral with the intervention of the Great Powers. Such involvement was only natural, as the Suez Canal represented a major, and in some cases paramount, interest of the Powers.

The Tripartite Powers shared Israel's desire to refute Egypt's territorial claims over the Canal, but they nevertheless opposed its efforts to impugn the blockade in the Security Council. Unaffected themselves by the blockade, the Powers feared that the issue, if pressed, could cause them considerable harm. In addition to generating further Arab animosity towards the West, it could create a precedent for contesting

America's status in the Panama Canal, endanger the supply of France's colonies in the Far East, and obstruct Britain's efforts to renegotiate its treaty with Egypt. Consequently, the Powers' policy towards the blockade was similar to that towards the Egypt–Israel border, namely, to preserve the status quo until circumstances permitted a comprehensive solution to the Arab–Israel conflict.[8]

The Powers' policy, however, was not always tenable. Having publicly deplored the blockade as a violation of the spirit, if not the letter, of the EIAA, the Powers could not fail to support Israel if it succeeded in bringing the issue before the Security Council. Thus, in September 1951, when the Israeli ambassador presented the Council with a formal complaint about the blockade, the Powers' delegates tried to have it referred to the EIMAC. But the EIMAC, in view of the civilian nature of the blockade, found it had no jurisdiction over the matter and returned it to the Council. There, the Powers had little choice but to support Israel with a resolution condemning the blockade as inconsistent with the EIAA and ordering 'free and open transit through the Canal without discrimination, overt or covert.'[9]

Over the next five years, the blockade would reflect the growing assertiveness of Egypt in the Arab–Israel conflict. This development stemmed from factors endogenous to the Arab world: domestic pressures and regional rivalries. The process, however, would be greatly accelerated by Israel, which launched a series of diplomatic and military measures against the blockade, as well as by the Powers, whose increasing intervention in Middle East affairs provoked both Egypt and Israel alike.

THE FREE OFFICERS INHERIT THE BLOCKADE

Egypt refused to comply with the 1951 resolution, and Israel's repeated attempts to appeal the matter to the Security Council were rebuffed by the Powers. The US and Britain were reluctant to address the issue at a time of renewed efforts to resolve the Anglo-Egyptian dispute. With the collapse of those efforts in the spring of 1952, however, the two Powers communicated to Israel their support for a UN review of the blockade. Then, in July, the Egyptian revolution provided the Powers with another excuse for delaying the debate on the grounds that it would prove counter-productive to Israel's efforts to establish contact with the new regime. Ben Gurion accepted this rationale. He ordered Israel's complaint to be withdrawn from the Security Council and, through the Americans, sent a message to General Naguib explaining that the démarche had been planned before the coup and was not directed at the Free Officers.[10]

For the Israelis, the blockade was another barometer of the new regime's interest in improved relations. Initially, the Officers seemed content with maintaining the status quo, neither relaxing nor tightening the restrictions. Then, suddenly, on 31 October, Egyptian customs authorities seized the *Rimfrost*, a Norwegian freighter en route through the Canal to Haifa with a cargo of Ethiopian meat. Noting that the *Rimfrost* had made the same voyage before without problem and that the incident coincided with Naguib's attempt to dominate Arab opposition to the reparations treaty, the Israeli Foreign Ministry concluded that Egypt now included foodstuffs on the contraband list. This was a serious development – Israel depended on Ethiopia for 70 per cent of its meat imports – and warranted a complaint to the Security Council.[11]

The *Rimfrost* seizure, while undoubtedly raising Egypt's prestige in the Arab world, threatened to undermine the Free Officers' efforts to foster an international image as reliable caretakers of the Canal. In exploring ways of averting a Security Council debate, the regime discovered that the customs officials had acted on the assumption that the *Rimfrost*'s cargo was Sudanese. The release of an Ethiopian cargo would prove far less difficult to explain to the Arab world. The seizure was subsequently overruled by an Egyptian prize court and the *Rimfrost* was allowed to continue its journey. Lieutenant Colonel Gohar in the EIMAC even apologized to Lieutenant Colonel Gaon. These gestures, however, did not satisfy Ben Gurion. Ignoring the Powers' warnings, he proceeded with the complaint to the Security Council. The result was a diplomatic embarrassment for the Israelis. At the opening session on 6 January 1953, the Egyptian delegate readily admitted to having erred in the *Rimfrost* incident, thereby rendering additional debate superfluous.[12]

Egypt had managed to escape condemnation in the UN, but it could not maintain the status quo in the Canal. Over the course of the following year, the RCC became increasingly dependent on the blockade as a means of establishing its domestic position and of advancing its regional ambitions. The Arab states, unable to respond to the growing number of Israeli border actions, also stressed the blockade and urged Egypt to tighten restrictions. In addition, 1953–54 witnessed an economic crisis in Egypt with the collapse of the regime's fiscal reforms. By expanding the blockade, the RCC hoped to deflect attention from its failures and from its growing inability to comply with the boycott.[13]

Shortly after the *Rimfrost* affair, the Officers tightened restrictions in the Canal. Henceforth, captains had to sign pledges that their ships would not call at Israeli ports after passing through the Canal; vessels blacklisted

43

for carrying Israeli cargoes were refused port facilities, even water, at the Canal's termini. The survivors of the *Tirennia*, a Finnish ship which sank in the Red Sea on 27 January 1953, were denied shelter by Egypt because the rescuing vessel, the Norwegian *Olaf Ringle*, was on the blacklist.[14]

Observers at the Israeli Foreign Ministry saw these measures as auguring the extension of the contraband laws to either East African foodstuffs or oil shipments from the Persian Gulf. Thus they were surprised when, on 2 September 1953, Egyptian officials seized the Greek freighter *Parnon* in the Canal, claiming that its Israel-bound cargo of asphalt constituted war material. Foreign Minister Sharett immediately petitioned the Powers to convene an emergency session of the Security Council. Once again, however, the Powers resisted; such a debate would interfere with their efforts to mediate the controversy over Israel's project to divert the Jordan river. They did, however, exert heavy pressure on Cairo, making it clear that they would have to support Israel's case if the *Parnon* were not released.[15]

The RCC again backed down and freed the *Parnon*. It could not, however, repeat the success of the brinkmanship strategy employed in the *Rimfrost* incident. Sharett hailed the *Parnon* affair as a great moral victory. The Arab press, on the other hand, responded with a spate of anti-Egyptian editorials. The RCC's National Guidance Minister Salah Salem had to call a special press conference to refute charges that the *Parnon*'s release represented a breach of Arab unity.[16]

The RCC acted swiftly to restore its prestige. At the end of November, it announced that henceforth the contraband law would include not only foodstuffs, but cotton, chemicals and precious metals 'likely to strengthen the war potential of the Zionists'. To supervise the full application of these restrictions, the RCC also created a new boycott committee comprising the chiefs of the Coast Guard and Aviation Control and chaired by Mahmud Riad.[17] A month later, on 20 December, Egypt seized the Italian freighter *Franca Maria* in the Canal and impounded its cargo of Ethiopian meat destined for Israel.

The RCC's démarche was directed at the blockade not only of the Suez Canal but of the Tiran Straits as well. Prior to this time, the Tiran blockade had existed only in principle. Since 1949, Egypt had leased from Saudi Arabia the Strait's two islands, Tiran and Sanafir, in order to 'keep the Jews out of the Gulf'. But Israel, though quick to exploit the Tiran blockade for propaganda purposes, had yet to develop a Red Sea port. In the absence of Israeli traffic, the Egyptian units stationed at Tiran were no more than a nuisance to neutral shipping. In July 1951 they fired on the HMS *Empire Roach*, and in November 1953 on the USS *Albion*, in both cases causing extensive damage.[18]

The situation changed dramatically in June 1952, with the dedication of Eilat. Israeli leaders, above all Ben Gurion, looked to the port to serve as Israel's gateway to Asia and Africa and as the key to the Negev's development. For the Egyptians, however, Eilat represented a post from which Israel could dominate Egypt's traditional markets, strengthen the territorial division between Egypt and the Arab world, and strike militarily at Egypt's vulnerable Eastern front. In addition to bringing political benefits to Egypt, the Tiran blockade was designed to strangulate Eilat.[19]

The Tiran controversy further complicated the debate surrounding the Suez blockade. Egypt claimed ownership of the Straits on the basis of 1906 Anglo-Ottoman treaty, which recognized Egypt's administration of the Sinai peninsula. Israel retorted that the 1906 Treaty made no mention of the Straits and that, in any case, Egypt had expressly waived any claim to sovereignty over Tiran in a 1950 note to the US State Department. Egypt also contended that the Straits, as part of Egypt, were covered by the EIAA, but that Israel could not appeal the blockade to the EIMAC as the port of Eilat, having been occupied illegally in violation of a 1949 UN truce, was not Israeli territory. Israel asserted that while the EIMAC had jurisdiction over Eilat, it had none over the Straits; the EIAA not only predated Egypt's occupation of Tiran, but insofar as it affected an international waterway, the Straits blockade was solely a matter for the UN.[20]

Unlike the Suez Canal, the Powers had virtually no interests in Tiran. As a result, Egypt had no hesitation in deploying its army above the Straits and Israel felt no restrictions in attempting to break the blockade by force. In January 1953, Ben Gurion determined to test the Tiran blockade by dispatching a Danish freighter, the *Andreas Boye*, through the Straits to Eilat. The plan was to respond to the ship's seizure by simultaneously lodging a complaint with the Security Council and launching an air attack on the Egyptian shore positions. The plan proved abortive. Egyptian troops fired on and boarded the *Andreas Boye*, but released the ship before Israel could undertake any action, either military or diplomatic.

Israel nevertheless revived the tactic in November when, as part of its extension of the Canal restrictions, the RCC announced the tightening of the Straits blockade. Israel sent another ship, the *Maria Antonia*, through the Straits in the hope that Egyptian interference would serve as the basis for challenging both blockades in the Security Council. This time the Egyptians obliged; the *Maria Antonia* was turned back at Tiran and Israel opened its offensive in New York.[21]

The Israelis, however, again encountered opposition from the Tripartite Powers. For all their differences on the issue, Egypt and Israel agreed to view the Straits and Canal blockades as one. In contrast, the Powers insisted on distinguishing between Suez and Tiran. While the former was an international problem to be considered within the framework of the UN, the latter was strictly an Egypt–Israel affair, subject to the decisions of the EIMAC.

Israel's strategy in the UN was to depict the Canal and Straits blockades as threats to international shipping. France and Britain agreed to sponsor a debate on the Canal blockade, their motive being to interest the US in a secret consortium of Maritime Powers to co-ordinate action in case Egypt closed the Canal. They refused, however, to include Tiran in the discussion. The Eisenhower Administration rejected the consortium proposal – it allegedly smacked of imperialism – and opposed consideration of the blockade until after resolution of the Jordan waters and British evacuation controversies.[22] Undeterred, the Israelis proceeded with their complaint, thereby creating a fait accompli which the Powers could not ignore.

The period of the Security Council debate coincided with Ben Gurion's retirement and Sharett's assumption of the premiership. Having publicly upheld the primacy of diplomacy in Israel–Arab relations, Sharett faced the first test of his convictions in the debate. These were already being questioned by Dayan and Lavon who, in view of rising tensions on the Egypt–Israel border, began to press for military action against the blockade. Sharett sent messages to Cairo by direct and indirect channels offering to cancel the complaint if Egypt lifted the blockades. The initiative brought some success. Egypt agreed to cease implementation of the November 1953 amendments and gradually to reduce restrictions, but in return demanded that Israel dismantle the kibbutz it had recently established in the Demilitarized Zone. Sharett could not meet this condition. The kibbutz, representing one of Ben Gurion's last acts in office and symbolizing the pioneering enterprise in the Negev, was inviolate.[23]

No less than in Israel, the debate occurred during a period of particular instability in the Egyptian government. Shaken internally by the widening rift between pro-Naguib and pro-Nasser factions, the RCC confronted mounting threats from the IDF, the Muslim Brotherhood, and, most menacingly, the British. The latter had broken off the evacuation talks and were now engaged in efforts to place the Canal under international control, thereby negating any Egyptian claims to Suez. In their public speeches as well as in private conversations, RCC leaders averred that the Israeli complaint was the product of British machinations designed to embarrass Egypt and to cast doubts on its ability to guarantee free shipping through the Canal.[24]

The RCC thus found itself in the grip of another dilemma. On one hand, the Egyptians needed to avoid another Security Council condemnation, but on the other, they could not slacken the blockade at a time of mounting domestic opposition and Israeli border provocations. The offer to relax the blockade quietly in return for withdrawal of both the complaint and the kibbutz presented an ideal answer, but the Israelis balked. The RCC was compelled to resort to its former brinkmanship policy. On 30 January 1954, just days before commencement of the debate, Egypt released the *Franca Maria* and assured the Powers that there would be no further seizures.[25]

The Security Council's consideration of Israel's complaint was scheduled to open in the first week of February, but immediately before that time an event occurred which altered the course not only of the debate, but of the entire Arab–Israel conflict. On 21 January, in voting on a Security Council resolution for Tripartite mediation of the Jordan river dispute, the Soviet Union, for the first time in relation to the Palestine issue, used its veto.

The event cast a heavy shadow over the impending blockade debate. The Israelis now had to dispel the Powers' fears of another Soviet move to curry Arab favour at the West's expense. Israeli diplomats tried to convince Western representatives that Moscow would support a resolution condemning the blockade – the Russians, after all, had an interest in free passage through straits – and intimated the possibility of Israeli military action in Tiran. The Powers were, in the end, persuaded but only on the condition that the resolution be sponsored by a minor Maritime country less likely to provoke a Soviet veto.[26]

The Security Council debate matched in opposition two seasoned diplomats, Israel's Abba Eban and Mahmud Azmi of Egypt. In public, they were formidable rivals. Eban accused Egypt of piracy and called for international sanctions against the blockade. Azmi contrasted the laxity of the blockade with the severity of Israeli border actions. Out of 32,000 ships inspected for contraband since 1950, he claimed, only 50 had been detained and no goods had been confiscated.

In private, however, Azmi and Eban enjoyed a good working relationship. Azmi, who exhibited understanding for Israel's position (his wife was Jewish), was also known to be close to the Egyptian government. Twice, in July 1951 and in March 1952, Eban presented Azmi with peace plans which, though not acceptable to the Egyptians, helped establish a direct line of communication at the UN. Thus the RCC turned to the Azmi–Eban channel in an attempt to avoid a condemnation by the Security Council. The effort, however, failed. Azmi repeated the offer to reduce restrictions in return for withdrawal of the complaint; no mention

47

was made of the kibbutz. For Eban, however, this was insufficient. 'If a man were brought into court for assaulting his neighbour,' the Israeli ambassador expounded, 'he could hardly win acquittal by a promise to beat him with somewhat lesser violence in the future.'[27]

In a final manoeuvre to dissuade the Powers from supporting the complaint, Azmi called for the re-examination of the 1888 Convention by its original signatories. This would have given the USSR, as successor to Czarist Russia, an entrée into the Canal's management. The Powers, however, were not intimidated. In the final week of March, they convened the Council to consider a resolution sponsored by New Zealand. The document contained a strongly-worded condemnation of Egypt for the two blockades, which were recognized as inseparable except that the EIMAC had the right to examine cases of seizure in the Straits. The vote, taken on 30 March, resulted in another shock for Israel and the West. The USSR, which had abstained on the 1951 resolution, again used its veto. The Soviet ambassador explained that the blockade was only one aspect of the conflict which could not be solved by denouncing one of its parties in a rehashed resolution.

The failure of the resolution, while representing a major diplomatic defeat for Sharett, succeeded temporarily in restoring the status quo in the Canal. With the renewal of the evacuation talks with Britain in the spring of 1954, Nasser endeavoured to play down the blockade. He quietly dropped the November 1953 amendments as well as the ban on providing port facilitites to blacklisted ships, and even reduced the size of the blacklist by 25 per cent.[28] Proof of Nasser's determination to deny Israel an excuse to interfere with the negotiations was the fact that, parallel to adopting these measures, he ignored several Arab League decisions expanding the boycott.[29]

For the Israelis, however, the relaxation of the blockade was immaterial. Though reduced, the basic reality of the blockade continued to inflate the costs of shipping and insuring Israeli cargoes through the Canal. The blockade also remained the backbone of the Arab boycott, which in 1954 managed to curtail oil shipments from the Persian Gulf sheikhdoms to Israel and to restrict greatly Israeli trade with East Africa. But the blockade's political significance, rather than its economic impact, was still paramount in Israeli thinking, as a symbol of the Arabs' refusal to end the state of war and of the Powers' willingness to appease that position. With the UN effectively disqualified as an arena for challenging Egypt's policy in the Canal, Sharett viewed the evacuation talks as providing a last opportunity for resolving the blockade policy by diplomatic means.

THE EVACUATION

The Israelis, as noted in Chapter 1, considered Britain's evacuation from the Canal Zone as a dire threat to the status quo. In their estimation, the event would not only tilt the strategic balance in Egypt's favour, but would allow Egypt to issue a total ban on Israel-bound shipping through the Canal. While they could not openly oppose the evacuation in principle – Israelis were fond of flaunting their own victory over British imperialism – they privately worked to portray Egypt as incapable of guaranteeing free shipping in the Canal after Britain's departure. Israeli diplomats appealed to the Powers to make the evacuation conditional on, *inter alia*, the complete lifting of the blockade.

Israeli leaders, who had already weathered the failed evacuation talks of 1950–51, knew that the approaching expiration of the Anglo-Egyptian treaty in 1956 necessitated further efforts to reach an agreement, and preferred that the negotiations should occur during a time when Egypt's bargaining position was weakest. Thus, in the period of domestic instability which followed the Egyptian revolution, the Israeli Embassy in London actually pressed Whitehall to renew the talks. It abruptly abandoned this course in April 1953, however, when the RCC, now more firmly established, invited Britain to the negotiating table.[30]

The withdrawal of 38,000 British soldiers from the Canal Zone, ending Britain's 70-year presence in the country, was the RCC's priority goal. Even before the revolution, Egyptian leaders had come to view the evacuation together with the Sudan issue as the *sine qua non* of Egyptian independence and national fulfilment, vital not only to domestic stability but to regional primacy. The Free Officers inherited this conviction and reinforced it with their youth and militarism. With the signing of the Anglo-Egyptian agreement on Sudan in February 1953, the RCC concentrated its full energy on the evacuation.

The RCC was wary of Israel's intention to obstruct the evacuation and was convinced that a secret Anglo-Israeli alliance existed to that end. Egyptian leaders believed that Israeli attacks on the Syrian and Jordanian borders were co-ordinated with Britain in an effort to intimidate Egypt and weaken its resolve on the Suez issue. Their suspicions indeed seemed confirmed when, following a breakdown in the evacuation talks on 6 May 1953, Winston Churchill, Britain's Prime Minister, condemned Egypt for exercising Nazi-style terrorism and praised Israel as 'the most important state in the Middle East'.[31]

Fear of Israeli interference in the evacuation led Egypt to be more solicitous of Israel's apprehensions. In contrast to the US and Britain, which tended to dismiss Israel's complaints and to prefer a total separa-

49

tion of the Palestine and Suez problems, Cairo often referred to the evacuation issue in its direct and indirect contacts with Jerusalem (see Chapter 5). Repeatedly in these communications, Egyptian diplomats assured their Israeli counterparts that their government would address the question of peace once the evacuation talks were completed. On one occasion it was suggested that the new Anglo-Egyptian treaty might include an Egypt–Israel non-belligerency pact.[32]

The Anglo-Egyptian negotiations resumed on an informal basis on 30 July 1953 and quickly foundered on the questions of the status of British technicians remaining in the Zone after the evacuation and the conditions under which the base would be reactivated. Israel's interests were not raised during these discussions. The Israeli Foreign Ministry repeatedly appealed to Britain's Foreign Office to make the treaty conditional on guarantees for Israel's safety and shipping rights. The Israelis even proposed the transfer of the Canal Zone base to Gaza as a means of maintaining the buffer.[33]

Sir Anthony Eden, Britain's new Prime Minister, rebuffed Israel's entreaties. Convinced that the evacuation would increase the danger of Israeli, rather than of Egyptian, aggression, he instructed British representatives to do no more than assure the Israelis that their interests would not 'be lost from view' in the talks.[34] The complete failure of Israel's lobbying efforts, coupled with the frustration of its initiatives against the blockade in the Security Council, seriously eroded the credibility of Sharett's diplomacy-over-militancy approach to dealing with the Egyptians.

The Anglo-Egyptian talks broke down on 21 October and resumed after an eight-month hiatus. Finally, on 27 July 1954, Egyptian and British negotiators signed the Heads of Agreement, a document containing the guidelines for the evacuation. In addition to its failure to take into account Israel's security concerns, the Agreement made no reference to the blockade or to Israel's demand for free passage. Over the following three months, during which time Egypt and Britain hammered out the details of their final treaty, London attempted to soften the blow by making vague assurances to Israel of measures to bolster its security; nothing, however, was said of the blockade. Conscious of these omissions, British officials began to fear that Israel might 'commit some folly' to torpedo the evacuation.[35]

ISRAEL AGAINST THE EVACUATION

On 28 September, 1954 the Israeli flagship *Bat Galim* entered Port Tawfiq with a cargo of Ethiopian meat and wood destined for Haifa.

Overriding the objections of senior IDF officers who still favoured military action against the blockade, Sharett had planned the voyage as a final attempt to resolve the issue through diplomacy. The inevitable seizure of the ship would provide the grounds for another complaint to the Security Council, thus calling international attention to the omission of Israel's interests from the evacuation talks.[36]

The mission, at first, went according to plan. After reaching the port, where Egyptian officials actually toasted its crew on the occasion of the Jewish New Year, the *Bat Galim* entered the Canal, only to be stopped an hour later by a customs patrol boat. The ship and its cargo were impounded and its crew of ten arrested and charged with shooting two Egyptian fishermen at the mouth of the Canal.

The initiative came as no surprise to the Egyptians – Israel had often threatened to send such 'test cases' through the Canal – but nevertheless caused them much discomfort. The *Bat Galim* had sorely embarrassed the RCC at a crucial juncture in its relations with the West. To make matters worse, rising tensions on the Gaza border and mounting opposition from the Muslim Brotherhood greatly hindered the RCC's ability to practise brinkmanship as it had in the *Rimfrost* and *Parnon* affairs. In an effort to save face, Gohar submitted the shooting charge to the EIMAC which, after dispatching a team of investigators to the scene, dismissed it as 'unsubstantiated'.[37] As a Security Council debate on the episode now seemed inevitable, Nasser appealed to Sharett through indirect channels, offering to return the crew and cargo overland in exchange for retracting the complaint.[38]

Israel rejected Nasser's proposal and insisted that the *Bat Galim* be permitted to complete its voyage to Haifa. Trusting that Soviet opposition to the evacuation agreement (see Chapter 3) would deter Moscow from exercising its veto, Israel requested the Security Council to consider a more strongly-worded version of its 1951 resolution. But the US and Britain again acted to preclude such a debate. A new resolution, they contended, would indeed be vetoed by the USSR, and succeed only in undermining their efforts to enlist Egypt in a Middle East defence network. While urging Cairo to release the ship, the two Powers warned Israel of the damage which the test case would cause to its regional and international relations.[39]

Anglo-American opposition notwithstanding, the Security Council began consideration of the Israeli complaint on 3 November 1954. From the outset it appeared there would be no room for compromise, with Israeli and Egyptian delegates evoking their traditional arguments against and in defence of the blockade. During the session, however, Mahmud Azmi suffered a heart attack – a member of the Israeli delega-

51

tion tried, unsuccessfully, to revive him – and while the event in itself presented a serious setback to Egypt–Israel relations, it nevertheless afforded the Western Powers time to explore alternative solutions to the *Bat Galim* question.

The Powers' efforts, however, proved futile. Egypt and Israel rejected proposals for submitting the case to the International Court of Justice or for allowing the ship to continue through the Canal under a pretext of quarantine. Nasser confidentially offered to release the boat, even to resolve the entire Canal question, at some point in the future, but, citing his domestic and regional constraints, refused to consider a moderation of the blockade policy. Sharett still insisted on the continuation of the *Bat Galim*'s voyage to Haifa and the total lifting of the blockade, and warned the Powers that Israel would not remain passive indefinitely.[40]

As in the past, just when the deadlock seemed most intractable, Egypt blinked. Cairo suddenly announced on 24 December that it would release the crew through the Red Cross and the ship and cargo through the EIMAC, the latter two in accordance with the EIAA and the Distressed Vessels Agreement. The move, designed to demonstrate that Egypt had acted in accordance with agreements accepted by other Arab states, also placed Israel in the role of the intransigent party. Jerusalem could utilize the good offices of the Red Cross but, in view of its insistence that the Canal was not Egyptian territory, it could not accept the EIMAC's involvement. The legal implications did not, however, disturb the US and Britain, which were now anxious to placate Egypt in the period before Iraq's adherence to the Baghdad Pact (Chapter 3). Rather, they praised the decision and acted to remove the issue from the Security Council. The Israeli press viewed the return of the crew on 1 January 1955 as a great victory, but Sharett realized that his Egyptian policy had suffered another serious defeat. On 26 August 1956, Egypt incorporated the *Bat Galim* into its own navy.[41]

The conclusion of the *Bat Galim* affair, while representing a milestone in Egypt–Israel relations, was overshadowed by another, more pivotal event: the trial in Cairo of ten Egyptian Jews accused of spying for Israel.

Since the Palestine war, Israel had maintained an espionage group, Unit 131, in Egypt, which incorporated young, idealistic Jews from Cairo and Alexandria. With the signing of the Heads of Agreement, IDF intelligence, backed by political elements opposed to Sharett's policies, instructed 131 to take 'measures that will lead to the undermining of [Anglo-American] diplomatic relations [with Egypt]'. Under the guidance of Israeli agents, the Egyptian Jews conspired to firebomb American and British institutions as well as public places in Cairo and Alexandria. The objective was to create chaos in Egypt, thus raising

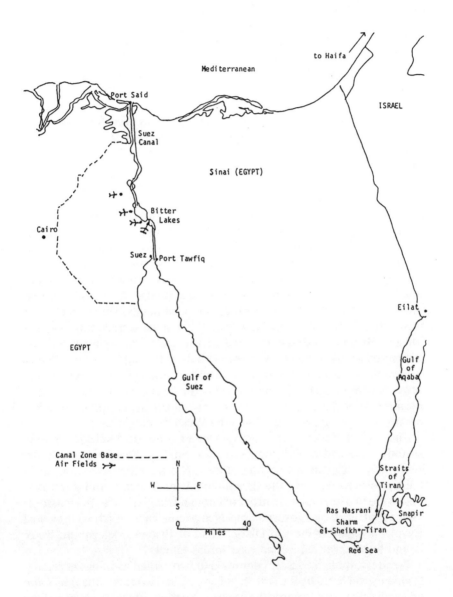

The Suez Canal and the Straits of Tiran

ORIGINS OF THE SECOND ARAB–ISRAEL WAR

Western doubts over the RCC's ability to protect the Canal after the evacuation.[42]

The ring carried out several attacks, though without causing any significant confusion. Then, at the end of July, one of the arsonists was arrested after a bomb exploded prematurely in his pocket. With the ring exposed, 150 Jews were arrested and ten eventually charged. An Israeli spy, Max Binnet, was also captured; two other Israeli agents escaped.

The operation greatly perplexed the Egyptians who for some time remained unsure of its exact purpose. No official statement was issued until 6 October, when Colonel Zakariah Muhi al-Din, the Interior Minister, announced the arrest of a group of Zionist spies. Their mission, according to the Egyptian press, was to disseminate Communist propaganda and bomb hospitals.[43]

Only in November, following months of intensive interrogation, did the RCC uncover the connection between the espionage ring and the evacuation. The revelation, however, placed Cairo in a predicament, for while the arson attempt might be used to divert attention from the *Bat Galim* affair, severe punishment of the accused might serve Israel's original goal of tarnishing Egypt's image in the West and perhaps provoke an IDF retaliation. Further complicating the situation was the fact that the episode coincided with the regime's crackdown on the Muslim Brotherhood and the trial of several of its members for the attempted assassination of Nasser in October. It would be impossible to demonstrate firmness towards the Muslims and leniency towards the Jews. A compromise solution was found involving a show trial, open to the international press, whose sentences would satisfy Egyptian and Arab opinion but not appear over harsh by Western standards.[44]

The trial of the ten defendants – Binnet committed suicide while in custody – coincided with the Security Council's discussion of the *Bat Galim* affair. Egyptian delegates at the UN often referred to the ring in their efforts to discredit the Israeli complaint. Foreign Minister Fawzi linked the two operations in order to impugn Israel's right to free passage: 'Ships controlled by a government which planned acts of sabotage against Egypt,' he told Sir Pierson Dixon, head of Britain's delegation, 'were bound to be regarded as bad risks in the Canal.'[45]

Privately, though, Nasser continued to fear Israeli warnings of retaliation, duly conveyed by the British, if Egypt failed to release the *Bat Galim* and show clemency towards the accused. Such an attack would humiliate the regime at the height of its battle with the Muslim Brotherhood and the Baghdad Pact. To avert this danger, Nasser communicated to Israel his willingness to relax the blockade for a six-month trial period, in one case offering to allow oil shipments to Israel on foreign-flag ships providing the cargo and its destination were suitably camouflaged. He consistently rebuffed, however, suggestions for permitting several Israeli ships through the Canal as the first step in a staged lifting of the blockade or for returning the *Bat Galim* through offices other than the EIMAC.[46]

The trial of the Egyptian Jews, discussed in greater detail in Chapter 5, would have a profound impact on all aspects of Egypt–Israel relations. The sentencing and execution of two of the ring's members in January 1955 capped a series of Israeli policy failures in the areas of arms acquisitions, regional defence and border security, resulting in Ben Gurion's return to government and in the Gaza raid of 28 February. In the wake of that attack, Nasser retracted his offer to relax the blockade, and thereafter continued to escalate it in response to Israeli border actions and the requisites of domestic and regional affairs.

Meanwhile, Israel's policy towards the blockade underwent a fundamental shift. Not unlike his attitude to contacts with Nasser, Ben Gurion was sceptical of the efficacy of UN debates on the blockade, and suspected them of being counter-productive. Furthermore, the campaign against the blockade had, in Ben Gurion's estimation, lost its significance once Egypt gained control over the Canal Zone base. The perception of Israel's growing vulnerability to Egyptian attack, its worsening isolation in international and regional affairs, and the expanding arsenal of the Arab states, led Ben Gurion to seek resolutions of all the outstanding issues in Egypt–Israel relations, including the blockade, by other means.

EGYPT–ISRAEL RELATIONS AND THE SUEZ CRISIS

1955 witnessed a steady increase in the *formal* restrictions in the Canal, particularly in the blacklisting of ships accused of having carried contraband to Israel. In practice, however, the blockade's application remained erratic, with Israel–Asia trade through the Canal actually expanding over the year.[47]

Then, in July, Egypt indicated that it intended to tighten the Tiran blockade by forbidding Israel-bound ships entry into the Gulf. The move, which came during a period of greater Egyptian assertiveness in foreign affairs, including the Palestine issue, may also have been prompted by signs of an impending Israeli attack (see Chapter 6) on the Straits. Nasser's determination to implement the decision was no doubt reinforced by the escalation of border fighting at the end of the summer and by the enthusiastic response which his Fida'iyun policy received in the Arab world. On 12 September, Egypt transferred responsibility for the Straits blockade to the Arab boycott office; air travel to and from Israel over Tiran was banned and ships' captains were required to submit inventories of their cargoes 72 hours before entering the Straits (Appendix IV).

Nasser's action deeply disconcerted the Israelis. Most damaging was the ban on overflights, which severed one of Israel's principal air routes to Africa and the East. Together with the announcement of the Egypt–Czech arms deal (Chapter 4) which followed shortly thereafter, Nasser's decision on Tiran further convinced Ben Gurion of Egypt's intention to wage war and hardened his resolve to launch a pre-emptive strike.

The situation gave rise to a bifurcation in Israeli policy-making. While Ben Gurion generally concentrated on preparing an attack on Tiran, Sharett, as Foreign Minister, continued his attempts to challenge the blockade through diplomacy. The Greek freighters *Konitea* and *Panagia*, which sailed from Haifa in February and May 1956 respectively, were both stopped by the Egyptians in the Straits. These test cases, however, were no more successful than their predecessors; complaints on the seizures submitted by Israel to the Security Council failed to produce resolutions condemning Egypt.[48]

Throughout the first half of 1956, however, Israel's diplomatic efforts focused less on the blockade than on the Anglo-American offer to finance construction of the Aswan dam. The project, Israeli diplomats argued, rewarded Nasser for concluding the Czech arms deal. That transaction, together with Nasser's opposition to Anglo-American policies in the Middle East and his expanding ties with the Soviet Union, convinced Dulles to withdraw from the Aswan project. The Israelis knew of this decision well before its announcement on 19 July. The same, however, could not be said of Nasser's nationalization of the Suez Canal a week later, which caught the Israelis as well as the Americans completely by surprise.[49]

Nasser's move returned the blockade issue to the ambit of international diplomacy. As the only recent case in which free passage had been denied to ships in the Canal, the blockade on Israel became an important element in the Anglo-French charge that Egypt could not be trusted as the sole caretaker of Suez. Nevertheless, the Powers insisted on excluding Israel from their efforts to resolve the crisis. Israeli involvement, they explained, would necessitate inclusion of the Arab states, thus enabling Nasser to rally regional support for his action.[50] Ironically, then, the Powers' policy paralleled that of Egypt, which also endeavoured to exclude mention of the blockade from the Suez debate.

Israel applied for but was denied permission to attend the First and Second London Conferences (16–26 August, 19–22 September) and membership in the proposed Suez Canal Users Association (SCUA).

Dulles, architect of these efforts to deal with the Suez crisis, explained that as the Canal did not account for 50 per cent of its shipping, Israel did not meet the necessary criterion for participation. Israel's argument, that the blockade prevented it, *a priori*, from attaining that standard, failed to alter the Secretary's position.[51]

Their exclusion from diplomatic initiatives nothwithstanding, the Israelis saw great benefits in the crisis. It fulfilled Israel's long objective of establishing the blockade as inimical to Western interests, and raised the possibility that Nasser could be toppled by international sanctions. Over the course of the summer, the Foreign Ministry, now under the direction of Golda Meir, submitted numerous memoranda to Western capitals on the Suez issue. These contained proposals for test cases, including international convoys, to challenge the nationalization decree, and for an oil pipeline from Eilat to Haifa which would bypass the Canal. They also made it clear that Israel would not allow Egypt to emerge from the crisis with its blockade intact. 'Since Israel has been singled out for special treatment by Nasser,' Meir told Edward Lawson, America's ambassador to Tel Aviv, 'he must be singled out for special attention now that [the] world has [the] Canal problem under scrutiny.'[52]

Egypt, meanwhile, still strove to separate the blockade from the Canal crisis. In conversations with Western diplomats, Egyptian officials denied that the issues were in any way connected but pledged to reconsider the blockade policy after a solution had been found to the current controversy. Egypt also undertook to mollify Israel during this period. On 18 August Ali Sabri, Egypt's observer at the London Conference, announced that the Canal would be open to all Israel-bound cargoes except war materials. Two weeks later the RCC agreed to release the *Panagia* if it would return to Haifa. Cairo Radio even sent 'warm felicitations' to Israel because of its 'cautious' position on the Canal question.[53]

The relatively congenial atmosphere in Egypt–Israel relations dissipated rapidly in September, however, when Britain and France, despairing of Dulles's efforts to resolve the crisis, referred the issue to the Security Council. The manoeuvre, designed by its anticipated failure to provide moral justification for Anglo-French military intervention against Egypt, brought the blockade into the centre of the Suez controversy. The September 1951 resolution represented the only precedent of Security Council action on the question of free passage in the Canal.

The US State Department, together with the British Foreign Office, opposed Israel's participation in the Security Council debate on the grounds that it would invite involvement by Arab delegations. But with French backing and a pledge to restrict his comments to the blockade issue, Eban secured permission to address the Council. His speech, presented on 13 October, contained a detailed chronicle of the blockade and depicted it as an action directed against the interests of the Maritime Powers.[54]

The Security Council debate placed Egypt in a precarious position. Having resisted the pressures of the London Conferences, it now faced a forum whose deliberations would be difficult to reject and whose previous resolution on the Canal put Egypt at a disadvantage. In addition, any concession on the blockade would deprive Nasser of the significant propaganda gains he had made as a result of the nationalization, and contribute to growing resentment in the Arab world over his neglect of the Palestine issue since the outbreak of the crisis.[55]

While other Arab delegations attempted to justify the blockade – seven received permission to speak in reply to Eban's speech – the Egyptian ambassador, Lutfi, attempted to deflect attention from the issue by reviving the proposal for updating the 1888 Convention. Throughout the debate, the RCC remained adamant in its opposition to linking the Suez and the blockade disputes, and even rejected efforts by the Powers to arrange secret Egypt–Israel talks on the blockade.[56]

Egypt's efforts to distinguish between the blockade and the general Canal crisis ultimately proved unsuccessful. An Anglo-French resolution was drafted incorporating six points on the future governance of the Canal. Though the document made no direct reference to the blockade, it nevertheless called for 'free and open transit, without discrimination overt or covert' in the Canal, and for insulating its management from the internal politics of any country; a second section demanded the immediate guarantee of free passage through the Canal. Britain and France assumed that Egypt would fail this test of the blockade, thus strengthening their pretext for an invasion. Egypt, however, was spared the trouble of rejecting the resolution by the Soviet Union's veto of the second section.[57]

Ben Gurion regarded with indifference the defeat of the six points in the Security Council. Incredulous of the UN's ability to guarantee passage for Israeli shipping through the Canal, the Prime Minister was at that time finalizing plans for a military strike at Tiran. The plan might also have provided for a thrust towards the Canal with the objective of closing off sections of the waterway until the blockade was lifted. Such an operation, however, would have made tremendous demands on IDF logistics and manpower and, most precariously, risk embroiling Israel in a confrontation with the Maritime Powers. The Straits, by contrast, presented a limited target with few international complications, and one in which Israel's legal position was comparatively strong.[58]

Thus, in contrast to Israel's long-standing diplomatic policy of refusing to distinguish between the two blockades, its military planning did precisely that. Even after the signing of the secret accords at Sèvres on 24 October (Chapter 6), Israel left the task of occupying the Canal, and of ending the blockade, to Britain and France. Meanwhile, officials at the Israeli Foreign Ministry, who were never privy to this planning, continued to regard the two blockades as one. On 29 October, the day the second Arab–Israel war erupted, Israeli diplomats issued a circular to foreign delegations at the UN reminding them of the 1951 resolution and its relevance to both blockades.[59]

3

The Struggle over Regional Defence

Regional defence was a recurrent theme in the international and local politics of the Middle East in the 1950s. The seemingly anodyne notion that Middle Eastern states could unite for their common defence against external threats served as the catalyst for widespread instability, even violence, in a number of those states, and was among the underlying causes of the Suez crisis and the second Arab–Israel war. Involving such crucial issues as the future of the Suez Canal, the arms balance and a Palestine settlement, the struggle over regional defence became a prominent feature of Egypt–Israel relations and a major cause of the second Arab–Israel war.

Egyptians and Israelis shared several basic attitudes towards the regional defence issue. Neither country accepted the West's justification for establishing the Middle East defence organization, that is that the region was in danger of Soviet invasion. Nor did they believe that that network would exist for any purpose other than to perpetuate Western hegemony over the area. The similarities, however, ended there, for while both Egypt and Israel opposed the West's concept of Middle East defence, they did so for radically different reasons.

Israel's opposition stemmed mainly from strategic considerations. Despite their public proclamations of neutralism, Israeli leaders identified with the West and secretly sought an association with its plans for defending the Middle East. However, when it became evident that the West had no intention of including Israel in its scheme, and that the proposed defence organization would facilitate the arming of the Arabs, Israel came to view the entire regional defence effort as a serious threat to its security. Consequently, the Israelis abandoned neutralism in favour of more explicit demands for alliance with the West.

Egypt's motivation in rejecting the regional defence plan was essentially political. In contrast to the Israelis, the Egyptians openly declared their commitment to the West while in reality resisting its regional defence plans. In their view, the defence organization, by enabling Britain to maintain its forces along the Suez Canal as well as in other strategically important parts of the Middle East, not only obstructed

Egypt's immediate goal of national independence, but also its long-term objective of regional ascendancy. As a result, the Egyptians traded places with the Israelis, dropping their pro-Western stance in favour of neutralism.

The struggle for regional defence served as another example of the Powers' role in exacerbating Arab–Israel tensions. The Western Powers, it will be recalled, abrogated exclusive control over the issue of Middle East security. That claim was posited in the Tripartite Declaration of 1950 and in various UN resolutions. Ideally, the Powers were to have acted in concert in establishing a Middle East defence organization while at the same time working to maintain the status quo in the Arab–Israel conflict. These policies, however, proved mutually contradictory. Guided by their individual interests, the Powers acted unilaterally on the regional defence issue, provoked both Egypt and Israel, and removed constraints on the rise of Arab–Israel tensions.

FIRST ENCOUNTERS WITH MEDO

The British regarded the regional defence organization as the best, if not the only, means of preserving their strategic position in the Middle East in the post-imperialist era. Egypt's participation in that project, they believed, was vital. Though Egypt would have little to contribute in the way of military prowess, it had tremendous strategic significance as the site of the Suez Canal and its massive British base.[1] Under the Labour government of Clement Attlee, vigorous efforts were made to lay the foundations of the Middle East Defence Organization (MEDO). These, however, met with strong nationalist opposition throughout the Arab world, above all in Egypt.

The Egyptians, of course, had no interest in perpetuating Britain's presence along the Canal or, for that matter, in Sudan. Accordingly, the Wafd government of Nahhas Pasha rejected Britain's approaches, and in October 1951, after 19 months of abortive talks on the Suez and Sudan issues, abrogated the Anglo-Egyptian treaty of 1936. To emphasize further their opposition to MEDO, the Egyptians insisted that Middle East defence was the sole prerogative of the Arab Collective Security Pact (ACSP). Created by the Arab League in April 1950, ostensibly to co-ordinate Arab defence against Israel, the ACSP in fact aimed at frustrating Hashemite ambitions in the Fertile Crescent and at ensuring Egyptian leadership of the Arab world.[2]

Exasperated with the Egyptian reaction to MEDO, the British turned to the United States. America's adherence to the pact, Whitehall predicted, would make it more palatable to the Egyptians, and thus open the way for the agreement of other Arab states as well. The Truman Administration, however, exhibited an ambivalent attitude towards MEDO. While convinced that the organization was essential for thwarting Soviet inroads into the Middle East, the Americans were repelled by Britain's imperialist stigma. They argued that Middle East defence was Britain's responsibility, just as the US had assumed that burden in the Far East. Washington was willing to support MEDO politically and financially, but would not join the organization.[3]

The British also did not overlook the possibility of an Israeli role in regional defence. In contrast to their contempt for the Egyptian army, the British had a high esteem for the IDF, though they tended to play down Israel's geographic importance – Jordan was equally well situated to guard the approaches to the Canal. Other factors, however, definitely militated against Israeli membership in MEDO: the country's proclivity for neutralism and communism, and the dangers of an anti-British backlash in the Arab world. Nevertheless, intent on their quest for Middle East defence, the British were willing to explore opportunities for strategic co-operation with Israel.

Bound by its ideology as well as by its concern for Diaspora Jewish communities in both the US and the USSR, Israel was compelled to follow a middle path between East and West. Israeli leaders proclaimed their neutralism while quietly supporting the West on major Cold War issues, such as the Korean conflict. Ben Gurion himself remained ambivalent about Israel's global orientation, though he was specific with regard to Middle East defence. In principle, he opposed MEDO but, fearing Israel's exclusion from it, favoured some type of association with the organization. He also saw in the alliance possibilities for obtaining Western arms and security guarantees. Accordingly, he communicated to Britain Israel's interest in MEDO. Whitehall responded guardedly, and instructed General. Brian Robertson, Commander-in-Chief of Britain's Middle East forces, to include Israel in his schedule of strategic talks in the area.

Robertson met Ben Gurion and Chief-of-Staff Yigal Yadin in Febuary 1951. Israel, he was told, wanted a Commonwealth-type relationship with Britain; during an emergency, it would provide Britain with port and transit facilities. In return, Israel expected to receive economic and military aid and diplomatic support to achieve a peace treaty with Egypt. Because of internal political constraints, however, the arrangement would have to be informal if not clandestine. British officers who came to supervise defence preparations would be requested to wear civilian clothes.[4]

After further consideration, the Attlee government declined the Israelis' proposals for strategic co-operation. Though not opposed in principle to Israel's adherence to MEDO, the British determined that the liability of such involvement in terms of Arab reaction far outweighed the asset of Israel's contributions to Middle East defence. Much to Ben Gurion's disappointment, there was no follow-up to the Robertson mission.

In the absence of Egyptian membership in MEDO, Britain began to look to Iraq as the organization's power base. In addition to being a more compliant ally, Baghdad was deemed less vulnerable to Egyptian influence. Indeed, Whitehall consistently underestimated the impact of Egypt's opposition to MEDO, while exaggerating that of Israel. The fact remained, however, that the defence organization could not be viable without access to the Canal Zone; further attempts would have to be made to bring Egypt into the organization. But in view of Egypt's worsening political instability, the British chose to postpone such efforts until Cairo was again capable of addressing them productively.[5]

The period of the first encounters with MEDO established patterns of Egyptian and Israeli, as well of British and American, interaction on regional defence. Despite changes of leadership in each of the countries, their policies on the issue would remain essentially unchanged. The same may be said of France, which had been entirely excluded from Middle East defence by the Americans and the British. Insulted and fearful of British designs on the Levant, the French would not be reconciled to the situation, and thereafter sought all means of frustating Anglo-American defence plans for the Middle East.[6] Thus, on the eve of the Egyptian revolution, the lines were clearly drawn in the coming struggle over regional defence.

MEDO REVIVED

The Free Officers' coup of July 1952 rekindled the hopes of Britain and the US for Egyptian participation in MEDO. Their optimism focused on the Officers' apparent commitment to staying out of inter-Arab intrigues and to opposing the spread of communism. Such expectations grew in the weeks following the coup, when the Officers requested clarification of the Powers' policies towards regional defence.

The Free Officers' thinking on regional defence in fact differed little from that of their predecessors, and they were even more determined to rid the Middle East of Britain. Nevertheless, the regime had an interest in favourable relations with the West, particularly with regard to military aid. Consequently, in their early communications with the British and the

Americans, the Officers promised to consider enlisting Egypt in MEDO after the evacuation, but only in return for military aid.[7]

The newly-elected Eisenhower Administration was inclined to accept these remarks at face value. Dulles, determined to reshape American policy towards the Middle East, adopted a platform which was at once anti-communist and anti-imperialist; supportive of Britain's role in regional defence but also of emergent nationalist movements. Of the latter, the Free Officers appeared the most dependable – the CIA had aided their rise to power – and Egypt the sturdiest cornerstone for a regional defence structure. Specifically, Dulles believed that Egyptian leadership of MEDO would diminish some of the organization's imperialist taint. As an incentive to such co-operation, the Administration offered arms to Egypt (see Chapter 5) and urged Britain to reach an early agreement on the evacuation issue. Dulles assured the Officers that he would oppose any regional defence scheme which excluded Egypt and which did not take account of the ACSP.[8]

In Britain, the Conservative government, which entered office at the time of Nahhas's abrogation of the Anglo-Egyptian treaty, regarded these developments with growing unease. While welcoming the renewal of American interest in MEDO, Churchill was disturbed by Eisenhower's courtship of Egypt, particularly by way of the ACSP, arms, and the evacuation. Such resentment caused serious strains in Anglo-American relations over the course of 1953. Goodwill was restored only after Washington agreed to make the arms sales conditional on Egypt's co-operation in resolving the Suez and Sudan disputes and in establishing a regional defence network. The British nevertheless continued to suspect the existence of a tacit US–Egyptian bloc against their Middle East interests. Even more to Whitehall's discomfort, that alliance seemed to be pushing Britain into a strategic relationship with Israel.[9]

Unaware of the gulf which separated the US and British positions on regional defence, the Israelis acted as if the two Powers were united with Egypt in excluding it from MEDO. In reaction to the upsurge in American interest in MEDO, Israeli diplomats approached the State Department and the Foreign Office with requests for full and open membership in the organization. The Powers together rejected these requests; they favoured an all-Arab organization which would have the right to decide whether or not to include Israel. To allay Israel's fears, however, they claimed that the establishment of MEDO would bolster the West's influence in the region and thus its ability to negotiate an Arab–Israel peace.[10]

The argument only infuriated the Israelis. 'This is the first instance of a Middle Eastern country knocking at the door of regional defence,' Eban complained to Dulles in Washington, 'and being denied admission.'[11] Their fears were compounded by the sharp deterioration in Israel's relations with the communist bloc. In February 1953, during a wave of anti-Semitism in Eastern Europe, a bomb exploded at the Soviet embassy in Tel Aviv, prompting Moscow to suspend diplomatic ties with Israel. Now the West appeared bent on completing Israel's international isolation and effecting its encirclement by an armed Arab alliance. In vain attempts to persuade Britain and the US to reconsider their positions, Israeli representatives argued that the Arabs had neither the inclination nor the ability to contribute to regional defence, and that the weapons they would acquire through MEDO would be used to fight not the USSR but the Jewish State.

Unlike the Israelis, the Egyptians were well attuned to differences between American and British thinking on regional defence and were quick to exploit them. By continuing to suggest to Washington that it would affiliate with MEDO after the evacuation, the RCC sought to generate American pressure on Britain to moderate its demands vis-à-vis the Canal. At the same time, the Officers resumed the efforts of the previous regime to achieve international recognition of an Egypt-dominated Arab pact. Throughout 1953, they declared the primacy of the ACSP in the area of regional defence, and undertook extensive efforts to transform that document into a viable military alliance. Thus, at a summit of Arab chiefs-of-staff in September, Egypt's General Abd al-Hakim Amer pressed for the unification of Arab armies under Egyptian command as the first step in the creation of a comprehensive Arab defence organization.[12]

The RCC's efforts to establish a purely Arab pact invariably assumed an anti-Israel mien. In promoting the idea, Egyptian propaganda was able to capitalize on popular resentment and fear of Israel. Underlying this rhetoric, however, was a genuine anxiety over alleged Anglo-Israeli collusion in MEDO. The organization, the Egyptians believed, served not only British imperialism but also Israeli expansionism. Not by accident, they noted, did Britain's revival of MEDO coincide with Israel's aggressive actions in the al-Aujah DZ.

Egypt's apprehensions were mirrored in Israel. There, the government watched as the US and Britain conducted, apparently at Israel's expense, a race for Egypt's favour, while Egypt constructed an Arab alliance dedicated to Israel's destruction. Egypt's devotion to that objective was, in Israel's view, revealed in the growing hostility of its propaganda, its aggressiveness on the border and, most poignantly, in its decision to tighten the Suez blockade.

In fact the perceptions of both the Egyptians and the Israelis were

65

fundamentally wrong. Nevertheless, the foundations had been laid for the Egypt–Israel struggle over regional defence.

EN ROUTE TO THE NORTHERN TIER

Since the July revolution, the Officers' pledges of future co-operation with MEDO had succeeded in focusing American pressure on Britain to conclude an evacuation agreement. Beginning with Secretary Dulles's visit to the Middle East in May 1953, however, the Administration began to accept the fact that Egypt would never join the organization.[13] Though Dulles never completely abandoned the hope of arriving at some form of understanding with the RCC, he began to concentrate on a Middle East defence network centred on the states bordering the Soviet Union. This was the so-called Northern Tier concept, involving Iran, Turkey and Pakistan, with Iraq acting as the alliance's anchor in the Arab world.

The bases of the Northern Tier alliance were established in April 1954 with the signing of a Turco-Pakistan defence treaty and the conclusion of a US–Iraq arms deal. Though piqued by America's entry into their exclusive sphere of weapon supplies (see Chapter 4), the British favoured the Northern Tier notion. Subsequently, they began to encourage Baghdad to adhere to the Turco-Pakistan pact.[14]

The Israelis viewed with trepidation Iraq's impending inclusion in a Northern Tier. Their major concern was that Iraq would, through the treaty, receive considerable amounts of Western weaponry which it could then use in waging a 'second round'. At the same time, however, the Israelis were hesitant to assail the West – after all, Iraq had yet to accede to the treaty – or Turkey, whose recognition they cherished. Lacking alternatives, Israeli diplomats again appealed to the State Department and to the Foreign Office for entry into the emerging pact. The Anglo-American position, however, remained unchanged: Israeli membership would doom whatever chances existed for Arab and Muslim support for the organization and thus had to be deferred until after the settlement of the Palestine conflict. Even then, the Powers again explained, Israel would benefit, as the pact would divide the Arab world and make it more susceptible to Western pressure for peace.[15]

The advent of the Northern Tier alliance was dreaded in Egypt no less than in Israel. Internally divided between pro-Nasser and pro-Naguib factions, and facing rising opposition from the Muslim Brotherhood, the RCC had also to face a marked improvement in Iraq's position in the Arab world. The latter resulted, first, from the US–Iraq arms deal and Egypt's preoccupation with the evacuation issue, and, second, from the fall of the anti-Hashemite Shikshakli regime in Syria and the restoration of stability in Jordan under the new king, Hussein. These events had spurred Iraq to revive its perennial campaign for Fertile Crescent unity centred around Baghdad.

Such challenges to the RCC's regional ambitions demanded a response, but, like Israel, Egypt had few options. To maintain American pressure on Britain on the evacuation issue, the RCC had to sustain the myth of its future co-operation with the pact, thereby limiting its ability to denounce Anglo-American policies openly. Criticism in the Arab world also had to be muted because of Pakistan's status as a major Muslim power. Egypt thus resorted to propaganda attacks against Turkey, which was portrayed as promoting the pact as a means of weakening the Arabs' steadfastness against Israel. Simultaneously, Egypt attempted to enlist Jordan, Yemen and Saudi Arabia in a Red Sea Defence Group, which, characteristically, was directed against an Israeli threat to the Gulf of Aqaba.[16]

Thus, even at this early stage, the Powers' manoeuvrings on the regional defence issue had succeeded in provoking both Israel and Egypt. The Egyptians, seeing a clear Anglo-Iraqi challenge to their regional hegemony, and suspecting clandestine Anglo-Israeli duplicity, sought to recruit Arab allies by increasing their belligerency towards Israel. The Israelis, faced with such enhanced hostility and the threat of an Anglo-American-Arab pact, were increasingly apt to break out of their isolation by military means.

The evacuation agreement, secured in principle in July and ratified in October 1954, inaugurated Egypt and Israel's struggle over regional defence. Though Nasser had received a certain degree of Western recognition of the ACSP and was now free to pursue a pan-Arab pact, he had paid a heavy price. He had agreed to allow British troops to re-occupy the Canal Zone in the event of an attack on a number of Middle Eastern states, among them Turkey. The provision effectively linked Egypt to the Northern Tier, thereby undermining Nasser's argument against Iraq. Furthermore, having compromised the purely Arab nature of the ACSP, Nasser could no longer use the pact as an instrument for extending Egyptian influence over the Arab world. Not surprisingly, Iraq, now under the aggressive leadership of Nuri al-Sa'id, began praising the ACSP as the best protection against Israel. In response, Nasser distanced himself from the ACSP and instead called for a new Arab alliance, completely detached from the West and directed exclusively against Israel.[17]

If the evacuation agreement was only a qualified victory for Egypt, it represented a total defeat for Israel. While ignoring Israel's economic and security concerns vis-à-vis the Canal, the agreement had excluded

Israel from those Middle Eastern countries whose security was linked with the Canal base and had extended unprecedented Western recognition to the ACSP. The treaty had also created a wave of competition between Iraq and Egypt, the former recently armed with American weapons, the latter soon to be in possession of the Canal Zone's stores and infrastructure, over which could better lead the fight to liberate Palestine. Though the British government, largely in reaction to charges from the Labour opposition that it had ignored Israel's interests in the evacuation, made oblique promises to ensure Israel's security, it refused to commit itself to any concrete measures to this effect.[18] As such, the treaty reinforced Israel's sense of regional and international isolation and strengthened the hands of those in its leadership who advocated blocking the evacuation at all costs.

For the US and Britain, however, the evacuation agreement represented a panacea for a range of Middle East problems. In addition to opening the way to Iraqi membership in the Northern Tier pact, the treaty was expected to provide the foundation for an Arab–Israel settlement and, ultimately, for a regional defence organization embracing all the Arab states. With Egypt's position thus weakened, it was reasoned, the RCC would be more amenable to accepting the conditions attached to American arms sales and, given the proper territorial incentives, to entering into a non-belligerency treaty with Israel. The conclusion of a comprehensive solution to the Arab–Israel conflict, expected to follow the Egypt–Israel agreement, would remove the essence of Arab animosity towards the Powers and thus the final obstacle to Arab alignment with the West.[19]

These assumptions, which formed the basis of the secret Alpha peace plan (see Chapter 5), failed to take into account Israel's opposition to an arrangement in which Israeli territory, together with Western arms, would be granted to the Arabs as incentives for joining a pact from which it was excluded. Equally, the Powers underestimated Egypt's determination to resist any challenge to its campaign for regional pre-eminence. Israel's attempts to block the evacuation have been noted in previous chapters. No less portentously, Nasser rejected another American arms offer in August, and that same month rebuffed a proposal from Nuri linking co-operation with the West on regional defence with Western support for an Arab–Israel settlement.[20]

BETWEEN BAGHDAD AND GAZA

The regional defence controversy played a significant role in the rise of Egypt–Israel tensions in the winter of 1954–55. The Egyptians interpreted Israel's efforts to obstruct the evacuation as plots to hinder Egypt's ability to combat the Northern Tier. Adding to Nasser's frustration was the Arabs' refusal to side with him against the pact. Twice, in December 1954 and in January 1955, he attempted to elicit from Arab leaders gathered in Cairo an unequivocal denunciation of the alliance, but without success. Many of these figures were wary of Nasser's ambitions, while others, such as the Syrian Prime Minister Faris al-Khuri, were persuaded by Nuri's argument that the Northern Tier, by providing a conduit for Western arms, would prove a more effective defence against Israel. Nasser was left with little choice but to escalate the border situation with infiltration raids into Israeli territory and to intensify hostile propaganda. The Voice of the Arabs unleashed a steady stream of allegations, such as the existence of a secret Turco-Israeli pact to conquer the Arab world and Nuri's honorary membership in the Zionist movement.[21]

The mood in Israel, already tense due to the *Bat Galim* affair and the Cairo spy trial, was further inflamed by Egypt's actions. Then, on 20 January Jerusalem learned that the proposed Turco-Iraqi pact would contain a codicil calling for the resolution of the Palestine problem on the basis of the 1947 partition plan. What was once seen as primarily a military danger now appeared to be a political threat as well.

In view of the worsening security situation, Prime Minister Sharett abandoned efforts to secure Israeli membership in the alliance and instead began seeking bilateral pacts with each of the Tripartite Powers, beginning with the United States. He wrote to Dulles:

> The Middle East is becoming a patchwork of pacts from which Israel is excluded not only as a participant but even as a candidate for participation ... What we could welcome is the conclusion of a defence treaty ... such as would guarantee the territorial integrity of Israel and assure us an arms supply corresponding to that of the Arabs.[22]

As in the past, however, Dulles remained unresponsive to Israeli requests. If afforded, such a treaty would remove any chance of Egyptian co-operation with the West on the regional defence issue, and eliminate the incentive for Israeli co-operation with Alpha. Dulles responded to Sharett.

> We have steadfastly avoided involvement in regional disputes. If we presented to the Senate a treaty with Israel today, many Senators would feel that they were not being asked to guarantee stability but,

rather, to guarantee US involvement in a highly inflammatory dispute.

The British Foreign Office agreed with this position, while the French Quai d'Orsay explained that they could not enter into a defence treaty without full Tripartite approval.[23]

The struggle over regional defence was among the factors which combined to make February 1955 a major turning point in Egypt–Israel relations. That month, Nasser won the first of his battles in his war against the Northern Tier by effectively dislodging Syria from Iraq's orbit. The victory was due, in large part, to Nasser's shrewd manipulation of the Palestine issue. While his propaganda broadcasts continued to depict the Northern Tier pact as a Zionist–imperialist plot, Nasser acted to demonstrate his commitment to the Palestine cause by appointing Mahmud Riad, a renowned expert on the issue, as ambassador to Damascus. These measures had a marked impact on Syrian public opinion which proceeded to force al-Khuri's resignation. The government of Sabri al-'Asali, which took office on 21 February, promptly declared its allegiance to Egypt in all matters pertaining to regional defence.

Iraq moved swiftly to meet this challenge, and on 24 February signed its long-anticipated defence agreement with Turkey, the so-called Baghdad Pact. Egypt retaliated two days later by announcing plans for uniting its army with Syria's under a joint command; Yemen and Saudi Arabia expressed their intention to accede to the accord. On 28 February Israel launched its fateful raid into Gaza.

EGYPT TRIUMPHANT, ISRAEL EXCLUDED

The Gaza raid, which was widely interpreted in the Arab world as an attempt to weaken Egypt's resistance to the Baghdad Pact, appeared to confirm Nasser's suspicions of Anglo-Israeli collusion in the regional defence project. Nasser, nevertheless, was undeterred by the incident and was quick to exploit the momentum which the attack had given his campaign. While Egyptian propaganda broadcasts to the Arab world evinced the raid as further proof of the Zionist–imperialist conspiracy in the Northern Tier, Nasser moved to extend the base of his opposition to the pact outside of the Middle East.[24]

In his public statements, Nasser began to profess adherence to 'positive neutralism', a doctrine which mandated opposition to Cold War alliances and active resistance to the Powers' defence pacts. The policy, which enabled Egypt to find a common cause with the emerging Third World nations of the East, soon proved its efficacy at the Bandung Conference of non-aligned nations in April 1955. There, in addition to obtaining a condemnation of the Baghdad Pact, Nasser convinced the conference to deny Israel membership in the non-aligned group and to pass a resolution supporting the Arab position on Palestine.[25] In a single stroke, Nasser managed to associate neutralism with opposition to both Israel and the Northern Tier and, in the process, to establish Egypt's leadership of the neutralist movement in the Middle East.

While publicly pursuing the neutralist line, secretly Nasser aimed for a major arms deal (see Chapter 4) with the Soviet Union. Apart from its strategic ramifications, the transaction would have a tremendous political impact by breaking the West's monopoly over Middle East arms sales, one of the central pillars of the Northern Tier. Since the death of Stalin in 1953, the USSR had been supporting the neutralist movement as a natural foil to the West. Though it had criticized Egypt for signing an evacuation agreement which seemed to serve Britain's regional defence plans, the Soviets soon arrived at an appreciation of Egypt's role in resisting the Baghdad Pact. By representing a 'leapfrogging' of the Northern Tier, the arms deal would reveal the impotence of the alliance and demonstrate that modern weapons, in significant quantities, could be obtained without a quid pro quo in terms of regional defence.

Nasser's strategy registered impressive results. The arms deal, announced in September 1955, was followed in October by the revision of the Egypt–Syria agreement on joint command. Soon that agreement expanded to include Saudi Arabia and Yemen, with Egypt entering into five-year defence treaties with each of the three Arab states. Henceforth, aggression against one of the signatories would be considered an attack on both.[26]

The Israelis, meanwhile, could claim no similar progress in their efforts in the regional defence field. The sense of insecurity and isolation created by the Baghdad Pact and which had influenced the decision to launch the Gaza raid, only intensified with Nasser's successes abroad and in the region.[27] Furthermore, in response to the raid, the Powers had suspended all discussion of bilateral treaties with Israel. Yet, while Nasser increasingly looked to the East for the answer to the Baghdad Pact threat, Sharett continued seek his solution in the West.

Throughout the spring and summer of 1955, Israeli representatives attempted to revive the bilateral pact concept. The focus of the démarche centred on Washington, on the assumption that if US approval for the plan were secured, similar arrangements would follow with Britain and France. Interestingly, one of Israel's principal tactics in these talks was to support the notion of American adherence to the Baghdad Pact. According to this logic, the US would compensate Israel for its membership in

71

the pact with a bilateral treaty. The agreement would then serve to link Israel indirectly to the Northern Tier.

In pursuing this policy, Sharett overrode the objections of Defence Minister Ben Gurion and Chief-of-Staff Dayan, who argued that such a treaty could not be obtained without major Israeli concessions of territory and military manoeuvrability. These caveats were presently confirmed by Dulles, who indicated that the US could not agree to such a treaty unless Israel made the territorial sacrifices demanded by the Alpha plan and publicly abjured the retaliation policy.[28]

Sharett categorically rejected these conditions but nevertheless persisted in his efforts. These took on added urgency after the revelation of Egypt's arms deal with the Soviet bloc. Israeli representatives tried to convince Western officials that that transaction had been a direct consequence of the Baghdad Pact, and that a proper response for the Powers would be to extend bilateral guarantees for Israel's security. But the Powers, more inclined to blame Nasser's decision on the Gaza raid, remained opposed to the suggestion as long as there existed a chance of dissuading Nasser from concluding the deal.

Nasser remained adamant in his decision, however, and in doing so provided a fillip to Israel's demands. On 6 December the Administration informed Sharett that it would now give serious consideration to the proposal. Israel's victory proved ephemeral. Less than a week later, the US reverted to its previous position in reaction to the Tiberias raid, the IDF's large-scale assault on Syrian emplacements on the Golan Heights.[29]

THE STRUGGLE FOR JORDAN

The Tiberias raid, like that on Gaza nearly a year before, was seen in Egypt as another Israeli attempt to fortify the Northern Tier alliance by weakening its opponents. Ostensibly, Israel's objective was now to demonstrate the ineffectiveness of the Egypt–Syria alliance and, in the process, push Jordan into the Baghdad Pact.[30]

By the winter of 1955, the focus of the regional defence struggle had shifted from Syria to Jordan. The development came as another result of the continuing disagreement between Britain and the US over the latter's role in the Northern Tier.

In April 1955, as one of his first acts of office after taking over from Churchill, Prime Minister Eden announced Britain's accession to the Baghdad Pact. Pakistan and Iran adhered shortly thereafter, leading Whitehall to believe that the US would soon follow suit. However, with Arab sentiment clearly arrayed against the pact, and with efforts underway to achieve détente with the USSR, Dulles saw no benefit in taking such a step. US membership at this stage, the Secretary explained to Eden, would only drive Egypt deeper into the Soviet camp and necessitate the granting of security guarantees for Israel, thereby undermining the Alpha peace plan. Insisting that a chance still remained of Egyptian co-operation on regional defence, Dulles advised the Prime Minister to desist from further attempts to expand the pact and instead try to promote Egyptian interest in Alpha. Once an Egypt–Israel settlement had been obtained, he pledged, the US would join the Baghdad Pact.[31]

This rationale only antagonized the British. Accusing Dulles of placating Cairo at Baghdad's expense, Eden was eager to defy Washington's prohibition against expanding the Baghdad Pact. 'The stronger the Northern Tier,' he wrote in the margin of a telegram from the Cairo embassy, 'the better Nasser will behave.'[32] Eden also believed that Jordan would soon fall into Egypt's sphere if Britain failed to act swiftly in admitting Hussein into the pact. That accomplishment, Eden predicted, would not only demonstrate to the Arab world the pact's viability, but convince the Americans of the advisability of adhering to the treaty.[33]

The possibility of Jordan's entry into the Baghdad Pact posed a serious threat to Egypt. Its previous victories over the Baghdad Pact notwithstanding, two recent defeats on Egypt's own borders – to Israel in the DZ in November and in December to Britain with Sudan's declaration of independence – belied the RCC's claims to be the region's guardian against Zionism and imperialism. The loss of Jordan to the Baghdad Pact would prove even more deleterious to Egypt's image in the Arab world, and, by isolating Syria within the Hashemite bloc, seriously endanger the strategic alliance with Damascus. In contacts with both British and American representatives, Nasser conditioned his co-operation with Alpha on an Anglo-American pledge to freeze the membership of the Baghdad Pact.[34]

The struggle over Jordan presented Israel with a choice between two evils: Jordan's adherence to either the Baghdad or the Egypt–Syria pact. Optimally, Israel favoured Jordanian neutrality and, in its Arabic propaganda broadcasts, exhorted Amman to remain outside the alliances. Though Fida'iyun raids continued to emanate from the West Bank throughout the final months of 1955, the IDF refrained from retaliating for fear of forcing Jordan either way.[35] The Israelis' decision to keep their distance did not, however, mean that the struggle for Jordan would be outside the Arab–Israel conflict. On the contrary, the conflict became central to the contest as both Britain and Egypt seized on it in their efforts to prevail over Jordan.

Britain's Jordan offensive began in the first week of November 1955 with the visit of Turkish president Jalal Bayar to Amman. Bayar had

73

come not to convince Hussein, who already favoured the pact as a means of obtaining new Western arms, but the four Palestinian members of the cabinet. These individuals, who represented the politically dynamic sector of the population, held the key to Jordan's regional orientation. In his discussions with the four Ministers, Bayar depicted the Baghdad Pact as Jordan's only safeguard against Israeli aggression and as the best means of realizing the Palestinians' demands for repatriation. Israel, Bayar pledged, would never be admitted to the organization.[36]

Shortly after the Bayar visit, on 9 November, Eden delivered a highly-publicized speech at the Guildhall which set out Britain's conception of a future Arab–Israel settlement. By stressing the need for Israeli territorial concessions and for a solution to the refugee problem, Eden aimed not only at responding to Dulles's alleged retreat from the Alpha plan (see Chapter 5), but also at assuring Jordan's Palestinians that alignment with Britain through the Baghdad Pact would surely advance their interests.[37]

The Guildhall speech served to prepare the ground for talks between Jordanian leaders and Sir Gerald Templar, Chief of the Imperial Staff, which opened on 7 December. Once again, Templar emphasized the benefits which would accrue to Jordan in terms of the Palestine problem if it adhered to the Pact and insured against future Israeli membership in the alliance.[38] His arguments, however, failed to persuade the Palestinians, who had to respond to the growing pro-Egyptian, anti-pact sentiment of their constituents throughout Jordan and the West Bank.

Egypt had done much to influence opinion among Jordan's Palestinians. Taking advantage of the sharp rise in Nasser's popularity in the West Bank which had resulted from the arms deal, Egyptian radio and propaganda leaflets informed the Palestinians that membership in the Baghdad Pact would remove whatever possibility remained of regaining their homeland and was tantamount to recognizing Israel. At the end of November, while representatives of the Baghdad Pact countries held a summit in Iraq, Nasser, together with the Syrian and Saudi ambassadors in Cairo, issued a statement which denied that meeting the right to discuss the Palestine issue. General 'Amer was subsequently sent to Amman with an offer of military aid to be used solely for the purposes of defence against Israel. Egyptian agents, aided by Saudi funding, helped to incite the large-scale demonstrations which greeted Templar on his arrival in Jordan. During the general's stay, Anwar Sadat met secretly with the Palestinian Ministers and convinced them to resign rather than allow Jordan to join the pact.[39]

The four Ministers resigned on 13 December, thereby blocking Jordan's accession to the Baghdad Pact. The event signified the high-water mark of British influence in Jordan and condemned the Baghdad Pact to a peripheral role in Middle East affairs. Continuing anti-British demonstrations produced, three months later, Hussein's dismissal of Sir John Glubb (Pasha), Commander of the Arab Legion and the symbol of British primacy in Jordan. With Glubb's removal, there was nothing to preclude Jordan's incorporation into Egypt's strategic sphere. In May, King Hussein travelled to Cairo to meet Nasser and representatives from Syria and Saudi Arabia to discuss Arab responsibility for Jordan's defence.

Egypt's victory in Jordan was very much Israel's defeat, though Israel itself shared responsibility for that outcome. Contrary to Arab perceptions, the Tiberias raid actually contributed to Jordan's rejection of the Baghdad Pact by arousing the anger and insecurity of the Palestinians. Israeli retaliations against the West Bank, which resumed in the summer of 1956, further accelerated Jordan's entry into the Egyptian camp. Egypt undoubtedly facilitated this process through its direction, unimpeded since Glubb's departure, of Fida'iyun attacks from Jordanian territory. By the autumn, Hussein could no longer resist pressures from his pro-Egyptian subjects nor could he refuse Nasser's offers of military aid. On 25 October the King placed his forces, alongside those of Syria, under Egyptian command.[40]

SUEZ: AN EPILOGUE

The struggle for Jordan brought to a climax the bilateral contest between Egypt and Israel over regional defence. Israel, the loser in that battle, subsequently determined to break the strategic arc of three Arab border states by knocking out its keystone, Egypt. Its ability to do so was greatly augmented by the Suez crisis which, by effecting a fundamental reordering of Middle East alliances, realized Israel's principal objective in the realm of regional defence.

The Powers' interest in Middle East defence, paramount since the beginning of the decade, greatly diminished in 1956. Though Eden continued to press for American membership in the Baghdad Pact, the Eisenhower Administration, disturbed by tensions in Anglo-Saudi relations and facing an election year in which Israel's exclusion from the pact might influence Jewish voting, was no more inclined to grant his request.[41] Election considerations also influenced America's rejection of Britain's appeals to 'put teeth' into the Tripartite Declaration (see Chapter 6), specifically by preparing plans for military intervention in the event of an Israeli attack on Jordan.

These developments, following in the wake of the USSR's penetration of the Middle East arms market and Nasser's rise to regional prominence, further exposed the myth of Tripartite tutelage of Middle East security. With the rapid breakdown of that system, France, hitherto excluded from regional defence by the US and Britain, began to cultivate strategic ties with Israel (see Chapter 4). The Franco-Israeli alliance was grounded on a common opposition to the Baghdad Pact as well as to Egypt.

The struggle over regional defence was eclipsed by Nasser's decision to nationalize the Suez Canal. In the shadow of that crisis, however, major transformations occurred in the traditional configuration of Middle East alliances. Britain, despairing of America's attempts to resolve the crisis by diplomatic means, allied itself with France in planning the invasion of Egypt. France then persuaded Britain to enter into a secret pact with Israel (Chapter 6), a move designed not only to topple Nasser but to save Jordan, by then essentially under Egypt's control, from Israeli attack.

Israel's long-standing assumption that guarantees for its security could be obtained from the other Powers only with prior US approval proved incorrect. On the contrary, while the US still deliberated over the issue, Britain and France acted decisively.[42] Thus, largely as a result of Nasser's successes in the region, Israel achieved its initial goal of a tacit alliance with Great Powers. Egypt, by exploiting popular fears of Israel, created specific alliances with a number of Arab states. In the end, Israel's motivation remained to safeguard its security; Egypt's, to establish its leadership of the Arab world. Fittingly, Israel's pact proved the most formidable militarily and Egypt's the most durable politically.

4

The Arms Race

The acquisition of modern weaponry was a major preoccupation – it might be said an obsession – of Egypt and Israel throughout the pre-Suez period. As in the issue of regional defence, Israel's overriding interest was strategic; arms acquisition was considered essential to the country's defence against external threats. Egypt's basic concern, especially under the military-minded RCC, remained political: to help establish the regime's legitimacy at home and its influence in the region. Though always intense, the two countries' search for weapons did not initially trigger an arms race. Such a competition, however, would emerge with the breakdown of the status quo. In time, it would dominate Egypt–Israel relations and ultimately constitute a primary catalyst for the second Arab–Israel war.

The arms issue, like that of regional defence, was *a fortiori* multilateral, featuring a high degree of international involvement. Middle East states, though wont to parade their armies as symbols of their independence, nevertheless remained totally dependent on foreign arms suppliers. These, for the most part, were the Western Powers – Great Britain and France and, to a lesser degree, the US – which together controlled the flow of almost all weaponry to the Middle East.

The Powers' policy towards Middle East arms sales was stated in the Tripartite Declaration of May 1950. That document, which purported to preserve the status quo, in fact aimed at maintaining the Powers' hegemony in the region. By limiting arms sales to the parties in the Arab–Israel conflict – it replaced a UN embargo instituted during the Palestine war – the Declaration placed formidable obstacles in the path of Arab–Israel violence. Furthermore, by stipulating that those weapons supplied be used solely for the purpose of national and regional defence, the Declaration safeguarded the Middle East arms market from outside competitors.

To secure the Declaration's objectives, the Powers created the Near East Arms Co-ordinating Committee (NEACC). With its headquarters in Washington, the Committee approved or rejected arms requests by Middle Eastern states on the basis of their estimated national and regional defence needs. At the same time, the NEACC acted to reduce competition between the Powers by ensuring that a Tripartite consensus be reached on all transactions. To this end, the committee observed the principle of 'habitual source', which recognized a Power's status as the traditional arms supplier for specific Middle East states.[1] Thus, Britain remained the 'habitual source' for Iraq, Egypt and Jordan; France, for Syria and Lebanon. The US, which historically did not have such a relationship with any state in the region, acted as the NEACC's moderator. Its task was greatly facilitated by America's ability to veto sales of 'off-shore procurement', that is arms manufactured in Europe but financed by the US and intended for use by NATO.

The NEACC system was particularly efficient in the area of arms sales to Egypt and Israel. Through the Committee, Britain was able to enforce a formal arms embargo of Egypt, levied in October 1951 in reprisal for Cairo's abrogation of the Anglo-Egyptian treaty. The Powers conducted an informal but no less total boycott of weapons sales to Israel which, in their view, was already over-armed.

The system, however, could not be sustained. Domestic economic interests, pressure from arms manufacturers burdened with Second World War and then Korean War surpluses, eventually drove the Powers to violate one another's habitual source spheres in search of arms buyers. Further undermining the system were the Powers' disagreements over the question of regional defence, and their attempts to separate that issue from both inter-Arab and Arab–Israel disputes.

The removal of the Tripartite arms limitations was one of the main causes of the breakdown of the status quo. Arab leaders, in need of arms for political ends, would receive Western military aid earmarked for regional defence, but then publicly justify the acquisition in terms of the struggle against Zionism. This would confirm the Israelis' perception of peril, and impel them to obtain more arms still. Egypt, confronted with both enhanced Israeli tactical and Arab political threats, would then seek absolute arms superiority in the region.

The rapidity of this process owed much to the technological innovations in weaponry in the 1950s. Of these, none was more destabilizing than the fighter jet. For the purchaser, such aircraft represented a quantum leap in prestige and offensive capability, and for the merchant, profits of unprecedented magnitude.

A harbinger of the system's collapse, and of the ensuing Egypt–Israel arms race, came in January 1952. The Truman Administration suddenly offered Egypt $1 million worth of 'parade items' – armoured cars, jeeps, and machine guns – to bolster King Faruq's faltering rule. The move reflected America's growing interest in Middle East defence, to which it believed Egypt's participation indispensable, as well as its ambition to replace Britain as Egypt's habitual source.[2] Britain and Israel strongly opposed the move, yet Washington was undeterred. Only the outbreak of the Egyptian revolution in July caused the Administration to pause and reconsider its decision to sell Egypt arms.

AMERICAN ARMS FOR EGYPT

The Free Officers, in one of their first foreign policy actions after coming to power, requested military aid from the United States. In doing so, they pledged to co-operate with the West on regional defence and to refrain from using the arms against Israel. The Truman Administration concluded that the new regime was earnest in proffering these guarantees and in November 1952 renewed its previous arms offer.

As in the issue of regional defence, there again emerged an enigmatic Anglo-Israeli alliance against the US and Egypt. Both London and Jerusalem vigorously protested about the American offer to Egypt, though on entirely different grounds. While the Israelis' basic concern remained security, the British feared an economic challenge to its habitual source status in Egypt. Prime Minister Winston Churchill retaliated by releasing 15 Meteor jets to Egypt and 14 each to Israel, Syria, Lebanon and Iraq, thereby defying President Truman's request that the planes be reserved for the Korean War effort.[3]

The Israelis observed this turn of events with mounting anxiety. The burgeoning Anglo-American arms race over Egypt, disconcerting in itself, had now resulted in a major increment to the Arab states' combined air power. To make matters worse, the US was trying to block the transfer of Israel's 14 Meteors in the NEACC. Sharett made strong representations to both Washington and London, demanding that the Powers ensure absolute arms parity between the IDF and the Arab armies or at least make military aid to Egypt conditional on the Officers' co-operation in a peace process. The effort was fruitless; the Powers, despite their differences over Egypt, were committed to maintaining a united front vis-à-vis Israel. Together they rejected Israel's demands, explaining that the arms, rather than increasing the chances for war, would contribute to peace by strengthening the West's position in the Arab world.[4]

While Britain and Israel protested, the Free Officers were far from pleased with the American offer. They objected to the Americans' insistence, under the Congress's Mutual Security Act (MSA), that a Military Assistance Advisory Group (MAAG) accompany the arms to ensure their exclusive use for defensive purposes. Also distressing was

79

the fact that Washington demanded payment for the weapons in dollars and refused to accept either Egyptian pounds or cotton, thereby threatening to deplete Egypt's foreign currency reserves. Most disappointing, however, was the size of the deal, which, despite indications of a significantly enlarged package, remained the same as that offered before the revolution. Under such circumstances, the Officers were extremely reluctant to purchase the American arms.[5]

America's first attempt to sell arms to Egypt was eventually frustrated by a combination of British opposition, American Jewish political pressure, and Egyptian indecision. Faced with so many obstacles, Truman opted to leave the question of military aid to Cairo to the incoming Eisenhower Administration. Though pleased with this outcome, the British were now on their guard for American designs on their habitual source sphere. The Israelis eventually received a total of 15 Meteors, but nevertheless viewed the episode as a major defeat. Not only had the Powers reiterated their opposition to absolute arms parity, but they had poignantly demonstrated the fact by providing the Arabs with an additional 58 jets. The Free Officers, alone, remained optimistic – the US had shown its willingness to break the British embargo – and determined to seek from Washington an offer which contained more arms and fewer conditions.

The chances for such an offer indeed seemed favourable by the beginning of 1953. The Republican Administration, professing 'evenhandedness' in the Palestine conflict and commitment to Middle East defence, regarded arms sales to Egypt as the bench mark of America's new rapport with the Arab world. The State Department had anticipated this change in policy and, in the period between Eisenhower's election and inauguration, drafted several large-scale arms programmes for Egypt. The objective was to convince the Egyptians that the offer was substantive, and the Israelis that 'nothing had happened'.[6]

Cairo was quick to exploit this situation. Ali Sabri, a leading member of the Free Officers, travelled to Washington, and there presented the Administration with arms orders worth $200 million. Dulles responded with a $10 million package, and considered the offer to be generous. It represented nearly half of all annual weapons sales to the Middle East.[7]

The fate of America's second attempt to sell Egypt arms was almost identical to that of the first. Britain vehemently protested over the deal which during 1953 led to marked strains in Anglo-American relations. Israel, as in the previous instance, sent urgent *aides-mémoire* to London and Washington, but received similar replies.[8] The ultimate failure of the transaction, however, resulted less from Anglo-Israeli opposition than from Egyptian discontent.

The RCC was again disappointed by the dimensions of the deal, especially in view of the fact that it did not include jets. Furthermore, in addition to the usual MSA restrictions, the US now made the sale conditional on the RCC's co-operation in resolving the Sudan and evacuation questions and in forming a regional defence organization.[9] The Officers thus rejected the offer, but in doing so found themselves in an embarrassing position. For months, the Egyptian press had been reporting the imminent arrival of American weaponry. By October 1953, the situation had become so awkward that Ahmad Hussein, Egypt's ambassador to the US, implored the Administration to sanction at least a symbolic shipment so that photographs of the arms' arrival could be displayed in Egyptian cities.[10]

Despite the Officers' rejection, Dulles and officials at the State Department remained confident that the Egyptian army would eventually be equipped with American weaponry. Meanwhile, in 1954, the Administration proceeded to offer arms to a number of Middle Eastern countries, in particular to Iraq. The US–Iraq arms deal in April, concluded in anticipation of Baghdad's adherence to the Turco-Pakistan defence pact, again brought protests from London and Jerusalem. Such opposition had been expected by Washington, though nothing prepared it for the virulence of Egypt's reaction. Cairo's Voice of the Arabs radio excoriated the deal as a Zionist–imperialist conspiracy and denounced the United States for its collusion in the plot.

Stunned by this invective, the Administration sought a means of mending its relations with Egypt. The signing of the Heads of Agreement on the British evacuation in July, by satisfying one of the conditions which America had placed on arms sales to Egypt, provided such an opportunity. The RCC, moreover, appeared receptive; it pledged to reconsider the MSA restrictions and to help minimize American Jewish opposition by reducing its anti-Israel propaganda. Thus encouraged, the American ambassador in Cairo, Jefferson Caffery, approached Nasser with a proposal for an arms package worth $20 million.[11]

In entering these talks, the US hoped that its arms deal with Iraq, which involved full compliance with the MSA regulations and a formal commitment to regional defence, would facilitate Egypt's acceptance of similar terms. But, on the contrary, that precedent severely limited the manoeuvrability of both the US and Egypt. To avoid making the Iraqis feel they had given too much for too little, the US had to secure written assurances of Egyptian membership in the Middle East defence organization and yet proffer a package no bigger than that received by Baghdad.

The situation proved untenable for Nasser. Faced with charges from domestic opponents that he had compromised Egypt's independence in the evacuation treaty, Nasser could not hazard a further qualification of Egypt's sovereignty. Nor could he, in view of the mounting Iraqi challenge in the region, accept an arms deal so similar to the one he had denounced. Furthermore, there was now less need for Egypt to accede to America's demands, for with the evacuation, Britain had ended the embargo. This created new possibilities for arms purchases, usually without conditions, in Europe. The US package, though twice the size of that proposed in 1953, was still too small to justify the political risks involved. Thus, on 29 August 1954, Foreign Minister Fawzi officially declined the American offer on the grounds of 'internal political considerations'.[12]

Loath to concede defeat, the Administration sent emissaries to Nasser to persuade him to reconsider. They offered to allow Egypt to purchase the weapons with US economic aid and to reduce the MAAG to a 40-man, non-uniformed group which would leave the country shortly after the arms' arrival. They also promised that the Administration would not make a counter-deal with Israel. Nasser, however, remained immovable. While refusing to support the Northern Tier, he presented the emissaries with a request for $100 million in armaments which, he argued, were necessary to protect Egypt from Israeli attack. Nasser warned that if the US could not meet Egypt's military needs, he would turn to another source, the Soviet Union.[13]

ISRAEL'S SEARCH THWARTED

Nasser's reference to the growing Israeli threat was an innovation in Egypt's traditional argument for arms. Though the Israelis had consistently opposed arms sales to Egypt and despite growing tensions in the border and blockade controversies, Cairo had previously taken only a minor interest in arms sales to Israel. The Egyptians may have known that the Israelis' arms search was even less successful than their own. By 1954, however, Israel had begun to register advances in the arms field which, though modest, augured the possibility of larger acquisitions in the future. With growing frequency, Egyptian representatives complained to Western interlocutors of the basic injustice of a Middle East arms balance in which Israel, a tiny country, received the same amount of weaponry as all the Arab states combined.[14]

Israel's repeated requests for arms from the Tripartite Powers before 1954 had met with almost total rejection. The consensus among the Powers was that Israel, whose forces exhibited high levels of morale and technical ability, already enjoyed a qualitative, if not quantitative, advantage over the Arab armies. The Powers also rebuffed Israel's contention of an Arab threat to its existence; the Arabs, the Powers believed, had more to fear from the danger of an Israeli attack. Finally, arms sales to Israel would have mitigated the primary value of such supplies to the Arabs, namely, to improve the West's image and to generate support for regional defence.[15]

The US, in particular, opposed arms transfers to Israel. Under instructions from Dulles, American representatives in the NEACC vetoed Israeli orders for spare parts and surplus items, and worked to obstruct transactions between Israel and other arms-producing countries, such as Canada. The Americans adduced Israel's alleged communist leanings, its inability to afford modern weapons, and its odious retaliation policy as the reasons for their opposition to arms for Israel.[16]

Israel's objective in armaments was, as stated, absolute parity with the Arab states, though Jerusalem's policy-makers realized that this was more a political line than a practical possibility. While small amounts of surplus material were purchased more or less clandestinely from private dealers, the IDF's arsenal remained precariously depleted well into 1953, the most serious deficiency being in jet power. While the Arab states had over 100 jet fighters – Egypt had acquired 41 before the embargo – Israel, after trying and failing to purchase Sabres from the US and Saabs from Sweden, had only its 15 Meteors.[17]

The reawakening of Anglo-American interest in Middle East defence, by affording the Arabs wider access to Western arms, compounded Israel's defence difficulties. One of the results of this development was the narrowing of the geographical scope of the Tripartite Declaration. Under the Eisenhower Administration, the US claimed that Iraq and Saudi Arabia, by virtue of the fact that they did not border Israel, were exempt from the Declaration's restrictions. Britain, for its part, argued that its treaty obligations to Jordan, Iraq and, after 1954, Egypt, had precedence over those stipulated by the Declaration, and necessitated higher levels of military assistance. Not to be outdone, France cited its presumed primacy in the Levant as a rationale for selling more arms to Syria and Lebanon. Israel, which had always preferred a total over a partial embargo of arms sales to the Middle East, increasingly encountered a situation in which it, alone, was subject to the Declaration.[18]

In response, the Israeli Foreign Ministry embarked on relentless press and lobbying campaigns in the Tripartite capitals. While these efforts gained some success in blocking sales of weaponry to Arab states – Jewish lobbyists in Washington frustrated a proposed US–Saudi tank deal in December 1953 – they failed to secure any arms for Israel. Paradoxically, Israel would eventually obtain weaponry as a result of the very process it feared – a Tripartite arms race in the Arab world. Thus, Britain's growing resentment of America's intrusion in its Middle East arms sphere was an important factor in its decision to sell 18 Centurion tanks and eight more Meteors to Israel in 1953. Far more significant in the long run was the attitude of the French who, angered by the loss of their Levant market to American and British suppliers working in the name of regional defence, sought compensation with arms sales to Israel.[19]

The Franco-Israeli arms relationship evolved gradually over the course of 1953–54. During that period, Israel was able to purchase small numbers of French tanks and guns and in return provided France with intelligence information on Egyptian involvement in Algeria and on British and American arms sales to Arab countries.[20] Israel's attempts to acquire substantive amounts of French weaponry, however, were consistently frustrated. The Quai d'Orsay, like its British and American counterparts, rejected the notion of arms parity between Israel and the Arab states, while the chronic instability of French governments precluded the fulfilment of several contracts.[21]

By the middle of 1954, however, serious setbacks in Indochina and North Africa, added to its exclusion from the Northern Tier alliance, led France to revise its attitude towards arming Israel. Key members of the military – Air Minister Diomede Catroux and Army Minister Pierre Koenig – looked to Israel as a means of reinforcing France's beleaguered position in the Middle East. Working closely with Shimon Peres, the Director-General of Israel's Defence Ministry, these officials managed to bypass the Quai d'Orsay. In July 1954, they signed a $15 million Franco-Israeli deal which included 30 Mystère-II fighter jets, AMX tanks, guns and ammunition.[22]

The contract represented a major breakthrough for Jerusalem. In theory, at least, a source had been found which was willing to defy the US and to sell arms at discount rates. Further encouraging signs were that the Americans, as if to follow France's lead, were moderating their position. In June, Dulles informed Abba Eban that the Administration, though it would not sell aircraft directly, would not oppose Israel's purchase of 24 F-86 Sabre jets from Canada.[23]

If the Israelis obtained any sense of relief from these developments, it was brief. Fierce opposition from the Quai d'Orsay and the State Department prevented the delivery of French arms, while Dulles in fact worked to block the sale of Canadian Sabres.[24] Then, as if to compound the Israelis' anxiety, Egypt and Britain reached an agreement on the evacuation. Not only was Egypt expected to acquire the vast stores contained in the Canal Zone but, with the British embargo lifted, it could obtain arms from Western suppliers. First among these stood France which, eager for allies in its opposition to the Northern Tier, promptly opened weapons talks with Nasser.

GENESIS OF THE EGYPT–CZECH ARMS DEAL

Nasser had indeed believed the evacuation would result in the complete rearmament of his military. His optimism, however, proved unfounded. Reluctant to destabilize the Arab–Israel balance, to deplete its own arsenals, and to remove an incentive to Egypt's adherence to the regional defence pact, Britain refused to sell arms to the Egyptian army or to provide it with any of the Canal Zone's weaponry.[25] France's offers, though substantial, nevertheless fell far short of Nasser's goal of attaining arms supremacy in the Midle East. Further frustrating the Egyptians was a sharp drop in the price of cotton, which made them even less able to pay for armaments. Nasser still could not persuade either the Europeans or the Americans to accept cotton in exchange for arms.

Such disappointments led Nasser to reconsider the possibility of obtaining arms from the Soviet Bloc countries. Though the Egyptians consistently preferred Western suppliers, their occasional threats to turn to the East were more than mere rhetoric. Since 1948 Cairo had periodically sought weaponry from the USSR. These efforts increased under the military regime, as first Naguib and then Nasser attempted to purchase arms either directly from the USSR or indirectly through its proxy, Czechoslovakia.[26]

Moscow constantly rejected these approaches, claiming that it had no interest in supporting so-called bourgeois nationalist movements. But the death of Stalin in 1953, and the subsequent rise of Nikita Khrushchev, opened the way to Soviet advocacy of Third World neutralism, including the Officers' regime. The transition was evident in the Soviets' voting at the UN and, more concretely, in the rapid improvement in Soviet–Egyptian commercial and diplomatic ties in 1954. The Soviet Union, no less than the Western Powers, looked to arms sales as a means of expanding their influence in the developing world and of disposing of mounting piles of surplus.

The ratification of the evacuation agreement in October 1954 removed the final obstacle to Egyptian purchase of Soviet arms – Britain would never have signed in the shadow of such a deal – and Cairo proceeded quickly towards that goal. In the third week of February 1955, when a Czech trade delegation arrived in Cairo, the British embassy received reports that its real purpose was to negotiate a cotton-for-arms deal between Egypt and the Soviet Union.[27]

The events of the final week of February gave further impetus to the

RCC's search for Soviet arms. Iraq, having received American weaponry, formally adhered to the Northern Tier alliance, thus making the decisive challenge to Egypt's regional ascendancy. The Gaza raid deeply embarrassed the Egyptian army, still the mainstay of Nasser's regime, and gave rise to demands from within its ranks for the means to retaliate against Israel. Though it involved neither tanks nor jets, the raid also demonstrated Egypt's lack of viable deterrence against Israel, especially as it coincided with reports – most of them highly inflated – of major Israeli arms purchases from the West. The redoubled Iraqi political and Israeli military threats, combined with the West's refusal to meet Egypt's requests, reinforced Nasser's determination to look for arms in the East.[28]

February's events also enhanced the Soviets' interest in selling Egypt arms. They, too, feared the Baghdad Pact, though more for strategic than political reasons, and believed the Gaza raid presaged the signing of a US–Israel defensive treaty. Khrushchev, however, having just participated in a rapprochement summit with Western leaders in Geneva, could not take the first step towards Egypt. The initiative would have to be Nasser's.

Nasser's approach came in March 1955, in talks between Salah Salem and Daniel Solod, the Soviet ambassador in Cairo. The results were apparently inconclusive, for the following month at the Bandung Conference, Nasser made a similar overture to Chou En-lai. The Chinese Premier, however, recommended that the USSR was in a better position to fulfil Egypt's arms needs, and so Nasser again turned to the Soviets. His efforts bore fruit; by the late spring, Egyptian generals were already studying the technical aspects of rearmament with Soviet equipment. At the USSR's invitation, Egypt submitted its official request in May, after which Egyptian and Soviet military delegations met regularly to discuss the deal's implementation.[29]

Throughout the period of his talks with the Soviet Union, Nasser persisted in his efforts to acquire arms from Western sources. Despite early difficulties, these yielded the Egyptian army an impressive array of munitions by the end of 1955: 70 tanks and 60 jets from Britain and France, and an additional 120 tanks and 50 jets from private agents in Belgium and Italy. The British were willing to sell Egypt additional arms to encourage Nasser to co-operate on regional defence, and the Americans in order to convince him to participate in the Alpha peace intitiative (see Chapter 5). For the US, however, the problem remained of the MSA conditions, which were still unacceptable to Nasser. He continued, nevertheless, to seek American arms.[30]

Nasser, in fact, would have preferred to receive arms from the US rather than the USSR, but the Americans' offer could not compare with that of the Soviets: an unprecedented $200 million worth of weaponry, including a significant number of jets. Though he had previously denied to Washington reports of his arms talks with the Eastern bloc, Nasser now warned Byroade that if the US failed to show greater largess, he would sign a contract with Moscow.

Dulles, however, did not take the threat seriously enough, nor was his Administration which was facing an election year keen on alienating Jewish voters by selling arms to Egypt. Byroade was instructed to tell Nasser that the US would 'give urgent and sympathetic consideration' to its arms requests. In July, Sabri submitted a $27.5 million order for tanks, guns and aircraft. Washington was willing to supply nearly half the equipment immediately, but still refused to waive the MSA restrictions and payment in dollars. Such concessions, Dulles determined, would only be made if Nasser committed himself to co-operate with Alpha.[31]

Nasser, however, had no intention of acceding to Dulles' terms, neither with regard to the MSA nor to Alpha. By June, Egyptian representatives in Prague had reached a final agreement on the Soviet sale and in late July they signed the contract. This described the transaction as one between Egypt and Czechoslovakia, thus reducing the chances of Western sanctions against Nasser and charges that Khrushchev had violated the détente achieved at Geneva. The package was, by previous Middle East standards, enormous: 600 artillery pieces, 500 armoured vehicles, 150 MiG 15s and 17s, 70 Illyushin-28 bombers, 20 torpedo boats, two destroyers, two submarines, small arms and ammunition.[32]

Definitive word of the Czech arms deal, as it would come to be called, reached Washington on 19 September. The official announcement came ten days later in Nasser's speech at the opening of an army exhibition. Nasser listed the factors which led him to pursue the deal: the Baghdad Pact, the ignominious conditions the West placed on arms sales to Egypt and, above all, the burgeoning Israeli threat. As proof of the latter, he cited the Gaza raid and Israel's acquisition of massive amounts of arms – 215 tanks and 70 jets – from Britain and France. Nasser was careful in stating that the Czech arms came with no conditions attached and would be used for defensive purposes only.[33]

In the following days, Western representatives hurried to Cairo in order to dissuade Nasser from concluding the deal. Nasser reiterated the explanations for his decision, with added emphasis on the Gaza raid, but pledged that the deal would be a 'one-time' transaction. Byroade, together with the CIA's Kermit Roosevelt and George Allen of the State Department, conveyed a number of admonishments. Among these were the threats of suspended economic aid and, above all, of an Israeli pre-emptive strike. Nasser did not deny this danger, but merely requested that his reasons for obtaining Soviet weapons, and assurances of their defensive nature, be conveyed to Jerusalem.[34]

ISRAELI EFFORTS FRUSTRATED AND FULFILLED

Nasser's assurances of the defensive nature of the Czech arms brought little consolation to Jerusalem. Israeli officials were acutely aware, as were Western policy-makers, that the deal had effectively nullified the Tripartite Declaration and had essentially eliminated any chance of restoring even a general arms balance between Israel and the Arab states. The Israeli Foreign Ministry not only expected the West to try to match the Soviets' offer to Egypt, but predicted that the deal would spur international competition for Arab markets. The immediate threat, however, came from Egypt. According to the Ministry's assessment, the Czech deal, which followed Egypt's assertive actions on the border and in the Tiran Straits, was the obvious next step in Nasser's campaign to lead the Arabs in the liberation of Palestine. Once it had absorbed those arms, Egypt would have no excuse for not fulfilling its repeated pledges for a 'second round'. Israel's task, then, was two-fold: to prevent inter-Power competition in arming the Arabs and to acquire sufficient weaponry to meet the Egyptian danger.

Formidable obstacles faced Israel in achieving these objectives. In September, just before the announcement of the Czech deal, the Powers voted in the NEACC to halt arms sales to Egypt and Israel in response to fighting in the Gaza and DZ areas. While the Czech deal did not, as the Israelis feared, move the Powers to lift the embargo on Egypt, neither did it lead them to renew weapon sales to Israel. The deal did, however, spark a rush of Tripartite arms offers to other Arab states, Soviet sales to Syria, and Egyptian arms transfers to Jordan, Saudi Arabia and Sudan.[35]

The Israeli government responded to these developments with urgent remonstrations to Western capitals. Sharett wrote to Dulles:

> Unless something drastic is done without delay to offset this menacing Egyptian [arms] superiority, Colonel Nasser will be [the] undisputed master of the situation, free to attack whenever he chooses. ... Israel's defensive position must and can be materially strengthened without further loss of time.

Other appeals intimated the possibility of an IDF pre-emptive strike, or of Israel itself purchasing Soviet arms. Messages were, in fact, sent to the USSR, but only to remind Moscow that it now bore the responsibility for the outbreak of a second Arab–Israel war.[36] As in the past, none of these representations brought results.

No more successful were Israel's own appeals for arms. On 16 November, Eban gave Dulles a list of weapons, including 72 Sabres, which Israel wished to purchase from the US. A less ambitious, though equally unprecedented request, was presented to British Foreign Secretary Harold Macmillan. Each met with a cool reception. Both Dulles and Macmillan were inclined to blame Israeli actions, and in particular the Gaza raid, for the Czech deal, and were wary of becoming embroiled in a Middle East arms race with the USSR. Moreover, they believed that by arming Israel, the West would drive the Arabs deeper into the Soviet camp. Israel could not, they explained, maintain an arms balance with the entire Arab world; peace, not weapons, would be the only guarantor of its security.[37]

In view of the implacable Anglo-American resistance, Ben Gurion again focused his energies on France. Following Peres's success in Paris in the summer of 1954, the Prime Minister remained sanguine of the French weapons source, especially as high-ranking members of the French military continued to show interest in arming Israel. However, a series of difficulties, beginning with a Tripartite arms embargo imposed on Israel after the Gaza raid and continuing with America's insistence that France first meet its supply obligations to NATO, precluded the full implementation of the first Franco-Israeli contract. Though the IDF did receive a sizeable number of French light tanks in 1955, not a single jet had been delivered; Nasser's claims of Israel's expanding air power were, in fact, baseless.[38] In time, Israel itself ceased pressing the deal, as the Mystère II was found to have serious aviational flaws and the IDF preferred to hold out for the more advanced Mystère IV. The French, for their part, showed no inclination either to oppose the Americans or to accede to Israel's requests, so that the issue of jet sales to Israel remained frozen.

The Czech arms deal served to break this deadlock in the Franco-Israeli arms relationship. Now, in addition to its on-going interest in promoting local opposition to the Baghdad Pact, France sought a counterforce to the enhanced Egyptian threat to Algeria as well as a replacement for its lost arms market in Syria. In September France indicated its willingness to sell Israel 12 Ouragan jets as temporary substitutes for the more advanced Mystères. The offer was expanded in October in Geneva at the Tripartite Foreign Ministers' summit, which Sharett attended in order to lobby for arms. While his importuning of Dulles and of Britain's Harold Macmillan met with little success, French Foreign Minister Auguste Pinay accepted Sharett's request for a $50 million package containing a dozen Mystère IVs and an additional 12 Ouragans.[39]

89

The Ouragans, planes vastly inferior to Egypt's MiGs, soon reached Israel but delivery of the Mystères, a more comparable fighter, was delayed by American and British opposition. Furthermore, in November, Paris lifted its arms boycott of Egypt in exchange for Nasser's commitment to refrain from interfering in Algeria. France was thus reluctant to jeopardize its restored relations with Egypt, whose recent defence pact with Syria made it an even stronger bulwark against the Baghdad Pact, with arms sales to Israel. No further transaction was possible, Paris now communicated to Jerusalem, without the public approval of Washington.[40]

Dulles, uncharacteristically, now found himself in a dilemma. He opposed arms sales to Israel on the grounds that it would remove an incentive for Israeli co-operation with Alpha and antagonize the Arabs. On the other hand, he realized that lacking both arms and a defence treaty, Israel was certain to launch a pre-emptive strike. To reconcile these problems, Dulles proposed that Israel seek weapons from France, Italy and Canada. The US would not oppose the deals, but neither would it publicly endorse them. Meanwhile, to reduce growing pressure on the Administration from pro-Israel groups, Eban would be told that the US would 'consider sympathetically' a modest Israeli request for arms.[41]

But secret American approval proved insufficient for the leaders of France, Italy and Canada, who saw no reason why the US should not share the brunt of the Arab backlash to arms sales to Israel. In addition, Dulles's offer to Eban, even if sincere, was retracted following the IDF's Tiberias raid in December. By the beginning of 1956, with Soviet arms in great quantities arriving in Egypt, the Israelis had yet to find an arms source.[42]

Confronting what he believed to be an imminent Egyptian threat to Israel's existence, Ben Gurion designated arms acquisition as the country's first priority. Throughout the first half of 1956, he sent numerous memoranda to Washington and spent many hours with President Eisenhower's special peace emissary (see Chapter 5) requesting arms. His emphasis throughout was that the US, in failing to provide Israel with the means to defend itself, would bear responsibility for the outbreak of war.[43]

These entreaties had little impact on Dulles. Though he continued to reassure the Israelis that their requests were receiving serious consideration, he remained immutably opposed to selling American arms to Israel. In the spring of 1956, when Eisenhower proposed that the US supply jets to Israel and even Nike missiles 'just to see if they work', Dulles vetoed the suggestion. However, mounting domestic pressure for some military aid for Israel continued to interfere with the Administration's efforts to sell arms to Arab countries, principally Saudi Arabia, and was already becoming a major issue in the approaching presidential election.[44]

In a further effort to address these considerations, Dulles devised Operation Stockpile. This called for the stationing of Sabre jets on Cyprus for use by Israel in the event of an Arab attack. To mitigate Arab reaction to the plan, Stockpile also provided for the supply of defensive arms, to be stored aboard a US frigate in the Mediterranean, to the Arabs. But unwilling to sell Israel the Sabres necessary to train its pilots to fly those on Cyprus, Dulles again turned to Canada.[45]

The Canadians, who produced the Sabres under an American contract, in fact favoured the sale. Prime Minister Louis St Laurent, however, refused to approve the transaction unless other Western countries joined in providing Israel with arms. The proposal became bogged down in negotiations between Ottawa and Washington, and agreement was only reached in mid-July after Dulles consented to release some jeeps and helicopters to Israel. But even this transaction failed to materialize, for with the nationalization of the Suez Canal, the deal was placed in abeyance. Reluctant to mix the Palestine and Suez issues, Dulles resolved not to announce Stockpile, and to suspend further consideration of supplying arms to Israel.[46]

Dulles's manoeuvrings on the arms question, meanwhile, led to a growing loss of patience in Britain and in France. Eden, who favoured a 'steady trickle' of arms to Israel in order to camouflage larger shipments to Iraq and Jordan, in March approved the sale to Israel of six Meteor jets. This provided France with a precedent for delivering 24 Mystère IVs to Israel in April 1956.[47]

The Mystère shipment was the culmination of months of work by Peres as well as the consequence of repeated appeals sent by Ben Gurion to French Prime Minister Guy Mollet. With a strong sense of socialist solidarity with Israel, and resentment over Nasser's alleged support for the Algerian revolution, Mollet looked with increasing favour on these requests. It remained only for France to fulfil its arms production commitment to NATO in June and Mollet would agree to additional arms sales to Israel. In a contract signed on 3 July, Israel purchased $51 million of French arms, including 36 jets, 210 tanks, and 100 guns.[48]

THE FINAL STRETCH OF THE ARMS RACE

The Czech and French arms deals triggered a desperate arms race between Egypt and Israel. Thereafter, Ben Gurion viewed Egypt's arsenal, as distinct from those of the other Arab states, as the greatest single danger to Israel's existence. Nasser, having isolated Iraq and eliminated his domestic rivals, now saw Israel as the most serious threat to his regime. With war increasingly regarded as inevitable in both countries, two questions remained: which would acquire the most arms in the least amount of time and which would be the first to be in a position to use them.

For the Egyptians, the race first necessitated more forceful opposition to Israeli arms procurements. Thus, the RCC strenuously protested against reports of American arms shipments to Israel and, in April 1956, organized mass demonstrations in Cairo to condemn Israel's receipt of French jets. Second, and more significantly, the race impelled Nasser to seek yet more arms. Though the US continued to impose an arms embargo on Egypt, the boycott was broken first by France and then by Britain; the former as a means of discouraging Egyptian interference in Algeria, the latter to regain some semblance of its former habitual source status.[49] The quantities and calibre of these arms, however, were small compared with those of the Czech deal – some forty tanks in all – causing Nasser to again look eastward.

Shortly after the arrival of the first shipment of Czech arms in December 1955, Nasser opened negotiations for a second deal with Moscow to include 100 MiGs and Illyushins. By May, the fate of these contracts appeared uncertain as rumours spread that the USSR would soon adhere to the Tripartite Declaration or would comply with a UN embargo of arms sales to the Middle East. Nasser took the precautionary step of recognizing Communist China which, lacking UN membership, would remain free to aid Egypt militarily.[50] The move proved unnecessary; that month, the USSR began expediting the second deal with the delivery of 11 Illyushin bombers. Together with these weapons, valued by Western sources at $250 million, came some 800 Soviet technicians and instructors. The undisguised presence of these personnel provided conclusive proof that it was the size of the package, and not the stipulation for a small, low-profile MAAG team, that led Nasser to reject the repeated American offers.[51]

These developments infuriated Eden and Eisenhower. Both claimed to have received private assurances from Nasser that the Czech deal had been a one-time transaction and would involve no Soviet advisers. Their umbrage figured prominently in the Anglo-American decision to withdraw from the Aswan dam project and in the imposition of a final Tripartite arms embargo on Egypt.

The IDF, meanwhile, received the first shipment of its newly-purchased French arms on 24 July. France had greatly understated the size of the package in its reports to the NEACC, and fear of American interference necessitated that the deliveries be made in secret. Thus,

French ships made nocturnal anchorings off Israel's coast (Operation Tide) to unload tanks, guns and other land equipment, while the Mystères were flown via Brindisi (Operation Dove) where they were registered as planes returning to Israel after undergoing repairs in France.[52]

Egypt's nationalization of the Suez Canal, which occurred at the height of these operations, further cemented the Franco-Israeli arms relationship. By the end of July, France was already considering Israel as a potential partner in military action against Nasser. Accordingly, it expressed a willingness to sell Israel an additional 24 F-86 jets and 10 Vauter bombers to counter Egypt's MiGs and Illyushins. With the crystallization of the alliance in September (see Chapter 6), France extended credit to Israel to pay for ordnance and spare parts and offered to loan Israel ten Dakota transport planes, 200 tanks and 200 half-tracks for its thrust into Sinai.[53]

Despite efforts to maintain secrecy, the arms activities of France and Israel soon became known to the US and Britain. Neither, however, raised serious objections to the shipments. Though concerned about the possible use of the arms against Jordan and the danger that, if revealed, news of the operations would fortify Nasser's position in the Suez debate, Eden was reluctant to antagonize his French allies during a period of joint military planning. He even approved a special shipment of Centurion tanks to Israel. The US Administration, concerned about its showing in the presidential election, chose to ignore the deliveries, and even acquiesced in the delivery of the 24 Canadian Sabres originally approved in July.[54]

The bilateral arms race concluded with the acquisition by Egypt and Israel of amounts and types of weaponry previously unknown in the Middle East or indeed anywhere in the developing world. According to Israeli calculations, the state of the Egyptian and Israeli arsenals in September 1956 was as follows:

Egypt

Tanks: 40 light, 410 medium, 60 heavy
Jets: 200 fighters, 45 bombers
Boats: 2 destroyers, 1 sloop, 3 frigates, 6 minesweepers, 4 submarines

Israel

Tanks: 155 light, 190 medium, 0 heavy
Jets: 114 fighters, 2 bombers
Boats: 2 destroyers.[55]

These figures, which in general conform to the picture which emerged from Western sources, show Egypt in a position of marked superiority in every area, especially in air power. They do not, however, represent the actual weaponry at each country's disposal at the time of the Sinai Campaign. On the eve of the invasion, Israel had only 66 of its jets in operational condition and did not expect to complete the absorption of its 60 Mystère IVs until March 1957. Egypt experienced tremendous difficulties in adapting to the sophisticated Russian techology – a large number of its MiGs reportedly crashed in training – and despite attempts to speed the training process for its pilots could fly less than a quarter of its jets by the time of the war. A similar situation existed with regard to armoured vehicles. Lacking manpower, Israel returned to France nearly half of the tanks it received for the purpose of the invasion. Egypt, also short of crews, began to transfer dozens of Soviet tanks to Syria.[56]

The arms imbalance between Egypt and Israel was, in the end, blurred by a number of circumstances peculiar to the second Arab–Israel war. Egypt withdrew significant portions of its forces from Sinai prior to the invasion and thus confronted Israel with only part of its military strength. Egypt's jet fighters, though on paper more numerous than Israel's, were grounded throughout most of the fighting, while many of the Illyushin bombers were removed by the USSR to prevent their capture.[57] On the other hand, Israel, while technically weaker than Egypt, received massive air and naval support from Britain and France. Thus, it is impossible to determine the exact influence which the Egypt–Israel arms race exerted on the outcome of the fighting; its role in triggering the war, however, remains indisputable.

5

Secret Efforts for Peace

We have seen that Egypt–Israel relations between the years 1952 and 1956 were characterized by a steady rise of tension and the gradual breakdown of the status quo. Parallel to that pattern, however, was another, covert process: the growth of contacts between Israel and Egypt. Indeed, there existed an inverse relationship between escalation and communication, as Egyptian leaders used the latter as a means of mitigating the former. Through such contacts, Egyptians and Israelis attempted to reduce tensions and to reach an understanding on peace. Their inability to achieve these objectives and the bitterness caused by that failure ranked among the primary causes of the second Arab–Israel war.

The secret contacts of 1952–56 represented a continuation of the exchanges which had taken place before the July revolution, even before the creation of Israel. Between the years 1946 and 1948, when Egypt officially opposed talks with the Zionists, Eliahu Sasson, Director of the Jewish Agency's Arab Affairs Department, held secret discussions with a number of Egyptian leaders: Prime Ministers Isma'il Sidqi and Ali Mahir, Foreign Minister Muhammad Lutfi al-Sayyid, and Arab League Secretary-General 'Abd al-Rahman 'Azzam. Sasson's purpose was to solicit Egyptian support for the partition of Palestine. The Egyptians were inclined to grant this request, but only if the international Jewish network – they were sure one existed – assisted in securing Britain's withdrawal from Suez and Sudan, and American economic aid for Egypt. Sasson, in reply, duly promised to rally his co-religionists to Egypt's cause. The Egyptians' belief in the power of World Jewry, and the Zionists' perpetuation of that myth, would constitute a recurrent theme in future Egypt–Israel communications.[1]

Sasson's efforts failed to achieve any concrete gains, nor did they prevent Egypt's drift into the Palestine war. Covert contacts between Egyptian and Israeli diplomats nevertheless continued during the fighting and increasingly focused on territorial issues, specifically that of the Negev. The Egyptians opposed Transjordanian designs on the desert – a vast, pro-British Hashemite bloc would then divide Egypt from the Arab

95

world – as intensely as they dreaded a strong Jewish state on their northern border. Beginning in September 1948, when the Egyptian army still occupied the Negev and Count Bernadotte, the UN mediator, had proposed the desert's transfer to Transjordanian sovereignty, Egyptian emissaries secretly approached Sasson with proposals for permanent armistice agreements. In these, the Egyptians insisted that all or parts of the Negev be annexed to Egypt or, together with the West Bank and Gaza, to an independent Palestine state.

The Israelis rejected Egypt's demands for the Negev, an area to which they attached great economic, strategic and ideological value, and which accounted for over half the partitioned Jewish state. Resisting intense pressure from the US and Britain to relinquish the Negev in return for retaining Western Galilee, an area not allocated to the Jewish State under the partition, Israel proceeded to drive the Egyptian forces out of southern Palestine. These actions, together with rising domestic opposition to Faruq's regime, removed whatever possibility had existed of a separate Egypt–Israel settlement. Even during the Rhodes Armstice talks, the Egyptians still sought some foothold in the desert, but without success. Israel's military initiatives, rather than diplomacy, had determined the fate of the Negev.[2]

The Negev issue, nevertheless, continued to constitute a central theme in Egypt–Israel contacts. In secret talks held behind-the-scenes at the Lausanne Conference in the spring and summer of 1949, the Egyptians again demanded the desert as a quid pro quo for any future settlement with Israel. The Israelis still rebuffed the notion of territorial concessions in the Negev, though in one instance expressed a willingness to sacrifice some Negev land in exchange for the annexation of Gaza to Israel. But the Egyptians, after initially conveying support for the plan, were forced to reject it out of fear of violent domestic repercussions to any agreement with Israel, especially one in which it acquired another part of Arab Palestine.[3]

After the collapse of the Lausanne Conference, Egypt–Israel communications expanded through both direct and indirect channels. The latter were conducted thorugh the good offices of the British Foreign Office and the US State Department. The Egyptians favoured this venue; it enhanced their image in the West while reducing the danger of exposure. The Israelis, however, certain that the Powers would demand of them more concessions than would the Egyptians, preferred direct exchanges. These occurred between Israeli and Egyptian diplomats in Europe, the United States and Turkey, and between Israeli officials and leading Egyptian figures. Thus, the Israelis held talks with Yasin Serag al-Din, Chairman of the Egyptian Parliament's Foreign Affairs Committee,

Prince Abbas Hilmi, a senior Egyptian Foreign Ministry official, and Ahmad Abboud, an industrialist closely connected with the crown.[4] Most involved on the Israeli side were Abba Eban through his personal rapport with Mahmud Azmi at the UN, Shmuel Divon, the Chargé D'Affaires at the Paris embassy, especially assigned the task of meeting with Egyptian and other Arab figures, and Gideon Rafael, an expert on Arab affairs at the Foreign Ministry.[5]

These contacts bore many similarities to previous discussions. The Egyptians still insisted on secrecy, and persisted in their belief in the power of World Jewry. On the other hand, the crystallization of the Arab–Israel conflict significantly raised Egypt's risk in holding such discussions. Thus, while formerly willing to speak in an official capacity and, on occasion, to pass written as well as oral communications, the Egyptians now stressed the personal nature of their remarks and refused to commit any of them to writing.

Their claims to officiousness notwithstanding, the Egyptians' comments on the question of peace were virtually uniform. In addition to disavowing any desire for war, they expressed an interest in an agreement with Israel. In such a settlement, Israel would have to offer the refugees the option of return or compensation – most would undoubtedly choose the latter – and agree to international supervision of Jerusalem's Holy Places. These conditions represented a significant softening of Egypt's previous position, but on one issue the Egyptians still refused to compromise. Israel would have to cede the Negev either to Egypt or to Jordan. The desert, the Egyptians explained, would provide a buffer between Egypt and Israel, and territorial contiguity between Egypt and the Arab world.

Israel's concession of the Negev would not, however, result in an immediate settlement. The Egyptians often reiterated that any treaty was, for the foreseeable future, impossible due to their domestic and regional constraints. In the interim, the Israelis would have to accept a certain degree of friction in their relations with Egypt, and understand that such acts as the blockade and armed infiltration were political necessities for Egypt and not representative of any truly belligerent intention. Still, the Egyptians were interested in limiting friction, and to that end proposed that Israel dispense with celebrations of its 1948 victory and make financial gestures to the refugees.[6]

These positions differed sharply from those presented by the Egyptians to both the West and the Arab world. In conversations with Western officials, the Egyptians made their willingness to consider a settlement conditional on Israel's prior implementation of UN resolutions on Palestine, i.e., withdrawal to the partition boundaries, repatriation of the refugees, and internationalization of Jerusalem. Before Arab audiences, the Egyptians repeated their demand vis-à-vis the UN resolutions but scrupulously avoided any mention of a settlement. Rather, they expressly negated peace and often stressed the need for a 'second round' with Israel.

In contrast to Egypt, Israel's position on peace was consistent, irrespective of whether it was presented publicly or in private. Israel would compensate the refugees, establish a free port in Haifa, and facilitate air and land communications between Egypt and the Arab world. Repatriation of the refugees, apart from a small number admitted under a family reunification plan, and territorial concessions, except for minor border adjustments, were ruled out.[7] Accordingly, Israel periodically issued peace proposals designed to accustom the world to the territorial and demographic status quo, while spotlighting the Arabs' rejection of it.

Israel's main goal, however, was to achieve a separate peace treaty. The policy was predicated on the belief that by negotiating directly and individually with Arab leaders, Israel would have to make fewer concessions than if the Powers and other Arab states were involved. Thus, from 1949 to 1951, Israel conducted secret discussions with King Abdullah of Jordan and with Syrian leaders Husni Za'im and Adib Shikshakli. In each case, the goal was the same. As one American diplomat, commenting on the Syrian contacts, commented: 'The Israelis want peace, not peaceableness'.[8] The Egyptian contacts, however, were especially prized by the Israelis, as they represented recognition from the most powerful Arab state. Even Ben Gurion, who was often sceptical of the contacts' worth, believed peace had first to be made with Egypt.[9]

The Egyptians, thus, hoped to gain political and economic advantages from their contacts with the Israelis. Their main purpose, however, was to maintain the status quo and avoid another outbreak of hostilities. For this reason, escalation of tensions between Egypt and Israel almost invariably led to a rise in communications between the two. This correlation between confrontation and contact was illustrated in the first half of 1952, during which time friction mounted steadily on the Israel–Egypt border. With increasing frequency, Egyptian diplomats appealed to their Israeli counterparts not to take advantage of Egypt's worsening internal instability by attacking Gaza or Sinai. In February, several representatives to the Egyptian parliament even went so far as to call openly for a peace settlement with Israel.

In attempting to improve communications with the Israelis, however, the Egyptians encountered a growing number of constraints. The remarks of the Egyptian representatives, coming at a time of such high Arab–Israel friction, triggered a backlash of criticism in the Syrian and

Iraqi press. In reaction, the Egyptian government vigorously denied the statements had even been made. Through secret channels, the Israeli Foreign Ministry sought clarification as to whether the representatives were signalling a change in Egyptian policy. Its requests, however, went unanswered.[10]

The episode tended to reinforce the suspicion held by Ben Gurion and other Israeli leaders that the contacts were no more than a diversion to allow Egypt to prepare for the 'second round'. Communications, however, continued. In July, only days before the revolution, Serag al-Din met with Divon in Paris and reiterated the Wafd party's willingness to consider a future settlement in return for Israel's help in pressurizing the British.[11]

THE FREE OFFICERS AND THE QUESTION OF PEACE

The July revolution inaugurated a new phase in the history of secret contacts between Egypt and Israel. Much to the Israelis' satisfaction, the Free Officers indicated their lack of interest in the Palestine dispute, and retained as their civilian Prime Minister Ali Mahir, a veteran of the 1946–48 contacts. In the weeks after the coup, Naguib acted to reduce border friction and anti-Israel propaganda, and made a highly-publicized visit to a Cairo synagogue, reportedly signing its guest book in Hebrew.[12] These gestures, especially those made to the Egyptian Jewish community, were interpreted in Jerusalem as demonstrations of goodwill towards Israel, and served to dispel some of Ben Gurion's doubts vis-à-vis negotiations with the Arabs. Early in August, he instructed the Foreign Ministry to draw up a peace initiative aimed at Egypt's new rulers.

In a speech before the Knesset on 18 August, Ben Gurion congratulated the Free Officers and wished them success in realizing Egypt's national aspirations, and then formally invited them to peace negotiations. At the same time, Divon in Paris presented Ali Shawqi, his counterpart at the Egyptian embassy, with a plan for achieving an interim non-belligerency pact. The treaty would include border adjustments, programmes for economic and strategic co-operation, compensation for the refugees and an international trusteeship for Gaza. A similar proposal (see Appendix V) was sent by Israel to Cairo via the US State Department.[13]

Ben Gurion's announcement touched off a wave of speculation in the Egyptian press on the existence of a secret peace process. This embarrassed the Officers at a time when they were still encountering consider-

99

able resistance from the Wafd and from unallied units in the army. However, the moderate faction within the regime, led by Colonel Nasser, favoured issuing an ambiguous response to the Israeli approach. This, at least, would keep channels of communication open and assure both the Israelis and the Americans of the Officers' peaceful intentions. The suggestion, however, was rebuffed by the more activist group of Anwar Sadat and the Salem brothers. Anything less than a categorical rejection of the initiative, they argued, would be disastrous for the government's domestic and regional relations.

The Officers ultimately concluded that the Palestine issue was simply too low a priority for the risks involved, and determined simply to ignore the invitation. In their press conferences, the Officers denied that any invitation had been received. Only in November, after reports on secret Egypt–Israel talks continued to appear in the Syrian, Iraqi and Israeli press, did Mahir finally present Caffery, the US ambassador, with a formal reply. Egypt would not consider a settlement unless Israel first implemented all UN resolutions on Palestine.[14]

The Egyptian reaction, or rather lack of it, deeply disappointed the Israelis. Eban complained to the Americans of the 'zone of silence' which separated Egypt and Israel. Divon, less restrained, threatened to publicize his talks with Shawqi if Cairo failed to respond to the invitation.[15] By October, the Israelis were exasperated. Egypt had seized the *Rimfrost* in the Canal, increased border tensions and opposed the German reparations agreement, and, in a move described as defence against Israel, recruited former Nazi officers into its army. Yet it was precisely at this juncture that the Free Officers sanctioned a series of direct contacts with Israel.

On the initiative of Egyptian diplomats, discussions were held with Israeli representatives in London, Paris and New York. The Egyptians explained that they had been prevented from responding to Ben Gurion's offer by regional and domestic constraints, but that once these were removed, the Officers would work to find a solution to the Palestine problem. Until then, the Egyptians wanted to reassure Israel that they had no plans for war. The regime's public pronouncements on Palestine, it was explained, were for domestic consumption only, and its recruitment of the former Nazis was solely for the purposes of internal security.[16]

In the light of these exchanges, Ben Gurion concluded that Egypt still presented the best chance if not for a peace treaty, then at least for a tacit understanding on non-belligerency. He resolved to pursue the contacts but at the same time to go public with the peace plan which had been conveyed to Cairo. The initiative again proved abortive. The plan, entitled the Blueprint for Peace, was presented to the UN General

Assembly in December and there met with stiff resistance from Egypt and the Arab states. During the course of the debate, Eban held extensive talks with Azmi. The Israeli ambassador stressed the substantive nature of the plan – it was no mere tactic – and its amenability to Egypt's interests. Azmi, however, could not be persuaded; the plan violated Egypt's sovereignty by presuming to impose conditions on it. Despite sponsorship by eight nations, the resolution failed to receive the necessary two-thirds majority vote in the Assembly.[17]

Conflicting signals from Cairo continued to reach Jerusalem before the end of the year. At the same time that General Naguib was reportedly co-ordinating anti-Israel strategy with Syria's Colonel Shikshakli in Cairo, the Officers were still sending messages of goodwill, even of their desire for peace, to Israel.[18] In November, Ali Mahir presented the British embassy in Cairo with a plan for resettling Palestinian refugees in the Negev. A month later, Mahmud Fawzi, Egypt's ambassador to London, gave Hector McNeil of the British Foreign Office an outline for a step-by-step peace process. This stipulated a period of secret mediation, to be followed by direct talks, and finally a UN peace forum.

As Egypt's consul in Jerusalem from 1941 to 1944, and as representative to the UN in 1947, Fawzi had had extensive contacts with Zionists. Now, and increasingly in his future capacity as Foreign Minister, Fawzi served as the Free Officers' tool in 'testing out the waters'. His task was to solicit reactions to various proposals on peace, thus enabling the Officers to ascertain Israeli and Great Power attitudes towards the issue, and to formulate their policy accordingly. More importantly, by presenting a moderate position, Fawzi served to impress the Powers and to placate the Israelis. Fawzi, in fact, refrained from committing himself to his proposals, and when pressed to, invariably retracted them. McNeil, for example, passed Fawzi's plan to Jewish leader Nahum Golmann who, in turn, conveyed it to the Israeli Foreign Ministry. But before Jerusalem could respond, Fawzi withdrew from the initiative, claiming it was 'premature'. However, this would not be the last instance of an Egyptian plan for step-by-step mediation, nor of Fawzi's efforts to 'test the waters'.[19]

Such contradictions in Egyptian policy caused considerable confusion in Israel. Ben Gurion suspected that Egypt was deliberately misleading Israel in order to dissemble its preparations for the 'second round'. By contrast, Sharett, together with many of his protégés at the Foreign Ministry, retained a sense that the contacts represented a nonpareil form of Arab recognition and that, at worst, they could help reduce bilateral tensions. With that, Sharett recommended that Israel seek a full peace treaty with Egypt – it required as much energy as an interim agreement –

101

and parallel to that, however possible, avoid antagonizing the Free Officers.[20]

1953: YEAR OF EXPANDED CONTACTS

The Revolutionary Command Council had set for itself two goals which were indeed revolutionary: the restructuring of Egypt's economy and its complete liberation from Britain. In order to focus on internal reform, and to gain America's aid to put pressure on Britain, the RCC had to avoid confrontations with Israel. Yet the Officers also strove for more traditional Egyptian objectives: ensuring the regime's domestic rule and securing its leadership of the Arab world. Both these necessitated opposition to the West and, especially, resistance to Zionism. The policy of secret contacts, then, by placating Israel and impressing the West, offered a useful means of reconciling some of the fundamental contradictions in Egyptian policy.

Egypt's use of secret contacts would, however, become increasingly problematic over the next year, as Israel launched more aggressive operations and Britain, backed by the US, began building its Middle East alliance. These measures threatened the RCC's domestic and regional status, leading it to adopt a more assertive posture on Palestine. Fearing war, however, the RCC simultaneously sought an expansion of contacts with Israel. Such communications, moreover, would for the first time include official messages from the Egyptian government. This development indicated the RCC's interest in achieving, if not an immediate peace, then at least a continuous dialogue with the Jewish State. Its basic goal nevertheless remained to preserve the status quo.[21]

The contacts of 1953 were facilitated by US and British diplomatic channels as well as by several prominent go-betweens. Among the latter were UN negotiator Ralph Bunche, Pakistani Foreign Minister Zafrullah Khan, and Labour MP Richard Crossman. In meetings with Naguib, Nasser and Fawzi, now Foreign Minister, these intermediaries received the usual Egyptian viewpoints – flexibility on the refugee and Jerusalem issues, insistence on obtaining the Negev – with a generally more optimistic assessment of the chances for peace after the British evacuation. Israel's position was also consistent. In return for an end to the Egyptian blockade (i.e., not for a peace treaty), Sharett offered to compensate the refugees and suggested that funds for that purpose be obtained through international loans or the German reparations. The most tangible result of these exchanges was an agenda produced by Bunche dealing with the refugee problem, Jerusalem and territorial matters for use in future peace talks.[22]

More frank and substantive exchanges occurred in direct talks between Egyptian and Israeli diplomats. The year witnessed the opening of two main channels: in Washington, between Colonel Chaim Herzog, the Israeli military attaché, and the Egyptian attachés, Colonels Ghalib and al-Shaf'i, and in Paris, between Divon and the Egyptian press attaché, Abd al-Rahman Sadiq. The former, it will be recalled from Chapter 1, dealt principally with the border situation. The latter, undoubtedly the most important of any of the contacts, served as a conduit for more comprehensive communications between Sharett and Nasser.

Nasser's objective was to persuade Israel to cease its political and military pressure on Egypt. This, Sadiq imparted, was undermining the RCC's relations with the West, and especially with the US from which Egypt had requested arms and economic aid. Nasser wanted Israel to refrain from border retaliations, to desist from efforts to challenge the blockade in the UN and, in general, to stop depicting Egypt as an aggressor. On the positive side, Nasser requested Israel's assistance in directing American pressure on Britain to evacuate the Canal Zone. In return, Nasser promised to reduce some of the restrictions on oil shipments to Israel through the Canal and to limit its anti-Zionist propaganda. Apart from that, Israel would have to realize that peace, for the present, was impossible, and a certain level of hostility unavoidable.

Divon, in reply, explained that Israel's military and diplomatic position towards Egypt was only a reaction to the RCC's belligerency on the border and the blockade, and its propaganda attacks against Israel. If Nasser moderated his attitude, agreed to regular meetings between high-ranking Egyptian and Israeli officials, and lifted the blockade, Israel would instruct its Washington lobby to support aid for Egypt and, in addition, would secretly purchase $5 million of Egyptian cotton.[23]

The positions of the two sides were eventually presented as lists of demands and proposals; Israel's on 29 January and 3 June (Appendix VI), Egypt's on 13 May. These generally conformed with the substance of the Divon–Sadiq discussions, with the exception that the RCC, wary of becoming beholden to Israel, politely refused the cotton purchase. Nothing came of these suggestions, though the positive atmosphere which they generated may have contributed to the achievement that June of the Distressed Vessels Agreement between Egypt and Israel.

Beginning in July, however, Egypt–Israel relations entered a period of marked decline. That month, the RCC increased its anti-Israel propaganda with the inauguration of the Voice of the Arabs broadcasts and, in September, convened a summit of Arab chiefs-of-staff in Cairo, reportedly to co-ordinate military planning against Israel. Israel completed the transfer of its capital to Jerusalem and, in the following weeks, it began the Jordan river diversion project, launched the al-Burayj raid, and constructed a kibbutz in the DZ. Tensions reached a climax in October with the IDF's attack on Qibyah village in the West Bank and with Cairo's decision to tighten the blockade in the Suez Canal.

Untypically, the contacts between Egypt and Israel became erratic and strained in this period. The RCC rebuffed Israeli proposals for meetings between senior officers to discuss border affairs and for the dispatch of a high-ranking Israeli diplomat to Cairo.[24] The Officers' retreat from the talks might have been necessitated by the Arabic press, which continued to publish reports, leaked perhaps by more activist members of the RCC, on the contacts. These led to charges from the Syrian and Iraqi governments, as well as from the Muslim Brotherhood, that the RCC was 'soft' on Israel. Indeed, in March 1953, Naguib tried to defend his policy in a telegram to Lebanese leader Camille Chamoun:

> Egypt is convinced that instead of answering negatively to [Israeli] peace proposals, it is better to present many and far more ambitious demands, while continuing to stick to the demand for the implementation of the UN resolutions. In the event that these demands are met, then the Arab states will face an all new situation. If Israel rejects them – it will appear responsible for the resultant situation.[25]

Over the coming months, however, the RCC's need to curry Arab favour by taking stronger stands against Zionism and imperialism but still impress the West and reassure Israel, would steadily grow. As a result, the lull in communications proved merely temporary.

DENOUEMENT OF THE DIRECT CONTACTS

Even as Egypt–Israel relations deteriorated, the leaderships of the two countries underwent changes that would greatly influence the contacts between them. Ben Gurion's retirement in October 1953 and Naguib's removal in April 1954, brought to office the two men who had been most involved in the secret exchanges. During the period in which their terms of office overlapped, Sharett and Nasser engaged in an unprecedented number of communications and exchanged views on the most substantive issues. This development, though indicative of a greater willingness to communicate on the part of both leaders, did not reflect any particular readiness to compromise on basic positions. There is no evidence to suggest that the policies of Sharett and Nasser towards peace differed in

104

any way from that of their predecessors. Rather, the distinction was merely tactical, and owed less to these leaders' moderation than to their inability to arrest the degeneration of the status quo.

Fundamentally, the breakdown of the status quo can be seen as a result of Egypt's and Israel's failure to achieve some resolution of the blockade and border controversies. The various attempts to ameliorate these situations through direct channels, in the Azmi–Eban talks at the UN and in the proposed Riad–Tekoah meeting, all failed. The Israelis had come to doubt Egypt's sincerity in reaching any understanding. The Egyptians suspected that Israel intended to transform talks on tension reduction into political negotiations.

By the spring of 1954, the RCC was even less inclined to negotiate with Israel. Nasser, who had only begun to consolidate his rule at that time, still faced domestic opposition from the Muslim Brotherhood and regional challenges from Iraq. In an effort to bolster his position, Nasser began to stress Egypt's Arab identity and its leadership of the pan-Arab movement. The démarche was officially announced in Nasser's speech marking the second anniversary of the July revolution:

> Egypt has started a new era of relations with the Arabs ... the aim of the revolutionary government is for the Arabs to become one nation with all its sons collaborating for the common welfare.[26]

The policy necessitated greater assertiveness in the struggle against Zionism, the *sine qua non* of Arabness, and strongly militated against efforts to defuse Egypt–Israel tensions.

The concomitant growth of Egypt's Arabism and anti-Zionism was manifest in its escalation of border violence and its attempts to tighten the blockade. Israel reacted resolutely to these actions by staging repeated retaliations and by challenging the blockade in the UN. These moves, in turn, provoked Egypt to demonstrate further its steadfastness on the Palestine issue.

The escalation of tension again produced an expansion of the secret contacts. A central theme in these exchanges was Egypt's position on Palestine after the future Suez evacuation agreement. In contrast to the public statements of National Guidance Minister Salah Salem, which pledged Egypt's aid in liberating Palestine once it had ejected the British, Nasser secretly assured Sharett of his intention to work for a settlement as soon as the evacuation commenced. Meanwhile, Nasser stressed, it was paramount that Israel do nothing to frustrate that process. Sharett responded that he would welcome Egyptian efforts for peace, and would not interfere with the evacuation, provided that it took into account Israel's vital interests.[27]

105

The Heads of Agreement of 27 July did not, as we have seen, address Israel's interests. Consequently, Sharett sent the *Bat Galim* through the Canal and Israeli intelligence activated its underground cell in Egypt. These operations brought Egypt–Israel relations to their lowest point since the 1948 war and, in the process, generated the most intensive round of direct contacts.

If gravely disappointed with the West's reaction to the *Bat Galim* test case, Sharett was shocked by the sabotage actions of Unit 131, which had not received his authorization. Politically, the danger now existed that Israel's involvement in the conspiracy would be exposed, causing a major international backlash and the government's certain collapse. Personally, Sharett deeply feared for the lives of the ten Egyptian Jews and the Israeli agent jailed in connection with the operation.

To limit the political damage, the Israeli Foreign Ministry embarked on a prodigious propaganda campaign, code-named Operation Alex. The object was to depict Egypt's charges of Israeli complicity in the plot as fabrications and to focus international attention on Egypt's alleged mistreatment of the suspects and of Egyptian Jews in general. Working through the World Jewish Congress, Israel also hired two European lawyers, Rene Gehant and George Wilson, as advisers to the Egyptian Jews, most of whom held either German or French citizenship. Through these representatives, Jerusalem was able to dictate to the Egyptian defence counsel, Ahmad Rushdi, his principal argument – that the defendants had not been working for an enemy country because the EIAA had ended the state of war between Egypt and Israel. Finally, Israel sent Roger Baldwin, Chairman of the International Human Rights Commission, to Egypt to observe the trial and to report on any improprieties in its conduct.[28]

These measures, though effective in mitigating the potential political repercussions of the trial, did little to remove the danger of death sentences. The possibility of such an outcome was significantly raised by the fact that the defendants were accused of espionage – arson was only a secondary charge – and by the recent hanging of six members of the Muslim Brotherhood implicated in an attempted assassination of Nasser in October. Faced with mounting criticism of its suppression of the Brotherhood from Syria and Iraq, Egypt had justified those executions by claiming that the condemned had been spying for Israel. In such circumstances, it was highly unlikely that Nasser could show greater leniency towards the Jews. Sharett's only option, then, was to appeal directly to Nasser and to persuade him of the deleterious effect of death sentences on the future of Egypt–Israel relations.[29]

In Egypt, meanwhile, the spy trial caused a serious rift within the RCC.

The activist faction pressed for handing down the harshest sentences, especially as these might defray some of the backlash to the regime's crackdown on the Brotherhood. Nasser, supported by Chief-of-Staff 'Abd al-Hakim Amer and Interior Minister Zakariya Muhi al-Din, favoured minimizing the punishment in order to preserve Egypt's image in the West, so recently improved by the signing of the evacuation treaty, and to deny Israel the grounds for retaliating militarily.[30] Ultimately, it was decided to try the case before a Military Tribunal, open to foreign observers and the press, and to respond favourably to Sharett's requests for direct communications.

The contacts, which began in late November, were both direct and indirect. The former took place between Israelis and Egyptians in Paris, most significantly through the Divon–Sadiq channel; the latter were conducted through the offices of two British MPs, Maurice Orbach and Richard Crossman. Though the exchanges were to concentrate on the *Bat Galim* and the Cairo spy trial, they soon expanded to incorporate all the outstanding issues in Egypt–Israel relations, including the question of peace.

The Israelis reiterated their interest in a comprehensive settlement and in regular negotiations between plenipotentiaries. Failing to agree to that, Egypt could still demonstrate its goodwill by fixing a six-month period during which Israel-bound oil shipments and a few Israeli-flag vessels could pass freely through the Canal. Israel, in turn, would mobilize its resources to obtain Western aid for Egypt. Sharett requested clemency for the accused in the Cairo spy trial – at one point he offered to trade them for Egyptian prisoners in Israeli jails – and, in a less entreating tone, demanded that the *Bat Galim* be permitted to continue its voyage through the Canal (see Appendix VII).

Nasser iterated that, while peace was still impossible in the present situation, he would give serious consideration to any peace plan which addressed Egypt's demand for territorial contiguity. He accepted in principle the six-month relaxation of the blockade, provided the destinations of the oil cargoes could be properly camouflaged, but excluded Israeli-flag ships from the agreement. As in previous communications, Nasser proposed a mutual reduction of border tensions and hostile propaganda. He would impose a curfew in Gaza and, as a further gesture to Israel, oust Salah Salem. Lastly, Nasser conveyed his intention to release the *Bat Galim* under the Distressed Vessels Agreement, but not to allow its passage through the Canal, and to show leniency towards the Jewish defendants, but only to a degree acceptable to Egyptian public opinion. Throughout the communications, Nasser expressed anger over Israel's interference with the evacuation of Suez and with its 'duplicity' with Egyptian communists and the Muslim Brotherhood. These acts, he charged, and not the blockade were the real reasons for the decline of Egypt–Israel relations.[31]

The contacts, though substantive, were ineffective in heading off a crisis. On 22 December the Israeli agent, Max Binnet, committed suicide in his Cairo cell. The incident, following the attempted suicide of another prisoner, Marcelle Ninio, gave rise to Israeli allegations that Egypt was torturing the defendants to extract confessions. Then, on the last day of the year, the Cairo Military Tribunal reached its decision: eight of the defendants were found guilty and two of them, Moshe Marzouk and Shmuel Azar, were sentenced to death. At the same time, Israel received an unprecedented written note from Nasser (Appendix VIII) expressing his gratitude for Sharett's recognition of Egypt's desire for peace and his hope that Israel shared that commitment.

The message, though unique, failed to mollify the Israelis. In his talks with Sadiq in Paris, Rafael accused the Egyptians of having reneged on their assurances against the passing of death sentences. The Foreign Ministry appealed to the Western Powers to intervene to save the lives of the two condemned men and, through the machinery of Operation Alex, managed to flood Nasser's office with thousands of telegrams from church, university and political leaders:

> In the case of ten Jews tried before military tribunal whose sentences are before you for confirmation strongly urge you in name of humanity and in interest of not increasing tension in Middle East show leniency and not confirm any death sentences.[32]

These tactics only infuriated Nasser. He rejected the appeals, refused to receive another visit by Orbach, and through Sadiq retracted his offers for relaxing the blockade and reducing tensions. The RCC, meanwhile, began countering Operation Alex by issuing its own pamplets detailing the activities of the Jewish saboteurs. Nasser finally confirmed the sentences on 27 January 1955; they were carried out four days later. In the Knesset, Sharett raged:

> The ruling clique in Egypt has decided to strengthen its position against its rivals at home and its opponents abroad by shedding Jewish blood ... Egypt will not be absolved ... the State of Israel will not forget the martyrs.[33]

Sharett's own words bespoke the collapse of his diplomatic strategy towards Egypt. His failure to break the blockade, to acquire arms and to meet the challenge of the Baghdad Pact, brought Ben Gurion back to the Defence Ministry, and with him a greater willingness to strike militarily.

The Gaza raid, which signified a major turning point in the overt areas of Egypt–Israel interaction, also had a powerful impact on the secret efforts for peace.

The Gaza raid completely surprised Nasser, who believed that the secret contacts represented Israel's guarantee against such actions. He ordered a suspension of communications with Jerusalem, but this again proved to be only a short hiatus. Though Nasser would remain embittered at Israel, and at Ben Gurion in particular, for the Gaza attack, he would renew the contacts in the spring of 1955, and subequently expand them in proportion to escalating tensions. By that time, however, the importance of such communications was overshadowed by the peace initiatives of the United States and Great Britain.

THE RISE AND FALL OF PROJECT ALPHA

Though they differed greatly on many issues relating to the Middle East, the Western Powers – France, the US and Britain – shared a common attitude towards the Arab–Israel conflict. All operated on the assumption that the conflict was the main source of anti-Western feeling in the region, and rejected both the Arabs' insistence on the *status belli* and Israel's demand for demographic and territorial integrity. Thus, the Powers were initially committed to a comprehensive change of the status quo. That commitment was expressed in the preamble of the Armistice and in UN resolutions on the refugees and the blockade.

The Powers, however, overestimated their ability to effect that change. The failure of the Lausanne Conference demonstrated the difficulties in achieving an Arab–Israel settlement. Unwilling to impose peace on the belligerents, but fearing the impact of a 'second round' on world peace and on their Middle East hegemony, the Powers resolved to preserve the status quo. This position attained its fullest expression in May 1950, with the issuing of the Tripartite Declaration. The Powers nevertheless remained eager to resume the search for a settlement and, to that end, US and British officials continued to devise proposals for peace.

At the US State Department, the general feeling was that Israel was more to blame for the conflict than the Arabs, and that its resolution would require Israeli, rather than Arab, concessions. The Department, however, was under the aegis of the Executive which, in turn, was constrained by 'domestic political considerations', a euphemism for American Jewish pressure. But the Republican Administration, being traditionally less reliant on American Jewish support, could be more even-handed towards the conflict. Dulles, whose memoranda indicate a marked antipathy to Zionism and its supporters, stressed America's need

109

to distance itself from Truman's support of Israel and to renew its relations with the Arab world.[34] The State Department welcomed this shift in US policy, and shortly after the 1952 elections, drafted a preliminary treaty between Egypt and Israel. The plan, which presaged all subsequent US proposals on the issue, called for extensive Israeli territorial concessions, repatriation and compensation of the refugees, and American aid for the Arabs.[35]

In addition to its balanced attitude towards the Arab–Israel conflict, the Eisenhower Administration also professed an abiding aversion to European imperialism. Ideally, the US would have preferred to pursue peace unilaterally, without the involvement of the other Powers. The question of peace was, however, integrally entwined with that of Middle East defence, to which the Administration attached great importance. France, lacking a real strategic presence in the area, could be excluded from any American initiative, but not so Britain. On the contrary, in view of their paramount role in Middle East defence, the British had to be full partners in all the Administration's efforts for peace.

The British Foreign Office, even more than its American counterpart, tended to favour the Arab position in the conflict. Yet, while not having to operate under domestic constraints, Whitehall did have to act in accordance with its long-established interests in the Middle East. Thus, the Foreign Office realized that peace was essential for safeguarding Jordan against Israeli expansionism, ensuring stability in Iraq, and for creating a Middle East defence organization. On the other hand, the British also understood that a settlement which failed to satisfy Arab demands would result in the isolation of Baghdad and Amman in the Arab world and generate additional resentment towards Britain in the region. As a result, British diplomats saw peace as necessitating even more extensive Israeli concessions than those envisaged by the State Department. Appropriately based on a formula favoured by Nuri al-Sa'id, their plan called for a compromise between Israel's current borders and those of the 1947 partition resolution. Israel would offer to repatriate any refugee wishing to return and compensate the rest and, in return for retaining Western Galilee, concede the entire Negev.[36]

Like Israel, the Powers were also aware of the opportunities for peace created by the Egyptian revolution, and thereafter closely monitored the course of the secret contacts between the RCC and Israel. Though the Free Officers repeatedly told the US and British ambassadors of their inability to negotiate with Israel under present circumstances, they nevertheless intimated their willingness to enter into a future treaty, as well as into a regional defence organization, provided Egypt could obtain the Negev. The regime's demand was received with sympathy in London and Washington, where territorial contiguity between the two halves of the Arab world was considered beneficial to Western strategic interests. Insofar as Israel had previously agreed to concede part of the Negev in exchange for Gaza, it was logical to assume that, with the proper inducements, it would yield even more of the desert.[37]

Joint Anglo-American planning for an Egypt–Israel settlement began in April 1953 and called for Israeli concessions in areas occupied in 1948 as well as in the Negev. The RCC soon made it clear, however, that no progress towards either peace or Middle East defence could be made before a solution was found to the Suez and Sudan controversies. This point was verified by Dulles in talks with Nasser and Naguib in May 1953. As a result, the Secretary of State re-ordered the Administration's priorities. Now an Anglo-Egyptian agreement would precede an Egypt–Israel settlement. Additional Arab–Israel treaties would follow, culminating in the creation of the Middle East defence organization.[38]

While striving for the first objective, Dulles did not intend to ignore the peace issue entirely. Rather, he recommended that a project be launched to 'nibble at the edges' of the conflict. Such an undertaking would reassert the West's monopoly over Arab–Israel diplomacy – an essential facet of its control over the entire Middle East – and prepare the ground for regional defence. The Secretary identified the targeted 'edge' in his speech of 2 June 1953, in which he proposed the solution of the refugee problem through a massive resettlement project. The concept reflected American thinking on the refugee issue going back to Lausanne, and was based on the plan prepared by Charles T. Main of the Tennessee Valley Authority. Main's thesis was that many if not most of the refugees could be resettled on reclaimed desert lands irrigated by the Jordan and the Yarmuk rivers. The project, to be known as the Jordan Valley Authority (JVA), would represent the first Arab–Israel agreement since the Armistice, and thus serve as a precedent for more comprehensive settlements.[39]

Eric Johnston, Chairman of the Advisory Board of the Technical Co-operation Administration, was assigned to secure Arab and Israeli acceptance of the plan. In October 1953, he embarked on the first of several tours, and the beginning of over two years' negotiation, in the Middle East. Though not a riparian state, Egypt was included in Johnston's itinerary in recognition of its ability to influence Arab opinion and, more significantly, of its centrality to future peace settlements.

The RCC accepted Johnston's invitation. Though they objected to the amount of water allocated by JVA to Israel, the Officers saw in the plan an opportunity for excluding Iraq from a regional project, for limiting Israel's ability to irrigate the Negev, and for acquiring American aid for Egypt. Furthermore, the resettlement of the refugees would reduce

111

Arab-Israel friction at a time when the regime feared being forced prematurely into a war. Thus, the RCC readily co-operated with Johnston, and established an Arab Technical Committee, chaired by Mahmud Riad, to formulate an Arab version of his plan.[40]

Johnston arrived to a far less enthusiastic reception in Israel. In addition to opposing Egypt's involvement in the project, the Israelis resisted the notion of a step-by-step approach to a settlement, in particular one which did not involve direct negotiations. They further resented the JVA's stipulation of international supervision for the Sea of Galilee, its exclusion of the Litani and Hasbani rivers, and the relatively small quantity of water it earmarked for Israeli agriculture.[41]

By the end of 1953, US policy towards the Arab-Israel dispute appeared to be nearing its objectives. The Administration had firmly established its even-handed reputation by adopting stringent measures against Israel's retaliation policy, and against its attempts to divert the Jordan river and to transfer its capital to Jerusalem.[42] The Arab states, led by Egypt, were still displaying receptivity to the Johnston mission. In the early months of 1954, they proposed an Arab counter-plan which, though it drastically reduced Israel's water share, seemed to recognize Israel's boundaries. Washington looked on these developments, together with the signing of the Anglo-Egyptian agreement on Sudan, as proof that mediation of an Egypt-Israel settlement could indeed begin after the evacuation.[43]

Events over the course of 1954, however, outlined the difficulties which the Powers' peace efforts would later encounter. In April, it will be recalled, the State Department failed to convince Cairo to sanction the Riad-Tekoah meeting. That same month, Washington received from Egypt the first indication that the JVA might run into political opposition in the Arab world. Finally, in November, Nasser refused to receive Jacob Blaustein, an American Jewish leader who had been sent by Dulles to explore Cairo's attitudes towards a settlement. Britain experienced similar disappointments. Nasser rebuffed attempts by Nuri al-Sa'id, backed by the Foreign Office, to solicit Egyptian co-operation on a peace initiative.[44]

These episodes did not diminish the optimism with which Whitehall and the State Department still viewed the chances for a peace process. These, they insisted, had actually increased. The RCC had communicated its commitment to co-operate with peace efforts after the evacuation, and other Arab governments had expressed their willingness to follow Egypt's lead; the US had established its 'even-handedness' in the Palestine dispute; and Israel was far more susceptible to international pressure. Britain's success in the Northern Tier, meanwhile, had 'shaken up Arab state relations', creating inter-Arab rifts which could be exploited.[45] This information served to obscure any evidence to the contrary, and in November, concurrent with the failure of the Blaustein mission, the US and Britain launched a major initiative, code-named Alpha.

In its principles, Alpha reflected previous Anglo-American planning for Arab–Israel peace. Ultimately, Alpha aimed at a comprehensive settlement of the conflict, though its immediate goal was a non-belligerency pact between Israel and Egypt. In recognition of the fact that the RCC did not have a pressing interest in peace and would incur considerable risks in negotiating with Israel, the plan provided for a number of incentives – 'gimmicks' as the State Department called them – for Nasser. Israel would have to repatriate 75,000 to 100,000 refugees and compensate those who preferred resettlement in the framework of the JVA. The Holy Places in Jerusalem would come under international supervision. Egypt would receive arms within the context of the Middle East Defence Organization and economic aid for construction of the Aswan Dam. The central feature of Alpha, however, remained Israeli territorial concessions. Israel would have to surrender land along the Jordan border to reunite villages divided by the Armistice and, more significantly, cede a large part of the Negev to provide territorial contiguity between Egypt and the Fertile Crescent.

Israel, by comparison, would receive neither membership of the defence organization nor, apart from an international loan for refugee compensation, economic aid. It would, however, secure termination of the secondary Arab boycott – blacklisting and the blockade – and US guarantees of its borders, but only after making the necessary territorial sacrifices.

The architects of Alpha, Francis Russell, the former First Secretary at the US embassy in Tel Aviv, and Evelyn Shuckburgh, Whitehall's Under-Secretary for Middle Eastern Affairs, recommended a strategy which had proved effective in mediating the Trieste dispute. A prominent mediator would shuttle between Cairo and Jerusalem and seek to narrow the differences between them. The first approaches would be to Nasser, to ascertain his willingness to accept such a plan and to lead the rest of the Arab world towards peace. Israel, meanwhile, would be 'kept in the dark', to prevent it from accepting Alpha prematurely thus forcing the Arabs to reject it, or launching a counter-initiative to sabotage the plan. In either case, the Israelis might demand the border guarantees without giving anything in return.[46]

After a short delay caused by the Gaza raid and the signing of the Baghdad Pact – the Arabs, it was feared, might associate those events

113

with Alpha – Nasser received his introduction to Alpha. This was conveyed by the new American ambassador in Cairo, Henry Byroade, a former Under-Secretary of State with extensive experience in Arab–Israel peace plans, and by Britain's Secretary of State, Harold Macmillan. Byroade and Macmillan revealed only general aspects of Alpha, placing stress on its stipulations for territorial contiguity. They informed Nasser that the US and Britain had succeeded in 'deflating' Israel by denying it arms and security guarantees, and 'injected realism into its thinking'. Egypt, they claimed, should take advantage of the situation while it lasted and, in the process, reap significant gains in terms of territory, aid and the leadership of the Arab world.[47]

Nasser's response reflected the long-standing Egyptian position on peace. While he did not reject the notion of a settlement, he could not at present commit himself to a negotiation process due to political constraints. Fawzi, who was also present during these dicussions, characteristically gave a more moderate reaction, and readily accepted most of Alpha's principles. Both Nasser and Fawzi, however, were united in rejecting the concept of an Egyptian corridor across the Negev – 'an artificial ambush trap for the future' – and in demanding the entire desert, including Beersheva. Regardless of whether it was annexed by Egypt, Jordan or a West Bank–Gaza Palestinian state, the desert would have to be ceded in full.[48]

Alpha's planners thus concluded that the key to the plan's success lay in the Negev. Further, they believed that Nasser's demands with regard to the desert represented only an opening bargaining position, and could be reconciled with Israel's interest in Eilat port. They considered numerous schemes for the desert – an Egypt–Israel condominium, a Western trusteeship, or an autonomous Arab administration – before deciding on the 'kissing triangles'. According to this concept, Israel would relinquish two triangular sections of the Negev, their bases on the Egyptian and the Jordanian borders. The apices of the triangles would touch – 'kiss' – several miles north of Eilat, thus linking the two halves of the Arab world. Later versions included a bridge over or a tunnel under the 'kiss' that would remain under Israel's control and ensure access to Eilat. 'Solomon,' according to one Foreign Office official, 'could do no better.'[49]

'Kissing triangles', however, proved no more acceptable to Nasser. He remained unswerving in his insistence on the entire Negev. Even Fawzi, who agreed to a major reduction in the number of refugees to be repatriated and even to let Israel annex Gaza, would not countenance Israel's retention of Eilat. To break the deadlock, the Foreign Office expanded the Negev concessions to conform to the 1947 partition boundaries – the so-called 'Northern Triangles' – but this, too, failed to persuade the Egyptians. The British and the American ambassadors alternately enticed Nasser with offers of economic and military aid and worried him with threats of an impending Israeli pre-emptive strike, but could not effect a change in his position on peace.[50]

The Israelis, meanwhile, had become extremely anxious over Alpha. The Foreign Ministry had learned of the plan almost from its inception, most probably from the CIA which resented State Department interference in its purview, and was quick in expressing its profound reservations. Prime Minister Sharett, in requesting details of the plan from Dulles, spelled out Israel's basic position:

> I would be failing in my duty of candour towards you if I did not make it clear beyond any possibility of misunderstanding that there can be no question for us of cessation of territory or the return of the refugees ... This does not of course exclude the technical demarcation of the frontiers at a peace settlement which may entail minor and mutual adjustments nor the continued application for the benefit of Arab refugees of the reunion of families scheme.[51]

Dulles responded by assuring Sharett that the US had Israel's interests in mind and requesting him to refrain from any actions which might frustrate the search for peace. As with his attitude towards Nasser's demand for the Negev, Dulles regarded Sharett's opposition to territorial compromise as an opening position. The Israelis, he had reason to believe, would at least agree to placing the territorial issue on the agenda, and would, if loans were available for that purpose, accept the principle of refugee compensation. There remained, then, a favourable chance for Alpha's success.

By the beginning of June 1955, however, much of Dulles's optimism had dissipated. Discouraging reports emanated from the Middle East. Violence on the Gaza border was rising, and Arab support for JVA falling. Ben Gurion, who the Americans believed to be more intransigent than Sharett, would soon return to the premiership, while Nasser had opened arms talks with the Soviets. The bulk of Dulles's concern, however, stemmed from domestic political factors. With election year approaching, Dulles feared that pressure on Israel would become too costly to the Republican Party, and would certainly be exploited by the Democrats. To avoid this situation, and to generate bi-partisan support for the Administration's policy, Dulles proposed to 'go public' with Alpha.[52]

Dulles presented the general concept of Alpha in a speech to the Council on Foreign Relations on 26 August. While stressing the need for

115

a solution to the Jerusalem and refugee problems, Dulles omitted virtually any reference to Israeli territorial concessions. Instead, he emphasized the need for Arab recognition of, and international guarantees for, Israel's borders.

As such, the speech was deplored by the Arab press, and formally denounced by the RCC. Privately, Nasser still refused to commit himself to a peace process, although he did express disappointment in the fact that Dulles's speech had not specified Israel's concession of the Negev. Fawzi remained sanguine; Egypt would co-operate with the plan provided that Israel pledged to concede the Negev and that the United States distanced itself from the Northern Tier. Israel, by contrast, welcomed the speech. Sharett described it as 'an emphatic effort to obtain in [the] Middle East a state of peace and co-existence between Arabs and Israelis' and Eban as 'a serious act of public statesmanship'. Jerusalem petitioned the State Department for further details of the plan.[53]

The sharpest reaction to the speech, however, came not from the Middle East, but from London. Eden and officials at the Foreign Office felt that they had been deliberately misled by Dulles. The American Secretary had submitted a number of drafts of the speech, all of which focused on the need for concessions in the Negev, yet, in the end, Dulles had delivered a 'watered down' version of Alpha. This, the British believed, had greatly reduced the chances of implementing Alpha and had jeopardized their position in Iraq and Jordan.[54]

Anglo-American collaboration on Alpha had never been free of tensions. Disagreements emerged on issues ranging from the size of Israeli concessions, to which of the Powers would pay the project's costs.[55] Dulles's speech, however, drove a permanent wedge between the US and Britain on the question of peace. Joint planning on Alpha would continue at the bureaucratic level until April 1956, but for all practical purposes the project had become defunct the previous October.

That month, while the West reeled from the impact of the Czech arms deal, British and American peace efforts received another blow in the Arabs' rejection of the JVA. Johnston had done much to conciliate the Arab position on the project, including a pledge that the plan would not prejudice a final settlement in Palestine, and thus obtained the approval of the Arab Technical Committee. Arab Foreign Ministers also favoured the JVA but, fearful of a popular backlash to an agreement which appeared to recognize Israel, insisted on submitting it for ratification by the Arab League Political Committee. There, on 15 October, the delegates voted to withhold acceptance of the JVA 'until an agreement safeguarding Arab interests is reached'.

The Political Committee decision typified the Arab position on peace.

Privately, Arab leaders were open to compromise, but publicly, because of political constraints, had to reject all efforts at conciliation. Egypt, in particular, illustrated this pattern: Nasser secretly backed the JVA, even after its rejection but, in the Political Committee forum, led the fight against it.[56] Israel, for its part, acted to intensify the pressures on Arab rulers. In the aftermath of the Arab League meeting, Sharett declared that Israel would resume work on the Jordan diversion project in three months. The announcement, in addition to increasing the chances for war, greatly reduced the chances for peace. Indeed, any Arab leader consenting to a settlement would seem to be buckling before Israeli *force majeure*.

The Powers, through their policies on arms and regional defence, also contributed to the deterioration of the status quo and the diminishing of chances for peace. Yet, at precisely this juncture, both Britain and the United States embarked on separate initiatives to achieve a settlement between Israel and Egypt.

THE GUILDHALL FORMULA

In accord with the correlation between escalation and communication, contacts between Egypt and Israel rose over the course of 1955. Renewed shortly after the Gaza raid, the contacts paralleled Anglo-American action on Alpha. These again involved a number of prominent intermediaries: the Black American Congressman Adam Clayton Powell, the *New York Times* publisher Cyrus Sultzberger, the Jewish activist Ira Hirshmann, and the Egyptian industrialist Ahmad Abud.[57] At first, the exchanges focused on the worsening border situation but by end of the summer they increasingly centred on the arms race. As much as Nasser was anxious to conciliate Israel and the West in view of rising Arab belligerency so, too, he sought to mitigate repercussions to one of the by-products of that process: the Czech arms deal.

The shift in emphasis from border to arms was illustrated in one of the most extensive mediation efforts of the period, that of Elmore Jackson. An American Quaker official with experience in Arab–Israel affairs, Jackson was approached by Ahmad Hussein, Egypt's ambassador in Washington, with an offer to mediate secretly the outstanding differences between Egypt and Israel. The initiative, Hussein claimed, had the blessing of both Fawzi and Nasser.

Jackson made three trips to Israel and Egypt between July and September. While wanting to address more substantive issues, the mission soon became bogged down in the border situation. Jackson sought an agreement whereby in return for Israeli constraint in the face of

117

Fida'iyun attacks, Nasser would relax the blockade and release the surviving members of Unit 131. The démarche failed, however, when Nasser reneged on a pledge to recall the Fida'iyun and Israel retaliated at Khan Yunis. By the first week of September, Nasser's attitude towards the mission changed dramatically. Instead of seeking calm on the border, Nasser now requested that Jackson secure him a personal meeting with President Eisenhower. The purpose, Jackson understood, was to press Egypt's case for American arms and, if that failed, to soften the anticipated Western reaction to an Egyptian deal with the Soviets. Eisenhower, however, denied the request, and subsequently Nasser lost interest in the mission.[58]

The Czech deal had a profound effect on regional and international politics in the Middle East. Viewed locally as triumph for Arab nationalism, and as a blow to Western hegemony in the region, Nasser's action greatly stimulated Arab opposition to the Baghdad Pact and to the pro-Western leaders of Jordan and Iraq. As such, the deal provided impetus to the Powers' efforts to achieve an Arab–Israel settlement. British and American policy-makers alike considered the deal a direct consequence of the Arab–Israel conflict – specifically of the Gaza raid – and a settlement as the only way of preventing further Soviet penetration of the Middle East. The Powers disagreed, however, as to the means for obtaining that settlement.

Eden and the British Foreign Office concluded that the Czech deal necessitated not only a peace initiative, but also efforts to strengthen the Baghdad Pact by adding Jordan to its membership. The idea, essentially, was to kill two birds with one stone. By 'going public' with a peace plan favourable to the Arabs, Britain would not only obtain goodwill in the region, thus regaining ground lost to the Soviets, but also placate Jordan's Palestinian population. Bitter towards Britain and now zealous for Nasser, the Palestinians opposed any attempt to enlist Jordan in the Northern Tier alliance.

Eden's plan retained most of Alpha's basic concepts. The refugees would be either repatriated or compensated, and Israel would receive guarantees for its borders. In contrast to Dulles's speech, however, and its stress on the benefits for Israel, Eden would emphasize the advantages for the Arabs. Resurrected was Nuri's old formula for a compromise between Israel's present boundaries and those of the partition resolution. This, it would be later explained, meant that Israel could retain Western Galilee, but only in return for relinquishing the Negev to Egypt. In preparing his initiative, however, Eden discounted reports from his Cairo embassy to the effect that Nasser had disavowed any interest in a settlement. Rather, he concentrated on Nasser's presumed eagerness to

118

soothe some of the West's rancour over the Czech deal and to take advantage of his ability to negotiate from strength.[59]

Eden presented his plan at the Lord Mayor of London's annual banquet at Guildhall on 9 November. The Foreign Office had anticipated Israel's reaction well. Ben Gurion, who had taken over the premiership on 1 November, described the speech as an effort 'to truncate Israel for the benefit of its neighbours'. Egypt's response, however, was unexpected. Though resistant to the notion of guarantees for Israel's borders and insistent on obtaining the entire Negev, Fawzi agreed that the plan should serve as a basis for indirect mediation. Nasser, still non-committal, nevertheless offered to sponsor an Arab League discussion of the speech.[60]

Eden believed that Guildhall had succeeded in reviving the Alpha project. Subsequent efforts to commit Egypt to a concrete course of action, however, were unsuccessful. Nasser not only failed to sponsor an Arab League summit on the plan, but effectively blocked Nuri's efforts to that end. In December, parallel to the collapse of Britain's efforts in Jordan, Nasser publicly castigated his own Deputy Prime Minister, Ahmad Khayrat, for telling a UN press conference that Egypt would accept British mediation. Thus, as with his attitude towards the Jackson mission, Nasser exploited the Guildhall plan to reduce the threat of a British reaction to the Czech deal. But once that danger had passed, Nasser demurred from committing himself to any aspect of a negotiative process.[61]

Foreign Office heads were quick to blame the Guildhall's failure on Israel. The IDF's actions in the Tiberias and al-Sabhah raids, they believed, were deliberate attempts to torpedo the plan. Much of Britain's bitterness, however, was directed at the United States. Though Dulles recognized Guildhall's value in terms of 'shock treatment' for Israel, he refrained from publicly endorsing the plan. In his view, Eden had greatly lessened the chances of a settlement by mixing the issue with that of regional defence. Furthermore, the timing of the Guildhall speech, from the Adminstration's point of view, was particularly unfortunate. It came at a time of Dulles's attempts to obtain bi-partisan support for his position on Palestine and, more importantly, to secure Israeli co-operation on Alpha.[62]

In the wake of the Czech deal, Washington redoubled its efforts to reduce Israeli opposition to the territorial and demographic aspects of Alpha. These, however, produced no significant progress. Sharett, who doubted whether Nasser would make peace even if Israel satisfied his 'whim' for the Negev, would neither commit himself to surrender territory nor to repatriate refugees, and certainly not in advance of negotia-

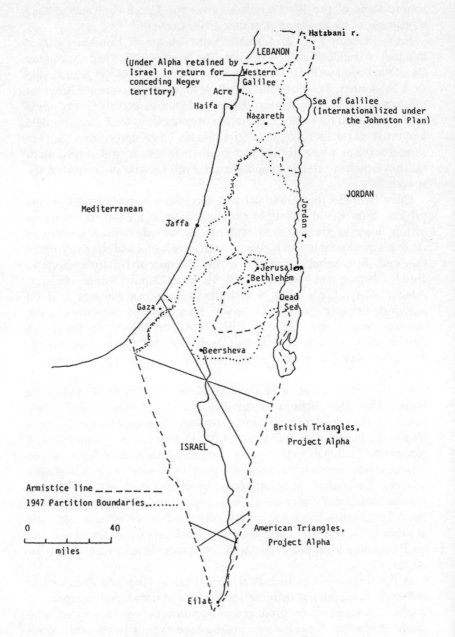

British and American Peace Plans 1953–56

120

tions. The Israeli Foreign Minister was especially swift in rejecting the 'kissing triangles' formula which, he claimed, gave territory to two countries which had no right to it, and which left Eilat 'hanging on a slender thread'. Such concessions, Sharett, argued, would be 'the beginning of a slippery slope leading to further Arab demands'. Nevertheless, Sharett accepted a negotiating agenda which included the territorial and refugee issues, and agreed to indirect mediation by any third party, except Britain.[63]

Despite their rigidity, Dulles thought he detected some 'give' in Sharett's responses, and saw advantage in the fact that Israel, in the wake of the Czech deal, had to negotiate from a position of weakness. More encouraging were the messages emanating from Cairo. Fawzi was again pressing the United States to undertake a peace intiative. State Department officials, previously doubtful of Fawzi's reliability, now concluded that he spoke with Nasser's approval. In the following weeks, their assumption appeared to be substantiated. Nasser offered to 'pilot' Arab League acceptance of the JVA, and suggested that measures be taken to reduce tensions in the area created by the Czech arms deal. Then, on 28 October, the Egyptian leader suddenly communicated his readiness to discuss a Palestine settlement, as well as other regional issues, with the United States.[64]

OPERATION GAMMA: AMERICA'S LAST GAMBLE

Nasser's *volte face* on the question of peace also reflected his desire to mitigate America's reaction to the Czech deal. This was especially critical in the light of the opening of negotiations with the US on financing the Aswan Dam. These immediately ran into difficulties as Nasser charged that the conditions for the aid impinged on Egypt's sovereignty. There remained, also, the need to mollify Israel – the situation in the DZ had seriously deteriorated – and to dissuade it from renewing work on the Jordan diversion project thus provoking a military clash with Syria. Lastly, Nasser sought to drive a wedge between the US and Britain over the Baghdad Pact. Throughout the coming discussions, Nasser insisted on linking the Palestine and regional defence issues, making his cooperation on the former contingent on American concessions on the latter.

Nasser's démarche generated considerable excitement in Washington where Dulles had yet to abandon the concept of Egypt as the cornerstone of America's Middle East policy. Tied to military aid and the finance of the Aswan Dam, and free of Britain's imperialist taint, peace talks could 'get Col. Nasser back on track' and act as a test of his sincerity.

121

Furthermore, progress towards a settlement would remove the Palestine issue from the 1956 presidential elections, relieve pressures on the US to sell arms to Israel, and lessen the likelihood of an Arab–Israel war. The Administration moved quickly to exploit the opportunity by launching a new initiative, code-named Gamma.[65]

Fundamentally, Gamma retained the principles of Alpha, especially with regard to the Negev and refugee issues, but much of its *modus operandi* derived from a previous project of the Central Intelligence Agency. In September 1954, the CIA, capitalizing on its close relationship with both Cairo and Jerusalem, attempted to arrange a meeting between Nasser and a high-ranking Israeli official. The operation, carried out by Kermit Roosevelt and James Angleton, had a number of code-names: Camelot, Chameleon, Mirage.

The CIA registered some initial success. By warning Nasser that the Israelis would use his refusal to meet with them as a means of undermining US–Egyptian relations, Roosevelt secured Nasser's approval of the meeting. Sharett, who in fact needed little incentive to co-operate with the operation, was informed of a State Department plan to force Israel to concede the Negev. Over the following weeks, the CIA facilitated exchanges of the two governments' standard platforms on peace. Sharett, meanwhile, appointed Yigal Yadin, the former Chief-of-Staff, as Israel's representative in the talks.

The proposed Nasser–Yadin meeting was delayed by the Israelis, who were angered by the *Bat Galim* episode and the Cairo spy trial. Israel, Sharett declared, 'would not negotiate under the shadow of gallows'. But when the Israelis attempted to renew the project in June 1955, Nasser ignored the approach. The State Department, Roosevelt explained to Sharett, had convinced Nasser that he had more to gain from Alpha than from the CIA's plan.[66]

Gamma represented a revival of the CIA operation in that it aimed at achieving a meeting between Nasser and a high-ranking Israeli, preferably Ben Gurion. This, however, would be a final, rather than a prelimary, stage in the peace process. Before that, the operation employed the Trieste formula stipulated by Alpha: a presidential emissary would shuttle between Cairo and Jerusalem, clarifying the two sides' positions and narrowing the differences between them, securing the support of other Arab leaders, and arranging low-level talks between diplomats. As his special mediator, Eisenhower appointed his close friend Robert B. Anderson, a former Deputy Secretary of Defence. Anderson's instructions contained incentives and disincentives for Nasser; unlimited economic aid and political support in return for co-operation but, in the event of opposition, economic and political sanctions. Similarly, Israel would be warned of severe repercussions if it failed to show flexiblity, but would also be offered arms in return for concessions.[67]

Preceded by personal letters from Eisenhower to Ben Gurion and Nasser requesting their co-operation, Anderson left for the Middle East in mid-January 1955. He operated under a tight schedule. Significant progress had to be made by 1 March, the day when Israel would resume work on the Jordan river diversion project (see Chapter 6) and when, with the opening of the presidential campaign, the Administration could no longer bring effective pressure to bear on Israel. Anderson's departure followed an upsurge of fighting on the Egypt–Israel border, but also of mediation attempts by prominent officials: Yugoslavia's Marshal Tito, Maltese Prime Minister Dom Mintoff, Canadian Foreign Minister Lester Pearson, USIA head Ted Straibert, and the British Members of Parliament, Cyril Banks and Richard Crossman.[68]

Anderson arrived in Egypt on 17 January and immediately encountered the difficulties that would plague his mission throughout. Nasser seemed less interested in talking about a settlement than about regional defence. 'My country,' he told Anderson, 'does not like to be confronted with surprises, such as the Baghdad Pact, which require counter-surprises.' The Egyptian leader also appeared obsessed with preserving the secrecy of the mission; if it were revealed, Nasser repeatedly claimed, his fate would be the same as King Abdullah's. As a result, the meetings took place late at night, with only Nasser, Roosevelt, and Zakaria Muhi al-Din present. On Nasser's insistence, Anderson could not fly to Israel directly, but only via Athens.

Apart from these obstacles, however, Nasser remained open to the idea of a settlement. The basis for this, he stressed, would be Israel's cession of the Negev on a line running from Hebron to Gaza. Though this represented an expansion of his previous demand for concessions south of Beersheva, Nasser indicated that if the Negev matter were solved, all other issues would be minor. He refused to consider a direct meeting with Ben Gurion, or to make any commitments to Israel, but agreed to sign a letter to Eisenhower, drafted by Anderson, summarizing the basic points of Egypt's position and abjuring any hostile intentions.[69]

No lesser challenges awaited Anderson in Israel. There, despite a warm reception, Anderson encountered pessimism from Ben Gurion and Sharett, both of whom charged that the mission was being used by the Administration to deny Israel arms, and by Nasser to gain the time needed to absorb his Soviet weaponry. While open to negotiation on all issues, including that of the Negev, Ben Gurion refused to rely on Nasser's secret assurances while the Arabs planned 'Israel's last stand'. He pledged 'to concede things Nasser never dreamed of' but only in direct

123

talks, and insisted that the US provide for Israel's security, lest it 'be guilty of the greatest crime in history'.[70]

Anderson returned to Cairo on 28 January to find Nasser willing to reduce tensions with Israel, including a relaxation of the blockade, and to solicit the support of other Arab leaders for a settlement. But he refused to meet with Ben Gurion until he had received guarantees of the territorial price Israel would pay. Such assurances, Nasser explained, were necessary in justifying a settlement to the Arab world. Ben Gurion, however, would make no commitments through Anderson but only directly to Nasser. Thus, by the beginning of February, Gamma was deadlocked.[71]

Responsibility for the stalemate, in the Adminstration's opinion, fell on Israel because of its demands for direct talks and arms and its opposition to territorial concessions. Indeed, in the following weeks, Egypt seemed even more eager to co-operate. Ali Sabri, now included in the discussions, met Byroade and Roosevelt and worked out a timetable for tension reduction and UN mediation of the border dispute. Accordingly, Anderson decided to concentrate his energies on achieving a breakthrough in Egypt. In doing so, however, he overlooked other dispatches from Cairo which showed a hardening of Nasser's position, and intimated that the Egyptian leader might be stalling for time.[72]

The Gamma talks resumed in Cairo on 5 March. Anderson arrived on the heels of a summit meeting between Nasser, Ibn Saud, King Hussein and Syrian president Shukri al-Quwwatli, and thus to an atmosphere hardly conducive to peace talks. More significantly, the motivation for Nasser's earlier co-operation with Gamma had diminished. The US appeared to have become reconciled to the Czech arms deal; negotiations on American aid for the Aswan Dam were nearing completion; Israel did not renew work on the Jordan diversion project and appeared weaker and more isolated than ever; Britain had failed in its effort to bring Jordan into the Baghdad Pact.

The influence of these factors was evident in Nasser's attitude towards Anderson. 'You continue to talk of the problems with Israel as if they were my problems,' Nasser now told the emissary. 'They are in fact your problems and you must settle them.' Nasser proceeded to make further co-operation on a settlement conditional on the curtailment of the Baghdad Pact, and rejected even a low-level meeting with either an Israeli or an American Jew saying 'He would still be Jew'. Nasser also rebuffed Anderson's requests that he support a renewal of the Johnston mission ('I could not openly urge the acceptance of a plan that would destroy the entire case for the refugees') and agree to a timetable for mediation. Nasser specifically derided the 'triangles' concept, suggesting that war would erupt the first time an Arab standing on the bridge would urinate onto the head of a passing Israeli.[73]

With this, Nasser terminated his dealings with the special emissary. The Israelis were willing to continue the talks, but only if they obtained guarantees of military aid. In summarizing his mission to Dulles, Anderson asserted that Nasser had deliberately misled the US on the settlement question. Time, Nasser believed, was on the Arabs' side, while a peace treaty would only impair Egypt's prestige in the Arab world. In the interim, Egypt believed it would continue to receive support from the US.[74]

On the last assumption, at least, Nasser erred. Though disgusted with Ben Gurion's incessant demands for arms, Dulles placed the blame for Gamma's collapse on Nasser. Again in co-ordination with Eden, the Secretary embarked on a punitive campaign against Egypt, code-named Omega. This called for the withholding of finance for the Aswan Dam, support for the Baghdad Pact and Nasser's rivals in the Middle East, and the 'building up' of Ibn Saud as leader of the Arab world.[75] It did not, however, mandate further efforts to reach an Arab–Israel settlement. Henceforth, Anglo-American intervention would not be directed at attaining peace, but at preventing war, which both Powers now viewed as virtually inevitable.

LAST EFFORTS FOR PEACE

Nasser's rejection of Gamma did not, however, mean an end to Egypt–Israel contacts. Thus, in January 1956, at the height of Anderson's mediation, a series of direct communications began in Brussels between the Egyptian ambassador, Ahmad Ramzi, and the Israeli consul-general, Yosef Ariel. In March, just after Gamma's demise, Nahum Goldmann received another Egyptian proposal, conveyed by Thomas Moore, MP, for a peace process.[76] The two initiatives coincided with the escalation of fighting on the Gaza border; both were attributed to Fawzi.

The Gaza situation provided the background for another, highly enigmatic, Egyptian initiative. In early April 1956, at the height of the Fida'iyun attacks, the Israeli Embassy in London was approached by Ibrahim 'Izzat, a young reporter for the Egyptian weekly, *Ruz al-Yusuf*. 'Izzat proposed that he be allowed to visit Israel and write a series of articles on the human side of the Jewish State. The Israeli Foreign Ministry readily agreed. 'Izzat toured the country for eleven days in April–May 1956, and received personal interviews with Sharett and Golda Meir. In these reports, 'Izzat repeated verbatim the substance of previous communications: Egypt's desire to preserve the status quo, but its need to maintain a certain level of tension; denials of Nasser's intentions to make war; and assertions of the defensive nature of the Czech arms. Sharett, typically, was very encouraged.[78] The same could not be said of Ben Gurion. He still regarded such exchanges as tricks to divert attention from Egypt's preparations for war. The 'Izzat episode only confirmed his suspicions. Although Israeli leaders had told the reporter of their desire for negotiations and peace, 'Izzat returned to Cairo and used their remarks as the basis of vituperative propaganda pieces against Israel.[79]

The US and Britain were also indifferent to these Egyptian manoeuvres. Thus, they dismissed Nasser's suggestion, made in late March, for separate JVA-type arrangements between Israel and each of the Arab countries. Much like Ben Gurion, Dulles and Eden had come to see ulterior motives behind Nasser's moves and plots to further Soviet influence in the Middle East. Having distanced themselves from the search for peace, both were now content to support the tension-reducing efforts of UN Secretary-General Dag Hammarskjöld.

Initially, at least, neither the Americans nor the British had much enthusiasm for Hammarskjöld's mission. Even if it succeeded – and the chances were deemed small – the mediation would open the door, by way of the UN, to Soviet diplomatic involvement in the Middle East. Presently, however, a Soviet démarche would alter the Anglo-American attitude towards the mission. On 17 April 1956, the USSR issued a communiqué calling for 'a peaceful solution [of the Arab–Israel conflict] in accordance with the national interests of all the countries concerned'. The statement reflected Moscow's concern that its military aid to Egypt would ignite a second Arab–Israel war. Yet, in the Powers' view, the announcement represented another Soviet effort to penetrate the Middle East, this time through diplomacy.[80]

Subsequently, Dulles and Eden looked to the Hammarskjöld mission as the best means of testing the Soviets' sincerity, as well as of checking their intrusion into the field of Arab–Israel peace-making. Moscow would be invited to participate in a quadrapartite effort to expand the Secretary-General's mandate to include more substantive issues in the Arab–Israel conflict. Soviet approval for such a course of action was in fact secured at a London summit meeting between Eden, Khrushchev and Bulganin at the end of April. Both sides agreed to support Hammarskjöld's mission and to work for a settlement 'on a mutually acceptable [to the Arab states and to Israel] basis'.[81]

In his capacity as Special Agent assigned to securing compliance with the EIAA, Hammarskjöld saw his task as one of narrowing the gap between the Egyptian and the Israeli positions, 'mediating ... by means of a midwife rather than those of a surgeon'. On the question of peace, the Secretary-General gave priority to the refugee issue; that, and not territory, was the Egyptians' primary concern. He also regarded Israel as the intransigent party, and the Egyptians, above all Fawzi, as open to compromise.[82]

Hammarskjöld's impressions were confirmed by his early efforts to implement a 'Suez–Sinai nexus'. This, as described in Chapter 1, was the proposed exchange of an Israeli withdrawal from the DZ for Egypt's lifting of the blockade. The Egyptians showed every indication of co-operating with the plan; Ben Gurion, in contrast, persisted in attaching conditions to Israel's compliance. By the end of May, the Secretary-General reported that the nexus was 'practically held in my hand ... All the balls are out in the field and they may still be put down into the holes'. With the nexus implemented, Hammarskjöld planned to tackle the refugee and Jordan river problems next.[83]

By the end of May, however, Hammarskjöld learned that for all Fawzi's flexibility, Nasser would never agree to the nexus. Then, on 4 June, the mission suffered another setback at the UN. The Soviets frustrated Britain's attempt to broaden the Secretary-General's mandate to include mediation of a peace settlement 'on a mutually acceptable basis'. The Syrians opposed the inclusion of the term – it implied recognition of Israel – and Moscow obliged. Disappointed by the limitation of his terms of reference, Hammarskjöld returned to the Middle East and to what appeared at first to be a pleasant surprise.

Though Egypt had publicly supported Syria's position at the UN, it now secretly presented Hammarskjöld with a staged peace plan. Drafted by Fawzi and similar to that given to Hector McNeil in 1952, the plan called for mediation by the Secretary-General and an international peace conference, to be held under the aegis of the United States, Britain, the Soviet Union, India and Pakistan.[84]

The US and Britain again suspected Egypt of acting to facilitate Soviet involvement in Middle East diplomacy. A better explanation, indeed one later surmised by Hammarskjöld, was that Nasser was seeking to improve his relations with the West, particularly in the aftermath of his recognition of Communist China. Nevertheless, the Powers agreed to support the mediation stage of the proposal, and Hammarskjöld opened exploratory talks in Cairo. These, however, failed to yield Egyptian agreement on any of the plan's stipulations. Furthermore, Nasser disassociated himself from the initiative, claiming it was ill-timed and 'too specific'. Even Fawzi, in a conversation with Hammarskjöld on 25 July, admitted that his plan was no more than 'thinking aloud'.[85]

The next day Nasser nationalized the Suez Canal. Thereafter, the US and Britain, anxious to separate the Palestine and Suez issues, distanced themselves from Hammarskjöld. Throughout the summer, in fact, there seemed little need of addressing the question of an Egypt–Israel settlement, as tensions between the two countries fell dramatically and the status quo seemed to restore itself.

Egypt–Israel tensions, however, suddenly rose again at the end of September, as the Suez crisis seemed to be heading towards resolution in the Security Council. Not surprisingly the contacts also increased. Goldmann was again approached, this time by Thawrat 'Ukashah, the Egyptian military attaché in Paris, who admitted he was operating on Nasser's orders. In Brussels, meanwhile, Ramzi warned Ariel that Nasser was under intense pressure from other RCC members to go to war, and implored Israel to refrain from provocations that would force his hand.[86] By the beginning of October the danger of large-scale violence was so great that Hammarskjöld pledged to renew his mediation mission. His efforts would indeed prove timely, but only after the second Arab–Israel war.

6

Descent to War

In the previous chapters we have seen how Egypt, impelled by the exigencies of domestic and inter-Arab politics, embarked on an increasingly assertive policy towards the Palestine issue. That process was greatly accelerated by Israel, whose political and military initiatives compelled Nasser to take the offensive, and by the Powers, whose intervention provoked both the Arabs and the Israelis and removed checks on the escalation of tensions between them. The interaction of these factors produced a chain of events – the Gaza raid, the Czech arms deal, the nationalization of the Suez Canal – which culminated in an international crisis. But that crisis provided the context, not the cause, of the second Arab–Israel war. The Anglo-French invasion of Egypt was conditioned on Israel's attack in Sinai, not vice-versa. Operation Musketeer merely determined the timing of Operation Kadesh which, in the eyes of its planners, had long been unavoidable.

Egypt and Israel's descent towards war in 1955–56 contrasted sharply with the previous two-year period, beginning with the Egyptian revolution. During those years, tensions arising from the border and blockade at times reached high levels, but were rarely so intense and comprehensive as to precipitate a full-scale confrontation. Rather than on the probability of war, the focus was on the possibility for peace. The situation, however, owed less to goodwill, or even to the absence of belligerency, than to the existence of formidable constraints on the leaders of Egypt and Israel.

Egyptian leaders preferred a Middle East devoid of the State of Israel, but were generally disinclined to translate that desire into action. Restraining them was the belief that the Egyptian army was incapable of winning, and the government of surviving, a war with Israel, and that renewed hostilities in Palestine would complicate Egypt's relations with the Powers. Nevertheless, the Officers strove to attain at least the appearance of an offensive capability. This, they hoped, would suffice to deter Israel while enhancing the regime's regional and domestic status. To achieve such a capability, however, the Officers had first to secure the British evacuation, procure modern arms, and gain ascendancy in the

Arab world. Respectively, these would guarantee freedom of action and a decisive weapons advantage over the IDF, and ensure, if war did come, that Egypt would not face Israel alone.

Israeli leaders believed that the Arab states were committed to their destruction and were inclined to respond with military action. Unlike the Egyptians, the Israelis had complete confidence in their army. Yet they, too, had to fulfil conditions before attaining an offensive capability. Israel needed the support of at least one Power, to guarantee against international sanctions and intervention, and arms, though less to strengthen its army than to safeguard its civilian sector from enemy attack.

In 1952–54, neither Egypt nor Israel had fulfilled the conditions under which they could launch a war. Over the next two years, however, the rapid deterioration of the status quo would spur them to meet those conditions. A race would develop in which the fulfilment of one country's condition would generate pressure on the second to follow suit and to consider pre-emptive action. Meanwhile, as a stop-gap measure to preserve its political status until it could meet its conditions, Egypt resorted to the Fida'iyun attacks. Israel, in order to maintain its deterrence capability until its conditions were fulfilled, conducted retaliation raids. These policies would only intensify the race and, as a result, hasten Egypt and Israel's descent towards war.

ISRAELI PLANS FOR THE CONQUEST OF GAZA

Egypt was the first to fulfil a condition for war in October 1954, with the signing of the evacuation treaty. This freed Nasser to play a more active role in regional affairs, but gave him access to the Canal Zone base. The latter, in particular, deeply worried the Israelis. Not only would Egypt receive 70,000 tons of equipment, 14,000 vehicles and infrastructure to support 80,000 men – these figures, in fact, proved greatly exaggerated – but, more importantly, it would acquire four airfields along the Canal. Using its newly-acquired British jets, Egypt could now launch a surprise attack, destroying Israel's air force on the ground and exposing its population to heavy bombardment.[1]

Egypt's success gave rise to calls within the Israeli cabinet and military for a pre-emptive strike against Egypt, beginning with the conquest of Gaza. Prime Minister Sharett succeeded in overriding these proposals, but the failure of his diplomatic strategy, together with the general escalation of Egyptian belligerency, significantly reinforced the position of those who favoured precipitous action.[2]

Ben Gurion, who while in retirement had strongly opposed the notion of invading Gaza, returned to government in February 1955 favourably disposed to the idea. The strengthening of Nasser's internal and regional position, he now reasoned, together with the Arabs' armament by the West, had turned time against Israel and justified the risks of a large-scale IDF action. By occupying Gaza, an area of Palestine vital to the RCC's legitimacy, Israel would bring about Nasser's downfall; the Western Powers would not intervene to save him, especially as the border clashes had provided Israel with a clear *casus belli*. In the wave of Fida'iyun attacks which followed the Gaza raid, Ben Gurion requested Chief-of-Staff Dayan to prepare plans for an assault on Gaza, to include the possibility of war with other Arab armies.[3]

The debate over the advisability of war was mirrored in Cairo as well. Immediately after the signing of the Heads of Agreement in July, activist elements in the army began to urge Nasser to undertake a military initiative against Israel. While willing to allow advocates of this position, in particular Salah Salem, to give public vent to their opinions, Nasser refused to take any action. The Egyptian army, he argued, was unprepared for war with Israel. It lacked the necessary equipment – the evacuation agreement had not, as anticipated, significantly augmented Egypt's arsenal – nor were the Americans willing to offer a sizeable arms package free of conditions. In addition, the regime now faced serious challenges internally from the Muslim Brotherhood and in the region from Iraq. The army's defeat at Israel's hands would surely be exploited by these elements for political ends.[4]

Israel's actions on the border and against the evacuation served to confirm Nasser's belief in Israel's aggressive nature. Nevertheless, he did not as yet consider the possibility of a major Israeli offensive against Egypt. His opinions in this respect were formed by reports filed by Egyptian military intelligence. These asserted that the IDF, though willing to conduct small retaliations, had neither the ability nor the inclination to engage in a full-scale war with Egypt. Trusting in this information, Nasser ordered Fida'iyun raids across the border. The attacks served to placate his activist colleagues while limiting the threat of a massive Israeli response. Such risks could be further reduced by direct and indirect contacts with the Israelis. Following the raids, Nasser made no effort to prepare for an IDF counter-strike. He merely reinforced his troops in Sinai and improved defences at El-Arish. These preparations, Nasser believed, were adequate for repulsing any Israeli thrust into Sinai and for driving the IDF deep into the Negev.[5]

Even then, Egypt's defensive preparations proceeded at a lugubrious pace, and were not completed until June, two months after the Fida'iyun attacks. By that time, however, such measures were superfluous. Ben

131

Gurion had already presented the Gaza invasion proposal for approval by the cabinet on 29 March. Sharett led the fight against the plan. Such an action, he argued, would result in Israel's complete international isolation, doom whatever chances remained of receiving Western arms and security guarantees, and invite Tripartite intervention. Furthermore, it would saddle Israel with thousands of refugees and bring it no closer to peace. Sharett's analysis proved convincing; the motion was rejected by a vote of eleven to five.[6]

Ben Gurion remained bitter over the defeat and vowed to implement the plan once Sharett was removed from government. Deterrence, in his opinion, had failed; Nasser was incorrigibly committed to the 'second round'. Israel, then, had only one option: the pre-emptive strike. The Gaza Strip, the scene of so many Egyptian provocations, presented a natural target for this action. But given the extent of opposition to the Gaza invasion in the Israeli cabinet, Ben Gurion turned his focus to another, no less vital objective.

OPERATION OMER: THE DRIVE TOWARDS TIRAN

Ben Gurion had always considered Egypt's blockade of the Straits of Tiran as a blatant act of war. By May 1955, he began to explore the possibility of breaking the blockade by force. His plan called for the dispatch of an Israeli-flag ship through the Straits; its certain seizure would justify the shelling of Egypt's shore positions from the sea. In early June, however, an IDF scouting party undertook Operation Yarkon, an inspection of the trail from Dahab, on the Red Sea, to 'Ayn al-Furtajah. The party determined that the route from Eilat to Sharm el-Sheikh was traversable for tanks. This discovery enabled IDF strategists to contemplate taking the Straits by land. Ben Gurion and Dayan promptly began planning an operation to this effect, scheduled for the spring of 1956.[7]

The RCC was again late in responding to this new Israeli threat. Guided by his own intelligence reports as well as by information supplied by Western diplomatic sources, Nasser continued to prepare for an Israeli strike into Gaza, which was expected some time in June.[8] That month, however, the detection of Operation Yarkon by Egyptian troops led Nasser to suspect that Tiran was now the IDF's objective. In July, the Egyptian army built fortifications on Ras Nasrani, the strategic heights overlooking the Straits, and went on high alert. The Egyptian batteries subsequently fired on HMS *Anshun* which they mistook for an Israeli vessel.

In addition to these military measures, Nasser also announced the

132

tightening of the Straits blockade. The move followed a significant hardening of Nasser's position on Israel, evidenced by Egypt's withdrawal from the Kilometre 95 talks and its dispatch of Fida'iyun into Israel. Given the explosiveness of the situation, such actions might be seen as reckless provocations of Israel. But the Arab world, and the struggle over the Baghdad Pact were Nasser's major concerns. To win that contest, Nasser had to demonstrate his steadfastness on Palestine and his refusal to be intimidated by Israeli reprisals. Until the Soviet arms were received and absorbed, however, he still could not risk a confrontation with the IDF.[9]

The outcome of the Israeli elections of 20 July served to intensify the war mood in Israel. The voting increased the Knesset seats held by the Herut party, whose members consistently called for a pre-emptive strike against Egypt, and returned to the premiership Ben Gurion, whose speeches conveyed support for such action.[10] But on entering office Ben Gurion demurred from proceeding with the Tiran operation. Rather, he proposed that Nasser be given a final opportunity to demonstrate moderation.[11] This wait-and-see period, however, proved short-lived. With the revelation of the Czech arms deal in September, Ben Gurion revived the notion of the pre-emptive strike.

The Czech arms deal fulfilled another of Egypt's conditions for war. Now Egypt enjoyed a decisive advantage over the IDF, in the air and on the ground. The event greatly strengthened the hand of those in the Israeli leadership who favoured pre-emptive action. A number of prominent officials formerly opposed to a military initiative, among them Abba Eban, Gideon Rafael and Mossad chief Issar Harel, now supported Ben Gurion on the issue. Support also came from an unexpected quarter: the United States. Though officially the Eisenhower Administration strongly opposed an Israeli action in the Straits, elements in the CIA, the Pentagon, and even Congress intimated to Israel that Washington would not be averse to an attempt to topple Nasser. Similar signals were received from London, which appeared to welcome any effort to oust Nasser as long as it did not involve Jordan and Iraq. It was the first sign that Israel, too, might meet one of its conditions for initiating a war – Great Power backing.[12]

Convinced that Nasser would attack in six to eight months, the estimated time needed to absorb the Soviet weapons, Ben Gurion instructed Dayan to formulate detailed plans for the invasion of Sinai. The Chief-of-Staff's report, dated 11 October, posited that although Egypt was receiving massive amounts of weaponry, it was at present weak, as indicated by its failure to respond to Israeli border actions. Israel, therefore, had to exploit the opportunity while it lasted by launching a two-pronged assault on the blockade. IDF infantry would drive down the eastern coast of Sinai to Sharm el-Sheikh and later link up with a paratroop brigade to be dropped in the Mitla pass; the air force would stage a lightning raid to destroy Egypt's jets on the ground. The operation, code-named Omer, would commence in December.[13]

Like the proposal for Gaza's conquest, that for Operation Omer sparked contention in the Israeli cabinet, with Sharett again leading the opposition. On this occasion, however, Ben Gurion did not insist on a vote. His reluctance to press the issue stemmed on one level from the absence of a unified government in Jerusalem – feverish coalition negotiations continued into November – but more fundamentally from his concern for Israel's new security situation. Especially troubling was Egypt's acquisition of long-range Soviet bombers which, if deployed in the Canal airfields, could easily reach Israel's population centres. Furthermore, the Egypt–Syria defence treaty, signed on 22 October, posed the danger of a two-front war.

In view of these factors, the Prime Minister decided to postpone Omer until Israel had obtained a large quantity of Western weaponry. Recent indications showed that the chances for such purchases had significantly improved as a result of the Czech deal, especially in France. The situation would be reviewed, Ben Gurion determined, after Sharett personally presented Israel's arms requests to the Tripartite Foreign Ministers. In the interim, the IDF would seek to establish clear superiority in the DZ and retaliate individually for each Egyptian provocation.[14]

Nasser, though disturbed by the outcome of Israel's elections and by Ben Gurion's return to the premiership, continued to discount the possibility of an Israeli invasion. Repeatedly warned by Western and Arab officials of the danger of an Israeli strike, Nasser still belittled Israel's military capabilities. To Byroade he boasted that the Egyptian army would draw the IDF into Sinai, and 'finish it off' in two months. 'I will face this [Israeli] threat with all my energies,' he told the American ambassador, 'and ... give you my conviction that we will defeat the Israelis if they launch an attack on us.'[15]

Nasser's confidence was again based on the optimistic assessments of Egyptian military intelligence. These now claimed that Israel would not dare attack Egypt once it possessed Soviet weapons. The West would not arm Israel for fear of the damage this would cause to its position in the Arab world, but rather would work to restrain Israel at all costs. Should Israel in any case resort to force, it would be more likely to strike at Jordan or Syria, the former to force Amman into the Baghdad Pact, the latter to discredit the Egypt–Syria treaty.[16]

These predictions appeared to be substantiated by the IDF's attack on

Syrian positions above Lake Tiberias on 11 December. That action, which resulted in part from Ben Gurion's desire to compensate Dayan for Omer's postponement, undermined the very effort for which the operation had been delayed – the acquisition of Western arms. This outcome might have moved Ben Gurion to implement Omer immediately but, instead, it merely reaffirmed his conviction that Israel could not act until it was adequately armed. Consequently, he ordered an end to retaliations against Egypt; the IDF remained passive throughout the Fida'iyun raids of April 1956. Nothing should interfere with Israel's search for weaponry.[17]

THE POWERS PREPARE FOR WAR

For all their efforts to sustain the status quo, the Powers remained acutely aware of the danger of renewed warfare between the Arab states and Israel. Such an outbreak, the Powers agreed, would most likely be initiated by Israel; the probability of an Arab attack on the Jewish State was considered minimal. In the Powers' analysis, Israel's growing need for land and natural resources and its activist ideology and dynamic society combined into an irrepressible urge to expand. The Arabs, on the other hand, were seen as weak and divided, incapable of mounting more than a propaganda campaign against Israel. Western military strategists concluded that the IDF could readily defeat one or all of the Arab armies in a matter of days.[18]

The assumption of eventual Israeli aggression was inherent to the Tripartite Declaration, and thereafter remained an important consideration in Anglo-American strategic planning for the Middle East. In theory, an Israeli attack would result in direct Tripartite intervention on the Arab side. In reality, however, a myriad of technical and political obstacles militated against joint action. Of the Powers, only Britain regarded intervention as a viable option. Its position was predicated on the knowledge that Jordan offered a tempting target for Israel, and that fulfilment of the Anglo-Jordanian defence treaty was essential for maintaining Britain's credibility in the Arab world. In several instances before 1954 RAF planes stationed in Jordan had scrambled to repulse IDF aircraft, and Whitehall had sent harshly-worded messages to Jerusalem warning of its commitment to Jordan's defence.[19]

The Powers' conception of the next Arab–Israel war underwent a gradual revision in the months after the evacuation agreement. Worsening tensions on the Egypt–Israel border, Nasser's political and diplomatic victories, the strengthening of the Egyptian army, all pointed to the possibility that Israel would switch its sights from Jordan to Egypt.

By March 1955, after the first wave of Fida'iyun attacks, the State Department and the Foreign Office both concluded that the IDF would soon occupy Gaza, igniting a war with Egypt. Intelligence reports of an Israeli military initiative, now aimed at Tiran, continued to reach London and Washington throughout the summer of 1955, and multiplied further after the Czech arms deal. While not, as noted earlier, unwelcome to some sectors of the American government, such a move was opposed by the Administration. Lacking any alternative leader for Egypt, Eisenhower and Dulles still hoped to cultivate Nasser as an ally. Eden preferred Nasser's downfall, but feared that an Israel–Egypt war would soon engulf Jordan and Iraq, thereby involving British troops in a direct clash with the IDF.[20]

The chances for the eruption of a second Arab–Israel war were greatly enhanced by the possibility that Israel would resume work to divert water from the Jordan river. Israel, it will be recalled, postponed renewal of the project until 1 March 1956 in order to give time to Nasser to obtain Arab approval of the JVA. With that date rapidly approaching, however, and no progress made on the Arab side, the Israeli cabinet was loathe to defer the project again. Such a decision, the Powers feared, would trigger a Syrian military response, thus activating the Egypt–Syria defence treaty and creating a situation in which other Arab countries – Jordan and Iraq – could not remain passive. Only through the application of tremendous pressure on Israel – sweetened by the promise of arms in return for its co-operation – did the US obtain an indefinite delay of the planned water diversion.[21]

The averting of a war sparked by the water controversy did not, by any means, eliminate the Powers' concern over the possibility of an Arab–Israel confrontation. Britain, again, was the most preoccupied with this contingency, in view of its treaties with Egypt, Iraq and Jordan. In the event of an IDF pre-emptive strike against Egypt, Whitehall predicted, Nasser would be too proud to ask for Britain's help, while Jordan and Iraq, by counter-attacking Israel, would forfeit their treaty rights to British assistance. The key, then, lay in convincing Nasser to accept Western intervention, and this, Eden believed, was possible only if the United States and Britain acted together.

Throughout the first two months of 1956, British military planners worked to secure American approval of a specific intervention scheme, code-named CORDAGE. This called for the shelling of Israeli ports and airfields, for blockading Israel's coast and occupying Eilat. The Americans, however, balked at these suggestions. While quick to assure Eden that the US would, in the event of an Israeli attack, respond under the Tripartite Declaration, Dulles added that military intervention was not possible due to Congressional constraints. Dulles agreed only to levy economic sanctions against Israel and to reinforce allied naval forces in the Eastern Mediterranean. Gravely disappointed by this refusal to 'put teeth' into the Tripartite Declaration, Eden continued to consider plans for military action against Israel. Indeed, the British army was still drafting them at the time of the Anglo-French invasion of Egypt.[22]

For all their differences over the intervention question, the Powers remained unanimous in their expectation of Israeli aggression. This assumption was severely shaken when, in early March 1956, Western diplomatic and intelligence sources began receiving reports of an impending Egyptian invasion of Israel. The Egyptian army, it was learned, had begun storing considerable quantities of supplies and ammunition along the border and was massing in Sinai. Battle orders, specifying Israel's destruction as the army's objective, were distributed to division commanders. The impression of an Egyptian intention to attack was further strengthened by the rise in hostile propaganda emanating from Cairo, Nasser's rejection of the Anderson mission, and a marked increase in Egyptian border provocations. 'We must strengthen ourselves to liberate all the Arabs,' Nasser declared in a speech delivered during this period, 'so that we may be able to restore to the people of Palestine their right to freedom and existence.'[23]

The impression of growing Egyptian belligerency was also registered by the British and the American ambassadors in Cairo. In conversations with Humphrey Trevelyan, Nasser began to intimate the possibility of Egypt occupying the Negev by force. With Byroade, he reiterated his belief that Israel, deprived of modern weaponry, posed no serious threat to Egypt; the IDF, Nasser noted, did not even dare to launch retaliations. On the basis of this information, the US and Britain concluded that Egypt intended to go to war, and probably no later than the summer.[24]

Egypt's preparations and Nasser's demeanour reflected a growing need to demonstrate an offensive capability. Prisoner to his own rhetoric and increasingly provoked by Israeli border actions, the Egyptian leader had lost his excuse not to act. The fulfilment of two of Egypt's conditions for war – the British evacuation and the Czech arms deal – inflated Arab expectations of Egypt's military prowess. Indeed, many Arab chiefs-of-staff, including Egypt's own 'Abd al-Hakim 'Amer, believed that Egypt now had the means to stage a military initiative. Nasser managed to withstand these pressures, explaining that the army had been slow in absorbing the Soviet arms and was still inferior to the IDF in air and naval power. Rather than initiating a war for which it was not yet prepared, Nasser insisted that Egypt continue to pursue the Fida'iyun policy.[25]

Throughout the spring of 1956, Egypt and Israel continued to prepare for battle, both politically and militarily. Nasser worked to conclude a second Czech arms deal and to consolidate the Arab strategic alliance. Ben Gurion concentrated on maximizing the new French arms source and on securing cabinet support for a pre-emptive strike by replacing Sharett with the more amenable Golda Meir. Such actions corroborated the evidence compiled by each country of the other's belligerent intentions, and served to spur the war-making process to its now unavoidable conclusion. On the same day, 31 March, the Egyptian War Ministry stated that 'the armed forces ... are capable of crushing and are determined to crush Egypt's enemies abroad', and Ben Gurion warned that 'Israel will crush it [Egypt] as it did in 1948 and in [the] Gaza [raid]'.[26]

THE LINKING OF OPERATIONS KADESH AND MUSKETEER

The question of the impending Egypt–Israel war which occupied much of the Powers' attention in the first half of 1956 fell into sudden abeyance with the nationalization of the Suez Canal. Paradoxically, Nasser had been emboldened to make that move by his confidence in the absence of an immediate Israeli threat. Egyptian intelligence estimated that the principal danger was of an Anglo-French attempt to seize the Canal. While Israel might take advantage of the crisis to launch a border action or to attack Jordan or Syria, it would not invade Sinai. The Egyptians assumed that the Powers, and especially Britain, would not risk their position in the Arab world by linking their cause with Israel's and, moreover, would prohibit Israel from implying such a connection. The IDF was deemed incapable of performing an incursion into Sinai's interior, either by land or by parachute drop. So sanguine was Nasser in these conclusions that even before announcing the nationalization he began to transfer troops from Sinai to the Canal.[27]

As Nasser's perception of Israeli intentions helped determine the timing of the nationalization, so too did the nationalization influence Israel's decision on when to attack Egypt. Though Ben Gurion now viewed the EIAA as inoperative, he remained resistant to Dayan's demands for taking advantage of the Suez confusion to conquer Gaza and the Straits. Such an initiative, he averred, would have to await Israel's acquisition of weaponry. The nationalization had greatly aided that effort by increasing the influence of those in Paris who advocated arming Israel as an obstacle to Nasser's ambitions. Thus, as a result of Nasser's action, Israel fulfilled the first of its conditions and appeared capable of meeting the second as well. As early as 13 August, the Israelis learned of Operation Musketeer, the planned Anglo-French invasion of Egypt. The reports, as Ben Gurion saw them, raised the possibility that Israel could

138

launch its strike with 'respectable company'. Allied with France or Britain, Israel would be safeguarded from international sanctions and intervention.[28]

Ben Gurion was optimistic of the chances for such an alliance. Discussions between Israel and France on ways of containing Nasser's involvement in North Africa and the Levant had already taken place in the spring of 1956. Shortly after the nationalization, Ben Gurion began exploring the possibilities of Franco-Israeli action against Egypt.

The French, at first, were reluctant to enter into a formal alliance with Israel. However, the failure of Dulles's diplomacy to resolve the Canal crisis, and the hesitancy of Britain to implement Musketeer, moved Prime Minister Mollet to reconsider his position. In August, he requested the use of Israeli airfields for France's jet fighters, and suggested that the IDF escalate border violence in order to destabilize Nasser's rule. By September, the French government had resolved to favour a more direct type of collaboration. In Paris, Foreign Minister Christian Pineau, Defence Secretary Maurice Bourgès-Maunoury, Chief-of-Staff Paul Ely and the Defence Ministry's Director-General Abel Thomas met an Israeli delegation consisting of Meir, Dayan, Peres and Transportation Minister Moshe Carmel. The French proposed either a joint thrust into the Sinai or a prior Israeli strike to be followed by Anglo-French intervention to 'protect' the Canal. In return, France would exert its leverage in the Levant against Syrian and Lebanese involvement in the war and, more importantly for Israel, work to secure British backing for these measures.[29]

Prime Minister Eden, however, not only withheld approval of the Franco-Israeli proposals but strenuously opposed them. In addition to recognizing the danger which co-operation with Israel presented to Britain's political interests in the Arab world, Eden was concerned that an Israeli attack on Egypt would invite Jordanian and Iraqi participation, leading to direct British involvement on the Arab side. Accordingly, he rejected France's suggestion, made at the end of August, that an Israeli assault on Tiran be excluded from the scope of the Tripartite Declaration. The following month, with the sharp rise in tensions on the Jordanian border, Whitehall again warned Israel that it would honour its duties under the Anglo-Jordanian treaty.[30]

The situation on the Jordan–Israel border continued to deteriorate. In a single month, beginning on 11 September, the IDF conducted four major raids into the West Bank. In response, Eden called for the introduction of Iraqi troops into Jordan. The move, which represented a unilateral extension of the Baghdad Pact, was a last-ditch effort to prevent Jordan from falling completely into Egypt's sphere – a process

139

which Israel had accelerated by its retaliations in the West Bank. However, in saving Jordan from Egypt, Eden risked sacrificing it to Israel, for Ben Gurion had declared that the entry of Iraqi forces would automatically nullify the Jordan–Israel Armistice Agreement. Whitehall's secret offers to Israel to reduce drastically the size of the Iraqi contingent and to restrict its movements to the Amman vicinity proved unavailing. With France refusing to intervene with Britain to protect Jordan, the possibility now arose that Britain would find itself allied with the Arabs in a confrontation with a Franco-Israeli front.[31]

Eden had to act swiftly to divert Ben Gurion's attention from Jordan. Equally urgent was the need to proceed with Musketeer. While the costs of maintaining a vast invasion force on Cyprus steadily mounted, so too did the political difficulties involved in such an attack as the Suez crisis faded from the world's attention and appeared to be heading towards an unsatisfactory resolution in the UN Security Council. Such a compromise, Eden believed, would prove unacceptable to France and, more odiously, allow Nasser to maintain his leadership of the Arab world.[32]

Relentless pressure from France, coupled with the realization that Israel, armed with French jets, could deal a harsh blow to British installations throughout the region, moved Eden to consider enlisting Israel in the attack on Egypt. At the beginning of October, he informed Ben Gurion that Britain would no longer regard an IDF thrust into Sinai as a violation of the Tripartite Declaration. By the middle of the month British and Israeli leaders, communicating via the French, began co-ordinating plans for the attack on Egypt. Though still aware of the dangers of such co-operation on Britain's position in the Middle East, Eden justified the risk by noting that Israel would no doubt exploit Musketeer to strike either Egypt or Jordan, thus giving the impression of collusion. Condemned in any event, it was therefore preferable to reap the benefits of Israeli involvement, for example by drawing Egyptian troops away from the Canal.[33] Once again, a combination of American and Egyptian policies had forced Britain into an unwanted alliance with Israel.

Active assistance from Britain was no less important for Israel. The alliance with France represented a major diplomatic and strategic achievement for Israel, but it did not suffice to protect Israel either from Western sanctions or from Egyptian aerial bombing of its population centres. To guarantee against these contingencies, Ben Gurion was willing to abandon his ambition for territorial gains on the West Bank – the plans for attacking Egypt all provided for an option strike against Jordan – and to pledge not to cross the Canal. In return, he expected Britain to destroy Egypt's air force during the Israeli invasion of Sinai

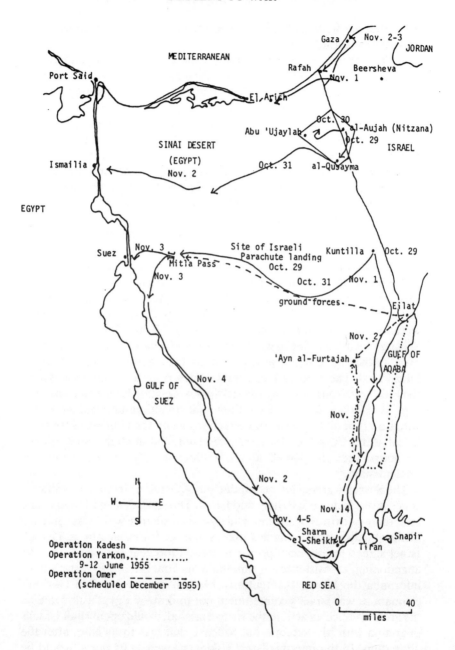

Israeli Strategic Planning for the Sinai Campaign

and, afterwards, to defend Israel in the face of the anticipated international backlash.[34]

Despite their general agreement on these points, Israel and Britain remained deeply divided on several fundamental issues. Ben Gurion, with his abiding distrust of the British, insisted that Eden's commitments to Israel both during and after the war be put in writing. He further rejected Britain's demands for a prior Israeli attack and for keeping the entire operation secret from the United States; the former, in the Prime Minister's opinion, would cast Israel in an aggressive light, the latter in a subversive one. Eden, with no less an antipathy for the Israelis, believed that Britain could fully disassociate itself from the IDF action and simply use it as grounds for reoccupying the Canal. He refused to sign a protocol which Ben Gurion could later use for political blackmail or to place his air force in a role which would clearly reveal the collusion. Indeed, throughout most of October, Eden continued to prohibit direct meetings between Israeli and British planners, and still insisted on French mediation.

A combination of time restraints and French lobbying, however, served to narrow the gap between the British and the Israeli positions. At the secret summit at Sèvres, which opened on 22 October, agreements were forged between Ben Gurion, Pineau and British Foreign Secretary Selwyn Lloyd according to which Israel would attack Gaza in the west and Tiran in the east and, at the same time, stage a paratroop drop near the Suez Canal. These operations would be described as retaliations against the Fida'iyun, thus reducing the risk of a large-scale Egyptian counterattack. Britain and France would then issue an ultimatum demanding the withdrawal of all Egyptian and Israeli troops to ten kilometres from the Canal. After Egypt's expected rejection of the ultimatum – an estimated 36 hours after the Israeli attack – Operation Musketeer would be implemented.[35]

The Sèvres Agreement, concluded on 24 October, involved significant concessions from both Britain and Israel. Though Eden and Lloyd would later deny its existence, Britain had signed an alliance with Israel and had further pledged not to join in Jordan's defence if Jordan attacked Israel. Israel agreed to conduct a prior paratroop drop near the Canal, thereby abandoning its insistence on simultaneous attacks, and to refrain from informing the US of its intentions. More hazardous, in Ben Gurion's estimation, was Israel's commitment not to destroy Egypt's air force on the ground – such an action, the British argued, would openly link Israel's operation with Musketeer – but to leave that task to its allies after the ultimatum. In the interim, Israel's skies, as well as its ports, would be protected by the French.

The Israelis had pressed for the earliest possible date for the invasion.

Ben Gurion saw Nasser's victory in the Suez crisis as proof of his ability to defy the Powers and thus to make war. The attack was therefore scheduled for less than a week after Sèvres, on 29 October. The timing seemed particularly propitious, as the US was preoccupied with its presidential election and the Soviet Union with growing unrest in Poland and Hungary; the Arab states had yet to conclude joint defence planning with Egypt. In Israel, too, the ground was prepared. On 15 October Ben Gurion had stated Israel's case before the Knesset, listing Egypt's policies in the blockade and on the border, its acquisition of offensive weaponry, and its repeated rejection of peace initiatives. Battle orders reflecting the influence of Omer and other operations planned against Egypt in the previous two years were issued to the IDF on 25 October and called for the elimination of Gaza's Fida'iyun bases and the conquest of Tiran. The operation was to be known as Kadesh, a Biblical name for Sinai.[36]

For all his past certainty on the question of war with Egypt, Ben Gurion now experienced serious reservations as to whether to proceed with Kadesh. First, Israel lacked a specific Egyptian provocation to initiate its action. He rejected France's proposal for feigning an Egyptian air attack on Beersheva and Britain's for sending another test case through the Canal, the former as unethical, the latter as too complicated to be arranged in time for the target date. Next, there was the danger of irreparable damage to US–Israel relations; Eisenhower had intimated as much in two letters of warning sent to the Prime Minister in the final week of October. And finally, there remained the operation's impact on Israel's position in the Middle East. Britain and France had agreed to let Israel retain Tiran and had not rejected Ben Gurion's plan, submitted at Sèvres, for dividing Jordan between Israel and Iraq and Lebanon between Israel and Syria. Nevertheless, Ben Gurion retained doubts as to whether the invasion would meet its basic objective – the collapse of Nasser's regime – or actually enhance Nasser's status as leader of the Arab world.[37]

Nasser, meanwhile, still played down the possibility of an Israeli strike. Despite intelligence reports from Paris of secret Anglo-Israeli-French talks, Israel had adopted a generally low-profile stance in the Suez dispute, which it had yet to exploit for diplomatic or territorial gain. Obliquely through Cairo Radio, and directly through the Ramzi–Ariel contact in Brussels, Nasser thanked Ben Gurion for his positive role in the crisis.[38]

The Suez crisis relieved Nasser of the need to adopt an offensive position against Israel by focusing domestic and regional attention on the struggle against Britain and France. By October, however, with little left but to settle the details of a political solution in the UN, and with the

143

danger of an Anglo-French invasion rapidly dissipating, Nasser once again had to turn to the Palestine issue. Egypt's Syrian and Saudi allies, already disgruntled by Nasser failure to consult them on the nationalization decision, now charged that he had acted to appease Israel during the crisis. Nasser's image had been further impaired by his failure to react to repeated Israeli raids into the West Bank, actions which, in turn, led to the proposed introduction of Iraqi troops into Jordan and a threat to Egypt's newly-won ascendancy in that country. In addition, Egyptian army commanders were arguing that the paucity of spare parts necessitated the immediate use of the Soviet arms, and that it was incumbent to act before Israel could absorb its French weaponry.[39]

Nasser reacted swiftly to the political threat in Jordan. On 25 October, the day the IDF received its orders for Kadesh, he concluded the treaty linking the Egyptian army with that of Jordan and Syria. Egypt and Israel had now fulfilled all their conditions for war; the question remained which would be the first to fire. Nasser remained reluctant to order a large-scale military initiative. While still possessing no concrete evidence of an Israeli intention to attack, he feared the repercussions of such a move when the Suez debate was continuing at the UN and while Anglo-French forces remained massed in the Eastern Mediterranean. Indeed, on the evening of 28 October, when IDF jets shot down an Egyptian plane *en route* from Damascus, killing ten officers – a second aircraft carrying Amer escaped – Nasser attributed the action to the British.[40]

Thus, for the final time, Nasser resorted to the stop-gap policy which had proved so effective in the past. Fida'iyun units, which had been withdrawn from Gaza during the crisis, returned and, beginning on 26 October, conducted several raids against Israeli settlements in the Negev. The attacks characteristically resulted in more Palestinian than Israeli casualties, but they nevertheless sufficed to persuade Ben Gurion that Nasser had not abandoned his ambition for war with Israel, and to provide him with the perfect pretext for launching Operation Kadesh. The status quo had fully broken down; the second Arab–Israel war had begun.

7

Conclusion

Israel's strike into Sinai began in the afternoon of 29 October with an armoured attack on Kuntilla and a paratroop drop in the Mitla pass. These manoeuvres were designed to appear as a large-scale probing action and thus minimize the extent of Egypt's initial reaction. The full force of the invasion came on the night of the 30th, with thrusts from al-Aujah to the Suez Canal and from Kuntilla towards Tiran, and the following evening, with the bombing of Egyptian airfields by Britain and France. Those Egyptian units which had not been withdrawn to the Canal area engaged the IDF in battle and in many cases, such as in the Mitla, fought fiercely. Throughout the Middle East, as elsewhere in the world, it was now known that this represented far more than a mere border clash, but was in fact the long-anticipated second Arab–Israel war.

The preceding chapters present a chronicle of relations between Israel and Egypt from 1952 to 1956. In addition to documenting an important episode in the modern history of the Middle East and to analysing the major issues in the Arab–Israel conflict, my primary purpose was to trace the origins of the second Arab–Israel war. These, it was posited, lay in the dynamics of the Arab world which, over the course of time, generated a growing momentum towards confrontation with Israel. The process, however, was greatly accelerated by the actions and policies of Israel as well as those of the Great Powers.

Following the 1948 Palestine war, there existed a status quo in Egypt–Israel relations and in the Arab–Israel conflict in general. In this situation of no war and no peace, the Israelis rebuffed the Arabs' demands on the three central issues – refugees, borders, and Jerusalem – while the Arabs denied Israel security and recognition. The Powers, for their part, deplored Israel's intransigence on the issues and the Arabs' obduracy on the question of peace. The Powers, Israel and the Arab states all opposed the status quo, but only in theory. In reality, all sought to maintain the stalemate until it could be replaced by a solution more compatible with their interests.

The status quo, however, could not be shielded from the destabilizing effects of Middle East and Great Power politics. Thus, following a short hiatus after the Egyptian revolution, tensions on the Egypt–Israel border resumed and controversy on the blockade and regional defence issues intensified. An arms race developed between Egypt and Israel and the two countries began their ineluctable descent to war.

The process of escalation stemmed from factors endogenous to the Arab world. Anti-Zionism had become integral to Arab identity in the 1950s, and activism in the struggle against Israel the *sine qua non* for establishing the legitimacy of post-colonial regimes. Arab leaders, chronically lacking in such legitimacy, exploited the conflict with Israel in order to discredit their political rivals and to detract from domestic problems. In doing so, however, they created expectations among their countrymen of an impending 'second round' with Israel, thus bringing tremendous pressure onto themselves. In the absence of the means to confront Israel militarily, however, and to obtain a political settlement acceptable to domestic opinion, Arab leaders resorted to acts of limited hostility, such as the blockade and support for armed infiltration. Such measures were designed to conciliate their constituents without upsetting the status quo with Israel.

The process was particularly evident in the case of the RCC. In addition to the problem of legitimacy, the Free Officers also had their military image to uphold and to face formidable political and economic challenges – factors which increased their need to stand steadfast on Palestine. Furthermore, the regime also strove for regional ascendancy, an aspiration blocked psychologically as well as physically by Israel. Thus, after demonstrating disinterest, if not moderation, towards the Palestine problem, the Officers proceeded to tighten the Suez blockade, to intensify border friction, and to increase hostile propaganda. All these measures were implemented within a year of the July revolution, during which time Israeli confrontations with Egypt also increased. Ultimately, the Officers' desire to maintain the status quo proved irreconcilable with political exigencies at home and in the region.

Despite early attempts to conciliate Egypt, Israel accelerated the process of escalating Arab hostility. In contrast to the generally passive position of the Arab states, Israel pursued a number of activist policies. Believing time to be on its side diplomatically and that the world would become accustomed to both its borders and its population, Israel undertook measures to reaffirm its territorial and demographic integrity. To this end, in 1953 alone, Israel began diverting the Jordan river and building settlements in the al-Auja DZ; it transferred its capital to Jerusalem and, in the UN, presented the Blueprint for Peace.

But if time worked for Israel politically, it was against it militarily, as the armed strength of the Arab world steadily mounted. Perceiving the

Arabs' acts of limited hostility as indicating an attempt to use that strength in a 'second round', Israel sought to deter the Arabs by conducting retaliation raids, such as that against the al-Burayj camp in August 1953. These operations, like those on the borders and in the UN, served only to provoke the Arabs. The effect on the process was clear: following Israel's actions in Jerusalem and on the Jordan, the RCC inaugurated the Voice of the Arabs broadcasts and hosted an Arab chiefs-of-staff summit to co-ordinate strategy against Israel. After the al-Burayj raid and the establishment of Kibbutz Ketziot in the DZ, Egypt increased its support for armed infiltration and expanded the Suez contraband laws.

Israel's policies also proved counterproductive in its quest for international acceptance of its borders and support for the resettlement of the refugees in Arab lands. The rise of Arab belligerency, and the hastened breakdown of the status quo, compelled the Powers to seek a settlement based on territorial and demographic concessions from Israel.

The Western Powers – the United States, Great Britain, and France – also expedited the escalation process. In principle, the Powers favoured Arab acceptance of Israel on the basis of a compromise between Israel's present borders and those of the 1947 partition resolution, and between the repatriation and compensation of the refugees. Thus, the Powers subscribed to the preamble of the Armistice Agreements, which called for a permanent peace in Palestine and sponsored UN resolutions providing for the refugees' rights, the internationalization of Jerusalem, and the end of the Suez blockade. However, reluctant to impair their relations with the belligerents by imposing a solution and fearing a 'second round' that would endanger world peace, the Powers undertook to preserve the status quo. This was the inherent intention of the Tripartite Declaration: to contain the Arab–Israel conflict and to protect it from outside intervention until conditions allowed for a negotiated settlement.

But like the Arabs and the Israelis, the Powers proved incapable of safeguarding the status quo. Pursuit of partisan economic and political interests led them to remove checks on Arab–Israel belligerency and to upset the region's delicate strategic equilibrium. Thus, the sale of Western weaponry to Iraq and to Israel spurred Egypt's search for Soviet arms, while Britain's withdrawal from the Suez Canal prompted Israeli provocations of Egypt – the *Bat Galim* and Cairo spy episodes. American and British policies on regional defence challenged Egypt's claim to regional primacy, effecting a hardening of its position on Palestine, and isolated Israel, making it more apt to respond to the Egyptian threat with force.

American policies in the Middle East, more than those of the European Powers, had the greatest destabilizing effect on the region. Under the guidance of Secretary of State John Foster Dulles, the United States pursued the contradictory goals of maintaining Britain's strategic presence in the Middle East and of supporting the aspirations of local nationalist movements. The result was to radicalize both the European Powers and the Arab nationalists, greatly exacerbating the conflict between them. America's policies on arms sales and regional defence also contributed to Israel's sense of isolation and frustration, and thus to its willingness to strike out militarily.

By the end of 1954, the rising current of anti-Israel sentiment in the Arab world, and its acceleration by Israel and the Powers, began to generate an irreversible momentum towards war. To counter challenges from Iraq and the Muslim Brotherhood, Nasser adopted more assertive policies towards Israel, thus providing Israel with the pretext for launching the Gaza raid of February 1955. Egypt reacted with the Fida'iyun attacks, the tightening of the Straits blockade, and efforts to dominate the DZ. These, in turn, triggered the Israeli reprisals at Khan Yunis (August 1955), Kuntilla (October 1955), and al-Sabhah (November 1955). The vicious cycle of border violence, combined with the struggle for regional leadership, led to the Czech arms deal of September 1955, the event most responsible for the outbreak of the second Arab–Israel war.

The Powers, meanwhile, continued to accelerate the process of escalation. As noted, the sale of arms to Iraq led to the Czech deal and to the penetration of the West's strategic monopoly over the Middle East by the USSR. Thereafter, in an effort to stem further Soviet penetration, the Powers removed additional checks on the Arab–Israel conflict and further upset the regional balance. Britain intervened to enlist Jordan in the Baghdad Pact (December 1955) and, together with the US, supported Hammarskjöld's attempt to reaffirm the ceasefire aspect of the EIAA (April 1956). The first act deeply antagonized Egypt, the second, Israel. Both contributed to the trend towards war.

The final stages of the process saw the fulfilment by Egypt and Israel of the conditions necessary for war. Having evicted the British, acquired a decisive quantity of arms, and entered into strategic alliances with Jordan and Syria, Nasser could no longer justify preserving the status quo. The Israelis, armed with French weaponry and Anglo-French guarantees of diplomatic support, sought to deter Egypt decisively by launching a pre-emptive strike. Britain and France, in an effort to restore the status quo ante in the Canal, removed the final check on Palestine tensions and completed the disruption of the regional balance by actively intervening in an Arab–Israel war.

Parallel to this process of escalation was another sequence of events involving secret efforts for peace. From 1952 to 1954, such efforts centred around contacts, direct and indirect, between Egypt and Israel. Over the next two years, these were overshadowed by diplomatic initiatives sponsored by the US and Britain. The impetus to achieve an Egypt–Israel accord did not diminish with the intensification of violence but, on the contrary, increased proportionately to it.

For the Israelis, the contacts represented a means of securing a settlement free of Great Power and inter-Arab interference and, as such, one more likely to preserve the territorial and demographic status quo. Apart from offering the refugees compensation and facilitating inter-Arab communication and commerce across its territory, Israel would not sacrifice territory unilaterally or repatriate large numbers of refugees in return for peace. The Egyptians, by contrast, derived various benefits from the contacts, such as Western goodwill, and in principle were not opposed to peace provided it brought them major territorial gains. But their main objective was to persuade the Israelis of Egypt's peaceful intentions, and dissuade them from conducting actions which would embarrass the RCC and push it prematurely into war.

The distinction between Israeli and Egyptian interests in the contacts was apparent in the preparations for the Riad–Tekoah meeting in April 1954 and in the abortive Kilometre 95 talks of July 1955. The Israelis wanted peace, the Egyptians quiet. For this reason, as tensions rose in their relations with Israel, the Egyptians become more eager for communications. By 1955–56, this desire had yielded a procession of independent mediators – Ira Hirshmann, Richard Crossman, Lester B. Pearson, and Elmore Jackson – as well as numerous direct discussions. Throughout, the Israelis continued to demand a full peace treaty, the Egyptians, a reduction in tensions through mutually-agreed measures.

The nature of Arab politics in the 1950s, however, strongly militated against any effort to reduce tensions with Israel, let alone make peace. Arab public opinion denounced the June 1953 Distressed Vessels Agreement and the October 1953 Johnston plan on the grounds that both indicated recognition of Israel. Though Nasser at one point (December 1954) proposed to relax the Suez blockade, it is hard to conceive how such a move could have been concealed indefinitely, and how it could have been presented to the Arab world without ruining Nasser's reputation. Nasser was willing to talk peace, especially through his Foreign Minister, but to act would have required risks no Arab leader of the 1950s could afford to take.

On the other hand, no responsible Israeli leader could have accepted, on face value, Nasser's assurances that acts of limited hostility were merely political ploys and not representative of a truly belligerent intent.

Less then a decade after the Egyptian invasion of Israel, with Radio Cairo exhorting the Arabs to war and the Egyptian army acquiring jet bombers purportedly for that purpose, the Israelis could not gamble on Nasser's secret sincerity.

Beginning in 1954, the US and Britain attempted to break the Egypt–Israel deadlock by conducting a series of initiatives: Alpha, Guildhall, and Gamma. These represented efforts to find a middle ground between the Israeli and the Arab positions. Israel was not required to relinquish all the territory it acquired in the 1948 war, nor to repatriate all the refugees, but neither were the Arabs requested to grant the Jewish State full peace and recognition. Egypt and Israel would also gain through the initiatives; the former, territorial contiguity with the Arab world, the latter, international guarantees for its borders. The underlying purpose of these plans, however, was to implement the Powers' vision of a Middle East defence organization. But in pursuing their own interests, the Powers overlooked those of Egypt and Israel.

Even if he could have agreed to a settlement with Israel – and this, again, was highly doubtful in the 1950s – Nasser hardly had an interest in supporting a regional defence organization designed to supplant Egyptian influence in the Middle East. Even if Ben Gurion agreed to include the question of refugee rights and border adjustments in the negotiating agenda, which appeared to be the case, it is unreasonable to assume that he would *a priori* concede much of Israel's territory and repatriate 100,000 refugees, even in return for border guarantees. The possibility of Israeli co-operation appears all the more remote when it is recalled that the proposed agreement failed to bring full peace with a single Arab state, to end the boycott, or to include Israel in a regional defence network.

Though equally unacceptable to both Israel and Egypt, it must be stressed that Anglo-American peace plans could have succeeded had they been approved by Nasser. Egyptian, and not Israeli, co-operation was essential. Only with agreement from Nasser could the Powers proceed to involve additional Arab countries in the initiative and, most importantly, place effective pressure on Israel. The point was noted, two years after Suez, by Viscount Hood, Britain's Minister in Washington:

> It was common ground that the heat should be turned on the Israelis only when we had brought the Egyptians to the point where the Arab agreement on Alpha terms seemed possible. The Alpha operation collapsed when the United States emissary [Anderson] reported that there was no hope of moving Nasser to the required point. Our guess is that Mr. Dulles would have been prepared to be very tough indeed [on Israel] if he had seen a chance of pushing the

settlement through. (From PRO, FO371/134298/1: Hood to Stevens, 12 December 1958)

In short, had Nasser accepted Alpha, Ben Gurion would have been forced to yield, and other Arab leaders would have joined the negotiations. The key to a settlement, like that to a war, lay ultimately in the Arab world.

As it happened, though, the secret peace efforts of 1952–56 never came close to reversing or even arresting the deterioration of the status quo. Rather, it appears that they, too, served to accelerate the process by creating false expectations among the interlocutors and sowing distrust and animosity between them. Just as IDF retaliations failed to deter the Arabs so, too, did Nasser's communications fail to mollify the Israelis. The Gaza raid, as well as the later waves of border violence in August–November 1955 and March–April 1956, all took place during periods of intense Egypt–Israel contact. In the end, it was Nasser's rejection of the most ambitious initiative, Gamma, which influenced America's withdrawal from the Aswan dam project. Nasser's reaction to that decision – the nationalization of the Suez Canal – triggered the final series of events which culminated in the second Arab–Israel war.

The pattern described above, of rising Arab belligerency intensified by Israeli and Great Powers policies, was unique to the 1950s. Nevertheless, aspects of the pattern were apparent in other phases of the Arab–Israel conflict, for example, in the periods preceding the wars of 1948 and 1967. Further research may reveal the extent to which the pattern is applicable to the conflict in general, and thus broaden our understanding of its dynamics. Caution, however, must be taken not to treat the Arab–Israel conflict as an immutable; not to view one period through the prism of another. Great changes have occurred in Arab–Israel relations since the 1950s, and certainly since the 1973 war and the treaty between Egypt and Israel. The historian's task is no longer solely to identify the pattern which terminates in war, but also the process which leads to peace.

Notes

CHAPTER ONE

1. References to the EIAA and the other Armistice Agreements are from the official Israeli texts published in Yemima Rosenthal (ed.), *Documents on the Foreign Policy of Israel*, Vol. III (Jerusalem, 1983). It is interesting to note that the size of the EIMAC differed from that of the other MACs which had only five members.
2. Egypt based its claim to the Negev on the UN Security Council resolution of 4 November, 1948. This called for the return of Israeli and Egyptian forces to the lines held on 14 October, a deployment which left most of the desert in Egypt's hands. Egypt substantiated its demand by citing the peace plan of UN mediator Folke Bernadotte, which also accorded the Negev to Egypt. Israel's claim to Gaza centred on the fact that the Strip, though not included in the partitioned Jewish State, was nevertheless a part of Palestine to which Israel had far greater right than Egypt. ISA, 164/9: Egypt's Demand for Territorial Contiguity, March 1953; 2439/1: Rosenne Note, 6 Aug. 1952; 2477/10: Shimoni to Eban, 13 Aug. 1952. See also David P. Forsythe, *United Nations Peace Making: The Conciliation Committee for Palestine* (Baltimore, 1972), pp. 54, 63. Rosenthal, op. cit., xi–xvii.
3. Information on conditions in Gaza from USNA, 784. 022/3–1650: Cairo to Acheson; 774.00/2–2354: Caffery to Department, 23 Feb. 1954. See also, James Baster, 'Economic Problems of the Gaza Strip', *Middle East Journal*, Vol. IX, No. 3 (Summer, 1955).
4. ISA, 2473/3: Intelligence Reports on Infiltration, 10 July 1952; 30 Dec. 1952. Ehud Ya'ari, *Mitzrayim vehaFidayeen* (Givat Haviva, 1975), pp. 9–11, 13. Yosef Ben Ze'ev, 'HaModi 'in beMa 'arekhet Sinai', *Ma'arachot*, No. 306–7 (Dec. 1986), p. 19. Ben Ze'ev, who served in IDF intelligence during the 1950s, contends that much of Egypt's sponsorship of infiltration was the work of Muslim Brotherhood sympathizers in the Egyptian army.
5. A considerable body of literature has accumulated on the subject of Israel's retaliation policy; for further reading see Shlomo Aronson and Dan Horowitz, 'HaIstrategia shel Tagmul Mugbal', *Medina uMemshal*, Vol. 1, No. 1 (Summer, 1971); Fred Khuri, 'The Policy of Retaliation in Arab–Israel Relations', *Middle East Journal*, Vol. 20, No. 4 (Autumn, 1966); M. Gur, *Plugah Dalet* (Tel Aviv, 1977), pp. 17–18; Aryeh Avineri, *Peshitot HaTagmul* (Tel Aviv, 1971), pp. 28–9; Rafael Eytan, *Raful: Sipur Shel Hayyal* (Tel Aviv, 1985), p. 56.
6. Egyptian attitudes towards Israel and the status quo in the period before the July Revolution are outlined in ISA, 2477/15: The Egyptian Struggle and Its Consequences, 22 April 1952; 2565/19: Divon Conversation with Azmi, 25 Jan. 1951. See also *al-Musawwar*, 25 Jan. 1952, which featured a survey of Egyptian leaders' opinions on Israel.
7. ISA, 2565/7/17: Questions for Discussion, Dec. 1950. David Brook, *Preface to Peace* (Washington, 1964), pp. 55 6.
8. Operation Yagev, as it is known in IDF annals, went unreported in the Israeli press. Egypt's *al-Misri*, however, claimed the following day that a large number of civilians had been killed and damage done to the extent of 25,000 Egyptian pounds.
9. By Israel's count, 231 infiltrators from Gaza had been killed and 206 captured in the year ending in March 1952. Israel also reported eight of its citizens killed and 17 wounded by infiltrators on the Egyptian border in the single month of May 1952. ISA,

NOTES

2439/1: Yearly Report on Infiltration, 12 March 1952; 2195/13: EIMAC Report, 10 July 1952. Ya'ari, op. cit. pp. 9–11. For references to Arab pressure on Egypt to increase border tensions see PRO, FO371/98474/16: Caffery to Eden, 11 July 1952. Patrick Seale, *The Struggle for Syria* (Oxford, 1965), pp. 107–8.

10. Anwar Sadat, *Revolt on the Nile* (New York, 1957), pp. 102, 123. Gamal Abdul Nasser, *Philosophy of the Revolution* (Washington, 1955), pp. 97–8; 'Memoirs of the First Palestine War', *Journal of Palestine Studies*, Vol. II, No. 1 (Summer, 1973). P.J. Vatikiotis, *Nasser and His Generation* (New York, 1978), p. 104. Miles Copeland, *The Game of Nations* (New York, 1969), pp. 66–7. Rasheed El-Barawy, *The Military Coup in Egypt* (Cairo, 1952), pp. 199–215. Mohamed H. Heikal, *Millaffat al-Suways* (Cairo, 1986), p. 163.

11. ISA, 2477/10: Simoni to Eban, 13 Aug. 1952. USNA, 774.00/7–3152: Hart Conversation with Eban, 31 July 1952 Yerucham Cohen, *LeOr HaYom uveMahshecha* (Tel Aviv, 1969), pp. 200–1. Captain Cohen held extensive talks with Nasser during the 1949 talks. His recollections of the future Egyptian leader were serialized in the Israeli daily *Haaretz* in January 1953.

12. USNA, 684A. 74/9–452: Jerusalem to Department, 4 Sept. 1952. ISA, 2439/1: Report of the Second EIMAC Meeting, 9 Sept. 1952. See also Jean Mandelstam, 'La Palestine dans la Politique de Gamal Abdel Nasser, Juillet 1952–Février 1955' (thesis, Paris, 1970), p. 113. ISA, 2477/10: Clipping from *al-Ahram*, 31 Dec. 1952.

13. ISA, 2439/1: EIMAC Reports, 5 Nov. 1952; 3 Dec. 1952; 2402/12: Egyptian Position in the EIMAC, 19 Nov. 1952. PRO, FO371/98475/154: Tel Aviv to Foreign Office, 22 Nov. 1952. Egypt's charge followed a proposal presented to Gohar by Col. Ramati, Israel's EIMAC representative. Ramati suggested that high-ranking Egyptian and Israeli officials meet to discuss ways of improving the border situation and of relaxing Egypt's blockade of Israeli shipping in the Suez Canal. See USNA, 674.84A/9–2752: Davis to Department.

14. Charges of Egyptian 'softness' on the Palestine issues are made in BBC, 308, p. 23; 309, pp. 33–5. The Officers' domestic and regional difficulties are discussed by Seale, op. cit., p. 214, and P.J. Vatikiotis, *The History of Egypt* (Baltimore, 1969), pp. 378–9. An assessment of the Republican victory's influence on Egypt's Palestine policy appeared in *al-Ahram*, 19 Nov. 1952. For references to Egypt's policy on the Reparations Treaty, see ISA, 90/25: Text of the Arab League Protest Note to Germany, 15 Nov. 1952. BBC, 308, p. 23; 309, pp. 33–5; 312, p. 25.

15. ISA, 2439/1: Analysis of the Situation in Egypt, 17 Dec. 1952; 2451/8: Rafael to Shiloah, 20 Nov. 1952; 39/22: Eban to Sharett, 7 Dec. 1952. Much has been written on Ben Gurion's approach to the Arab world and the retaliation policy, particularly in contrast to that of his Foreign Minister, Moshe Sharett. See, for example, Uri Bialer, 'HaKonflikt HaYisraeli Aravi B'aynei Ben Gurion ve'Zharett', *Medinah Ve'Memshal*, Vol. 1, No. 2 (Fall, 1971), pp. 58–70. Gabriel Sheffer, 'Sharett, Ben Gurion U'Milhemet HaBreirah', *Medinah Ve'Memshal*, No. 27 (Winter, 1987). Avi Shlaim, 'Conflicting Approaches to the Conflict with the Arabs', *Middle East Journal*, Vol. 37, No. 2. (Winter, 1983), pp. 180–201.

16. ISA, 2460/3: February 1953 Report, Washington Embassy; 36/3: Elath to Sharett, 6 March 1953; 2475/2: U.S. Middle East Policy, 8 March 1953; 39/22: Sharett to Eban. 9 March 1953. See also PRO, FO371/98475/54: Evans to Foreign Office, 22 Nov. 1952.

17. In January 1953, for example, Egypt first agreed to co-operate with Israel in a border marking project then, inexplicably, retracted the offer. See ISA, 2593/1: EIMAC Reports, 29 Jan. 1953; 18 Feb. 1953; 30 March 1953.Heikal, op. cit., pp.216–7.

18. USNA, 780.5/3–1353: Ankara (McGhee) to Dulles; 684A.86/2–1153: Dulles to Lodge; /4–853: Memorandum of Conversation between Byroade, Sharett and Eban. PRO, FO371/104477/1: Baker to Crosthwaite, 3 Feb. 1953; /3: Stevenson to Bowker, 16 Jan. 1953. ISA, 2403/12: Report on Crossman Visit to Egypt, 16 Jan. 1953; 2460/4: Eban Conversation with Dulles, 27 Feb. 1953; 2453/12: Israel's Replies to Nasser's Proposals, 13 May 1953; Ben Gurion to Sharett, 13 May 1953; 2477/20: Herzog to Foreign Ministry, 4 Feb. 1953; 12 March 1953; 22 April 1953. Heikal, op. cit., pp.216–17.

19. ISA, 2453/3: EIMAC Reports, 14 Feb. 1953; 1 April 1953; 11 March 1953; 25 June 1953; 2439/1: EIMAC Reports: 30 April 1953; 10 May 1953; 23 June 1953. BBC, 385, p. 28; 386, p. 21.
20. On the al-Burayj raid and its aftermath, see ISA, 2493/1: EIMAC Report, 27 Aug. 1953. USNA, 774.00/9–2153: Caffery Conversation with Gohar; 684A/85/9–853: Caffery to Department. For background on the origins of Unit 101 see Uri Milstein, *Historia shel HaTzanhanim* (Tel Aviv, 1985), pp. 22; 220–1. Dan Horowitz and Edward Lutwak, *The Israeli Army* (New York, 1975), pp. 108–9.
21. BG, Diary, 16 Oct. 1952. ISA, 2439/9: Sharett to Ministry of Finance, 30 July 1954.
22. USNA, 674.84A/9–1453: Jerusalem Consulate to Department; 683.84A322/10–553: Ludlow Conversation with Eliav; 774.00/9–2153: Caffery Conversation with Gohar.
23. USNA, 674.84A/10–453: Caffery to Department, /11–1053: Caffery to Department; /9–2953: Caffery to Department; 774.00/9–2153: Caffery Conversation with Gohar; 684A.85/17–1053: Caffery to Department. The formation of 250-man Civil Guard followed demands from Palestinians and Egyptian army officers in Gaza for a freer hand in matters of border security. The move might also have been necessitated by Jordan's creation of a similar unit in the West Bank or by the transfer of Egyptian troops from the Strip to the Canal after the breakdown of the evacuation talks. See Ya'ari, op. cit., pp. 12–13. ISA, 2439/1: Neuberger to Eytan, 21 Jan. 1954.
24. Sharett's views on retaliation are aired in ISA, 2195/3, a file containing correspondence between the Foreign Minister and senior Israeli diplomats on the retaliation question, and in PRO, FO371/121729/5: Nicholls to Shuckburgh, 31 Dec. 1955. The issue also appears frequently in Sharett's memoir, *Yoman Ishi* (Tel Aviv, 1978); see, for example, pp. 499, 529, 1679.
25. Moshe Dayan, 'Israel's Border and Security Problems', *Foreign Affairs*, Vol. 33, No. 2 (January, 1955). See also USNA, 784A.00/3–1754: Tel Aviv to Department.
26. On Nasser's inability to restrain his border forces, see ISA/ 2593/22: Avner to Rafael, 5 Oct. 1954; 2549/8: Eytan Conversation with Russell, 7 Nov. 1954. PRO, FO371/111107/208: Nicholls to Foreign Office, 14 Dec. 1954. Sharett, op. cit., 538. E.L.M. Burns, *Between Arab and Israeli* (Beirut, 1964), p. 78.
27. Sharett learned about the Nahhalin raid on the morning news. It also surprised the Egyptians, who were braced for an attack, and angered the British and the Jordanians. The latter were convinced that responsibility for the massacre lay with the Black Hand organization of Hajj Amin al-Husayni, the former Mufti of Palestine, based in Gaza. The Gaza-origin version of the massacre was not entirely discounted by some figures at the Israeli Foreign Ministry. See PRO, FO371/111099/28: Glubb to Foreign Office, 26 March 1954; FO371/111101/70: Tripp Minute, 20 April 1954. ISA, 2475/2: Bendor Conversation with Russell, 24 March 1954; 2460/3: Eban Conversation with Dulles and Byroade, 25 March 1954; 2439/1: Tsur to Eytan, 7 May 1954. Sharett, op. cit., 416. Further reference in Sir John Bagot Glubb, *A Soldier with the Arabs* (London, 1957), p. 320. E.A. Hutchinson, *Violent Truce* (New York, 1958), p. 69. For general information on border situation in early 1954, see USNA, 774.00/5–1954: Caffery to Department; ISA, 2439/1: Neuberger to Eytan, 21 Jan. 1954.
28. The series of events which led to Egypt's exit from the EIMAC began on 25 March when Egyptian soldiers allegedly kidnapped an Israeli soldier on his own territory. Egypt refused the EIMAC's order to return the soldier, whereupon an IDF unit tried to kidnap an Egyptian soldier. Egypt ambushed an Israeli patrol in retaliation. In all, three Egyptians and one Israeli were killed in these clashes for which the EIMAC held Egypt largely responsible.
29. USNA, 774.00/4–3054: Caffery to Department; 684A.85/4–654: Lodge Conversation with Azmi. ISA, 2457/3: Rafael Conversation with Russell, 16 April 1954; 2384/3: Herzog to Intelligence Wing, 22 April 1954; 2439/1: Minute, Foreign Ministry Discussion, 23 April 1954; 2453/20: Sharett to Eban, 9 April 1954. Sharett, op. cit., pp. 374, 378–9, 446–7, 477.
30. For US diplomatic intervention on the Syrian border see USNA, 683.84A/3–1953: Dulles to Middle East Embassies; /11–1452: Waller to Hart; /6–853; /10–1753: Caffery

NOTES

Conversation with Fawzi. British intervention on the Jordanian border in ISA, 40/1: Eban to Elath, 11 Sept. 1952. PRO, FO371/111105/183: Jebb to Foreign Office, 31 Aug. 1954.

31. Quote from PRO, FO371/104741/3: Evans to Knox Helm, 1 Dec. 1953. See also USNA, 684A. 86/4–754; Byroade to Dulles; 784A.00/3–1754: Tel Aviv to Department. ISA, 2457/2: Avner to Rafael, 20 Aug. 1954.

32. USNA, 674.84A/4–1754: Russell to Department; /5–454: Caffery to Department; /5–654: Caffery to Department; /4–2554: Caffery to Department; 684A.85/8–754: Dulles to Egyptian Embassy; /14–854: Caffery to Department; /4–2254: Caffery Conversation with Riad. ISA, 2439/1: Minutes of Foreign Ministry Discussion, 23 April 1954; 2453/20: Sharett to Eban, 9 April 1954 Sharett, op. cit., 453–4, 459, 465–7.

33. USNA, 674.87/8–2354: Acting Secretary of State to Egypt Embassy. ISA, 21/1: Tekoah to Sharett, 1 June 1954; 11 June 1954.

34. USNA, 684.84A/7–1254: Caffery Conversation with Riad.

35. PRO, FO371/111107/251: Nicholls Conversation with Sharett, 5 Nov. 1954. USNA, 684A.85/10–1554: Russell to Department. ISA, 40/17: Sharett Conversation with Nicholls, 5 Nov. 1954. ISA, 2593/22: Avner to Rafael, 5 Oct. 1954; 2549/8: Eytan Conversation with Russell, 7 Nov. 1954; 2460/3: Herzog to Sharett, 4 July 1954. Sharett, op. cit., 634. Ben Ze'ev (op. cit., p. 18) argues that the rise in infiltration towards the end of the year was due to the arrival in Gaza of members of the Muslim Brotherhood banished by Nasser. Though Ya'ari (op. cit., p. 13) takes issue with this conclusion, it was shared at the time by Sharett. See PRO, FO371/111107/208: Nicholls to Foreign Office, 14 Dec. 1954. Sharett, op. cit., p. 538.

36. BBC, 548, p. 27. On Egypt's border policy in January 1955 see PRO, FO371/115896/12: Stevenson to Shuckburgh, 26 Jan. 1955. Ya'ari, op. cit., p. 16.

37. Michael Bar Zohar, *Ben Gurion: A Biography* (London, 1977), pp. 217–8. Events in February and their effect on the border situation are described in Milstein, op. cit., p. 287. Sharett, op. cit, pp. 732, 800. Jacob Tsur, *Prélude à Suez* (Paris, 1968), pp. 68, 165.

38. For the Israeli perspective on the Gaza raid see Milstein, op. cit., pp. 288–90. Abba Eban, *An Autobiography* (New York), p. 179. S. Gafni, 'Hetz Shahur al 'Aza', *Maarachot* (Feb. 1977). Sharett, op. cit., pp. 804–22. The Egyptian reaction in FRUS, XIV, pp. 93–4, 119. ISA, 2951/10: Gaza Incident, Summary and Estimation, 22 March 1955; 2477/20: Shimoni to Foreign Ministry, 14 March 1955; BBC, 548, pp. 28–9; 549, pp. 21–2. See also *al-Ahram*, 1 March 1955; *al-Akhbar*, 2 March 1955; *al-Gumhurriyah*, 2 March 1955. Heikal, op. cit., p. 356.

39. PRO, FO371/115628/66: Cairo to Foreign Office, 5 March 1955; /45: Cairo to Foreign Office, 2 March 1955. Burns, op. cit., pp. 86–8, 92. Ya'ari, op. cit., pp. 19–21. Milstein, op. cit., p. 328. Eric Rouleau, *Sans Patrie* (Fayolle, 1978), p. 50.

40. ISA, 2454/5: U.S. Government to Israel Government, 30 March 1955; 2951/13: U.S. Government to Israel Government, 1 April 1955. Sharett, op. cit., pp. 892, 930.

41. Israel also rejected the 500-metre pullback proposal on the grounds that it represented no concession for the Egyptians; their bunkers were already that distance from the border and Gaza, in any case, was not Egyptian territory. ISA, 2451/1: Burns to Eytan, 5 May 1955; 2951/13: Burns to Sharett, 7 April 1955; /15: Tekoah to Sharett, 15 April 1955. FRUS, XIV, 135–8, 144f.

42. PRO, FO371/11900/145: Jerusalem to Foreign Office, 28 May 1955; 115901/152: Jerusalem to Foreign Office, 21 May 1955; ISA, 2951/13: U.S. Government to Israel Government, 21 April 1955; 2952/2: Herzog to Washington, 29 May 1955; 48/2: Western Europe Desk to Eytan, 3 June 1955. FRUS, XIV, 134–5, 158, 221–2.

43. The tension of the 7 June meeting was also the product of a statement made by Sharett on the eve of Burns's departure to Cairo to the effect that the Chief UNMO would be conveying a warning to Nasser. The remark infuriated the Egyptians as well as Burns, who demanded an apology. ISA, 2951/13: Tekoah Conversation with Burns, 11 May 1955; U.S. Message to Israel Government, 22 May 1955; Kidron to Foreign Ministry, 8 June 1955; /1: Anglo-American Message to Egypt, 3 June 1955; Burns Conversation with Eytan, 8 June 1955. FRUS, XIV, 160–1, 186–9, 236. Burns, op. cit., p. 79. Sharett,

op. cit., pp. 1066–7; 1070–1.
44. The Powers were also dissatisfied with Egypt's choice of Gohar, and urged Egypt to declare his status as a plenipotentiary of Foreign Minister Fawzi. ISA, 2451/1: Tekoah to Embassies, 18 June 1955; Eytan to Kidron, 12 June 1955; 2951/13: Lawson Conversation with Sharett, 11 June 1955; Kidron to Foreign Ministry, 13 June 1955. FRUS, XIV, 241, 247–8, 257–9.
45. Before resubmitting the issue to the Security Council, Burns proposed a compromise plan for the erection of obstacles on the ADL and the restriction of patrols to infantry on foot. Israel accepted the restriction but insisted on prior construction of the obstacles; Egypt rejected the obstacles entirely. PRO, FO371/115874/186: Cairo to Foreign Office, 24 Aug. 1955. FRUS, XIV, 299–300, 267, 347–8, 390. ISA, 2952/15: Tekoah to Embassies, 24 Aug. 1955. Sharett, op. cit., p. 1133. Burns, op. cit., p. 86.
46. Theories on the origins of the Fida'iyun attacks in PRO, FO371/115874/186: Cairo to Foreign Office, 24 Aug. 1955; 115905/306: Burns to Foreign Office, 29 Sept. 1955; /324: Glubb to Foreign Office, 12 Oct. 1955. ISA, 2455/10: U.S. Desk to Washington Embassy, 28 Aug. 1955; 2951/10: The Operation of Egyptian Gangs, 4 Sept. 1955. FRUS, XIV, 413. Glubb, op. cit., p. 381–2.
47. PRO, FO371/115904/252: Cairo to Foreign Office, 3 Sept. 1955; 115903/242: Tel Aviv to Foreign Office, 1 Sept. 1955; /245: Cairo to Foreign Office, 1 Sept. 1955. FRUS, XIV, 398–401, 416. See also ISA, 2951/14: Tekoah to Embassies, 26 Aug. 1955.
48. FRUS, XIV, 406–7, 416, 428.
49. Following Jackson's failure to secure a ceasefire, Ben Gurion declared his intention to boycott the cabinet, and Gen. Dayan his commitment to resign, if Sharett did not sanction the retaliation. The Khan Yunis raid, known in IDF history as Operation Elyakim (after a commander who died in the Gaza raid), was considered a major military achievement for the Israeli forces. See FRUS, XIV, 440. Dayan, op. cit., p. 151. Sharett, op. cit., pp 1153–61. Burns, op. cit., p. 88. Milstein, op. cit., p. 328. Elmore Jackson, *Middle East Mission* (New York, 1983), pp. 43–54, 82–5.
50. ISA, 2439/2: Tekoah to Eytan, 28 Oct. 1955; Kidron to Eytan, 3 Nov. 1955; 2474/16: Memorandum of Conversation, Pearson and Nasser, 2 Nov. 1955. PRO, PREM-11 947: Graham to Millard, 29 Sept. 1955; FO371/121734/87: New York to Foreign Office, 14 March 1956. FRUS, XIV, 496–7, 515–6, 563–4, 687–91.
51. ISA, 2439/2: Tekoah Conversation with Burns, 5 Nov. 1955; 2951/14: Kidron to Foreign Ministry, 4 Nov. 1955; /8: Burns Conversation with Nasser, 16 Nov. 1955; 2952/1: Tekoah to Embassies, 6 Nov. 1955; 1602/10: Record of Meeting, Prime Minister and Burns, 5 Dec. 1955. FRUS, XIV, 700–4, 804–7. PRO, FO371/121722/11: Cairo to Foreign Office, 15 Jan. 1956; /15: Cairo to Foreign Office, 19 Jan. 1956; 121733/47: Nutting Minute, 16 Jan. 1956. Burns, op. cit., pp. 134–5. Sharett, op. cit., p. 1351. David Ben Gurion, *Medinat Yisrael HaMehudeshet* (Tel Aviv, 1969), p. 474. Dan Hofstadter, *Egypt and Nasser* (Facts on File, 1973), Vol. I, p. 97.
52. References to the second phase of Hammarskjöld's mediation in ISA, 2440/11: Record of Conversation with Burns, 25 Jan. 1956; PRO, FO371/121733/69: Documents Relating to the Implementation of UN Resolutions on Egypt–Israel Relations, 5 March 1956. FRUS, XV, 7–8, 21–3, 42, 69. Brian Urquhart, *Hammarskjöld* (New York, 1972), pp. 136–54.
53. PRO, FO317/121772/20: Burns to Gohar, 17 Feb. 1956; /37: Burns to Foreign Office, 9 March 1956; 121734/117: New York to Foreign Office, 27 March 1956; 121736/141: Cairo to Foreign Office, 4 April 1956. ISA, 2952/1: Tekoah to Embassies, 12 Feb. 1956; /2: Tekoah to Embassies, 20 Feb. 1956; /15: Kidron to Foreign Ministry, 2 March 1956. FRUS, XV, 238–9, 283–4.
54. On the background to the Fida'iyun attacks of April 1956 see FRUS, XV, 350–1, 357–8, 478–9, 491, 498–9. Burns, op. cit., p. 60. Ya'ari, op. cit., pp. 21–5. Sharett, op. cit., pp. 1169–70, 1195. Ben Gurion, op. cit., p. 482. Heikal, op. cit., p. 434. Egypt's 'Voice of the Arabs' broadcasts claimed that the raids involved 50,000 Fida'iyun, hundreds of Israelis were killed and thousands fled in panic. See BBC, Daily Report 24, p. ii.
55. DDQ, 1980 322C: State Department Middle East Summary, 11 April 1956; 150A:

NOTES

Byroade to Dulles, 10 April 1956. DDE, International File, Box 8: Byroade to Dulles, 10 April 1956. FRUS, XV, 492–4, 498–9, 502–4, 514, 524, 528–9, 526–7, 538, 563. Burns, op. cit., pp. 142–5.

56. PRO, FO371/121735/117: Cairo to Foreign Office, 27 March 1956; 121739/225: New York to Foreign Office, 4 Aug. 1956; /219: New York to Foreign Office, 4 May 1956; 121710/71: Cairo to Foreign Office, 26 July 1956. ISA, 2448/5: Eytan to Eban, 22 June 1956; Ben Gurion to Hammarskjöld, 29 June 1956. FRUS, XV, 564–5. Heikal, op. cit., p. 436.

57. BG, Diaries: 7 Oct. 1956. ISA, 2456/3: Israel Policy After the Arms Deal, 10 Nov. 1955. FRUS, XV, 764–9, 845–6.

58. Ya'ari, op. cit., pp. 24–31. FRUS, XV, 781–3, 799.

59. DDQ, 1982 322: Dulles to Hammarskjöld, 10 Aug. 1956. PRO, FO371/121741/300: New York to Foreign Office, 1 June 1956; 121738/210: Damascus to Foreign Office, 4 May 1956. Urquhart, op. cit., pp. 154–6.

60. BBC, Daily Report 27, p. iii; 47, p. ii.

CHAPTER TWO

1. USNA, 774.00/12–1152: Cairo to Department. BBC, 320, p. 21; 322, p. 15.

2. ISA, 418/15: Israel's Oil Policy, 1951. See also PRO, 104207, a file which outlines Britain's attitude towards the boycott.

3. Quote from ISA, 2419/1: Special Survey of Blockade Amendments, 21 Dec. 1952. Egypt also violated the Arab League's ban on participation in athletic events with Jews. Egypt's national basketball team had two Jewish starters. See USNA, 974.53/12–2252: Caffery to Acheson. ISA, 26/2: Yaari to Katz, 8 March 1953. PRO, 104204/EII21/92: Egypt Boycott of Cyprus, 5 May 1953.

4. Egypt took bold steps to sever trade links between Sudan and Israel. Following the normalization of Israel–Sudanese relations in February 1950, Egypt seized Israel-bound cargoes of Sudanese cottonseed in the Canal and led an all-Arab effort to convince Khartoum to comply with the boycott. Officially, Sudan refused to co-operate with Egypt, but with the development of stronger trade ties with the Arab world, Sudan acted unilaterally to reduce its commerce with Israel. References in PRO, FO371/96962/2: Ledward to Chedwick, 21 June 1952. USNA, 974.5301/11–1750: London to Department. ISA, 164/9: Tsur to Foreign Ministry, 1 Sept. 1953. On the connection between Egypt's oil interests and the blockade, see ISA, 339/2: Zinder to Eban, 15 Aug. 1951. The document records an interesting Egyptian offer to lift the blockade in return for the internationalization of the Haifa refineries.

5. References to the 1888 Constantinople Convention from John Norton Moore, *The Arab–Israel Conflict* (Princeton, 1977), pp. 1001, 1003.

6. Apart from increased shipping and insurance costs, Israel suffered only potential losses, some $70–90 million per year according to Israeli estimates, in Asian and African trade. In conversations with Western diplomats, however, Israeli officials greatly exaggerated the blockade's impact on their economy. See ISA, 416/7: Amendment to September 1 1950 Law, 28 Nov. 1953; 418/15: Israel's Oil Policy, 1951; /26: Eban Conversation with Dulles, 8 Jan. 1953; 2453/3: Background on Boycott, undated.

7. The RCC apparently took the Eilat–Mediterranean Canal idea seriously. As late as September 1954, Cairo Radio declared that such a canal would be 'built over the Arabs' dead bodies'. Cited in BBC, 500, p. 33. See also ISA, 416/5: Yaari to Rafael, 20 Feb. 1953; 2452/1: Comay to Eytan, 15 Feb. 1953; 26/2: Ministry Discussions, 9 April 1953.

8. USNA, 974.5301/7–2850: Ross to Acheson; /10–950: Legal Department Memorandum. PRO, FO371/102897/7: Allen Minute, 9 Jan. 1953; 108524/19: Ledward Minute, 27 Jan. 1953; 108505/107: Millard Minute, 9 June 1954.

9. Moore, op. cit., p. 1006. ISA, 2452/3: Background on Boycott, Sept. 1951.

10. USNA, 974.5301/7–2852: Ross to Acheson; /8–652: London to Acheson; /9–852:

Acheson to London. ISA, 164/8: Eden to Elath, 17 Dec. 1952, 2546/2: Levin to Foreign Ministry, 22 Aug. 1952.
11. USNA, 974.5301/1–553: London to Department. ISA, 2452/3: Untitled, 12 Dec. 1952. See also Mandelstam, op. cit., p. 132.
12. PRO, FO371/102897/11: Bailey to Foreign Office, 27 Jan. 1953. ISA, 2439/1: EIMAC Report, 27 Dec. 1952; 2452/3: Eban to Foreign Ministry, 6 Jan. 1952. USNA, 974.5301/12–1952: Department to Tel Aviv.
13. In resolving to intensify the boycott of foreign firms with branches in Israel, the Arab League chose as a test case that of the Imperial Chemical Industries. While it was willing to pressure Libya and Sudan to comply with the boycott of ICI, Egypt refrained from doing so. ICI had major investments in Egypt. ISA, 26/2: The ICI Boycott, 20 Jan. 1953. PRO, FO371/104202/27: Amman to Foreign Office, 24 Feb. 1953; 108361/E11353/1: Morris Conversation with the Sudanese Ambassador, 23 July 1954; 108405/JE11353/1: Morris Conversation with Gazit, 10 March 1954. ISA, 416/7: Comay to Elath, 4 May 1953; Yaari Note, 12 Nov. 1953; 2460/8: Washington Embassy Protocol, 14 Jan. 1954; 416/7. See also al-Musawwar, 6 March 1953 and al-Ahram, 28 May 1953. References to Egypt's motivations in strengthening the blockade in ISA, BBC, 406, pp. 22–3.
14. ISA, 2546/2: Clipping from the New York Times, 28 Jan. 1953.
15. USNA, 974.5384A/9–2653: Cairo to Department. ISA, 164/9: Ben Hurin Conversation with Murphy, 17 Sept. 1953.
16. Israeli and Arab reactions to the Parnon release in BBC, 390, p. 26. Salem's press conference discussed in PRO, FO371/102733/12: Hankey to Foreign Ministry, 21 Sept. 1953. Salem explained, rather unconvincingly, that the release, like the exchange of deserters on the border, was sanctioned by the EIAA.
17. ISA, 2419/1: Survey on Amendments, 21 Dec. 1953; 416/7: Amendment of Boycott Law, 28 Nov. 1953; /15: Yaari to Katz, 27 Nov. 1953.
18. Israel was quick to exploit these incidents for their propaganda value, calling attention to the fact that the commander of the batteries, Albert Gayelin, was a former commander in the Nazi SS. USNA, 774.5/2–1554: Cairo to Department. Egypt claimed that the Empire Roach incident was an Anglo-Israeli plot to embarass Egypt; see al-Ahram, 15 July 1951.
19. Eliahu Elath, Israel and Elath (London, 1966), p. 5. Gunther E. Rothenberg, The Anatomy of the Israeli Army (New York, 1979), p. 79. Sharett, op. cit., p. 360.
20. In asserting its claim to ownership of the Straits, Egypt avoided the popular Arab position that the Gulf constituted an Arab–Muslim mare clausum in which the Jewish State had no rights. Carl F, Salans. 'Gulf of Aqaba and the Strait of Tiran: Troubled Waters', in Moore, op. cit., pp. 810–11. On occasion, Egypt also depicted the blockade as a means of stemming Israeli drug smuggling into the Gulf; see PRO, FO371/108504/63: Jebb to Foreign Office, 13 March 1954 and Mohammad Naguib, Egypt's Destiny (London, 1955), p. 150. Israeli policies described in ISA, 2419/1: Survey on Amendments, 21 Dec. 1953; 2419/5: Rosenne to Tekoah, 12 Nov. 1955.
21. BG, Diaries: 26 Dec. 1952; 3 Dec. 1953. ISA, 2395/13: The Andreas Boye Incident, 24 Jan. 1953.
22. ISA, 2460/3: Eliav Conversation with Ludlow, 4 March 1954; /8: Eban Conversation with Dulles, 15 Jan. 1954; 2382/2/12: Tsur to Sharett, 14 March 1954. PRO, FO371/108505/27: Foreign Office to UK Delegation UN, 9 Feb. 1954; 108522/10: Millard Minute, 2 March 1954; 108524/20: Leward Minute, 30 Jan. 1954; 108503/36: Jebb Conversation with Eban, 11 Jan. 1954; /14: Stevenson to Foreign Office, 1 Feb. 1954. USNA, 974.5301/2–1954: New York to Dulles, 19 Feb. 1954, /11–954: Suez Canal Advertisement in the Herald Tribune of 4 Jan. 1954. On the consortium concept, see PRO, FO371/102898/41: Briefing for the Minister of State, 18 April 1953. USNA, 974.5301/16–2653: Caffery to Department, 8 Sept. 1953.
23. ISA, 40/19: Bendor to Sharett, 23 Feb. 1954; 2403/12: Bevin Letter to Eytan, 25 Dec. 1953; 2531/27: Divon Conversation with Sadiq, 3 Jan. 1954. Sharett, op. cit., pp. 331–2.
24. USNA, 974.5301/11–2654: Cairo to Department, 26 Jan. 1954; /12–154: Caffery to

Department. PRO, FO371/108312/7: Egypt Blames Britain for Israel's Security Council Action, 12 Feb. 1954; 108503/12: Makins for Foreign Office, 27 Jan. 1954; /15: Stevenson to Foreign Office, 1 Feb. 1954. Public references by Egyptian officials to Britain's role in the Israeli complaint in BBC, 437, p. 24 and in ISA, 2475/9: Arabic Radio Review, 2 Feb. 1954.

25. USNA, 974.5301/11–2854: Egyptian Ambassador (Niazi) to Hart. PRO, FO371/108503/14: Stevenson to Foreign Office, 30 Jan. 1954; 108505/101: Boothby Minute, 2 Feb. 1954; /103: Tel Aviv to Foreign Office, 2 April 1954.

26. ISA, 2419/1: Sharett Note, 21 Jan. 1954; 40/19: Eliav to Foreign Office, 30 Jan. 1954; 2460/3: Eliav Conversation with Ludlow, 4 March 1954. USNA, 974.5301/2–1954: New York to Dulles; /2–1754: Waller Conversation with Ben Hurin; /3–2354: Ludlow Conversation with Hart. PRO, FO371/108504/68: Crosthwaite to Foreign Office, 6 March 1954.

27. Background on the Azmi–Eban relationship in ISA, 339/3: Eban to Sharett, 20 July 1951; 2453/12: Eban to Sharett, 19 March 1952. Sharett also wrote a letter of condolence to Azmi on the death of his wife, see ISA, 22410/10: Sharett to Azmi, 5 Aug. 1952. On the Eban–Azmi talks on the blockade see PRO, FO371/108504/60: Millard Minute, 5 March 1954; /63: Jebb to Foreign Office, 13 March 1954; /70: New York to Foreign Office, 10 March 1954. ISA, 2439.1: Eban to Sharett, 12 Feb. 1954.

28. Statistics on the exact number of ships reaching Haifa and Eilat in 1954 differed, but all indicated that shipping through the Canal to the two ports, even of cargoes of foodstuffs and construction materials, was generally unimpeded. During that year, Egypt also removed 25 out of 100 ships from its blacklist. ISA, 26/2: Untitled, 8 Aug. 1954; 2452/1: The Struggle for Freedom of Passage, 5 Jan. 1955. PRO, FO371/108503/187: Murray to Foreign Office, 29 Nov. 1954. USNA, 684.84A/9–2454: Jernegan Conversation with Eban; 974.5301/9–2154: Department to Middle East Embassies; /10–654: London to Department; /10–1854: Caffery to Department.

29. Egypt, for example, ignored an Arab League ban on airlines flying to or over Israel, fearing that such a move would lead airlines to choose Tel Aviv rather than Cairo for their Middle East stop-overs. See ISA, 416/7: Galezer to Eban, 22 April 1954.

30. ISA, 2403/12: Katz to Foreign Ministry, 7 April 1953; 2593/17: Gazit to Elath, 12 Oct. 1953; 2395/12: Gazit to Elath, 19 March 1953; 2419/1: Gazit to Elath, 9 Oct. 1953; 42/13: Eban Conversation with Dulles, 5 Aug. 1954. PRO, FO371/104753/23: Stevenson to Foreign Office, 3 Nov. 1953. Gideon, Rafael. *Destination Peace* (New York, 1981), p. 36.

31. USNA, 684.84A/7–954: Cairo to Department; 683.84A/9–2853: Caffery to Department. ISA, 2549/8: Divon to Rafael, 3 Jan. 1954. Egypt also emphasized the Anglo-Israeli duplicity theme in its propaganda broadcasts; see BBC, 363, pp. 23, 27–8; 354, pp. 27–9.

32. USNA, 780.00/5–2953: Caffery to Dulles; 774.5/3–2653: Dulles Conversation with Fawzi. ISA, 39/20: Arnon to Elath, 29 April 1953; 2593/18: Avner to Lourie, 16 July 1953.

33. ISA, 2593/17: Rafael to Sharett, 19 Jan. 1954. Israel hoped that the transfer of British troops to Gaza would provide greater security on its southern border and a boost to its ailing economy. Britain seems to have considered the idea seriously, but ultimately rejected it as financially and politically unsound. The notion resurfaced periodically in the first half of 1954 and appeared to have the support of Egypt – Cairo had first suggested the idea in 1950 – but, in July, Nasser indicated he would only agree to the creation of a British base in the Negev. Israel, subsequently, retreated from the plan. See 2451/3: Elath to Sharett, 13 March 1954; 360/8: Eban to Eytan, 2 April 1954; 2403/12: Elath Conversation with Crossman. British policy towards the Gaza base proposal is described in PRO files, FO371/96972–7.

34. ISA, 2593/17: Gazit to Elath, 12 Oct. 1953; 2395/12: Gazit to Elath, 19 March 1953; 2419/1: Gazit to Elath, 9 Oct. 1953; 2477/10: Gazit to Elath, 5 March 1954; 2460/3: Eban Conversation with Dulles, 15 Jan. 1954. PRO, FO371/111073/10: Fox to Falla, 26 May 1954. USNA, 684A.85/1–1554: Dulles Conversation with Eban.

35. PRO, FO371/108486/23: Eden to Elath, 23 Oct. 1954; 111075/225: Commonwealth Relations Circular, 4 Oct. 1954; /236: Falla Minute, 1 Oct. 1954. Fear of such a 'folly' led Britain to postpone for a day the release of the treaty's final text. The delay was intended to deny Israel the opportunity to launch a military action designed to undermine the treaty.

36. On the origins of the *Bat Galim* test case see ISA, 2384/14: Washington Embassy to Foreign Ministry, 12 Oct. 1954. Sharett, op. cit., p. 577. Milstein, *Historia shel HaTzanhanim*, p. 281. Moshe Dayan, *Avnei Derech* (Tel Aviv, 1976), pp. 121, 132.

37. The EIMAC team found no evidence of shooting – the *Bat Galim* was unarmed – nor of the existence of the two fishermen said to have been killed. It found the charge 'unfounded', but later changed the term to 'unsubstantiated' to save the Egyptians further embarrassment. Even among Egyptian diplomats there was a sense that the charge had been fabricated. See PRO, FO371/108505/117: Complaint of the Egyptian Ambassador, 29 Sept. 1954. ISA, 2452/3: Eban to Foreign Ministry, 7 Dec. 1954; /4: EIMAC Report on *Bat Galim*, 30 Nov. 1954; /48: Rafael Summary of Discussion, 20 Oct. 1954; 164/8: Elath to Sharett, 22 Nov. 1954.

38. PRO, FO371/108505/124: Makins to Foreign Office, 8 Oct. 1954; /150: Stevenson Conversation with Fawzi, 3 Nov. 1954; 108506/200: Bromley Minute, 11 Dec. 1954; /193: Makins to Foreign Office, 6 Dec. 1954. USNA, 974.5301/12–854: Memorandum of the Officer in Charge of Egypt, Anglo-Egypt and Sudan Affairs.

39. ISA, 40/17: Elath Conversation with Nicholls, 5 Nov. 1954; 2452/4: Kidron to Foreign Ministry, 27 Nov. 1954; 21/39: Sharett Conversation with Hoover, 17 Dec. 1954. PRO, FO371/108314/49: Stevenson to Foreign Office, 29 Nov. 1954; 108505/128: Dixon to Foreign Office, 13 Oct. 1954; 108506/191: Dixon to Foreign Office, 2 Dec. 1954; 108486/31: Terton Conversation with Elath, 9 Nov. 1954. USNA, 974.5301/10–1254: Lodge to Dulles; 684A.85322/10–454: Russell to Dulles. Britain was so opposed to the debate that it attempted to prevent Israel from gathering testimony from sailors aboard the *Empire Clyde*, a British ship which entered the Canal at the same time as the *Bat Galim*. France, while having little interest in Anglo-American plans for Middle East defence, also sought to avoid a debate in the light of the tense state of Franco-Egyptian relations. See PRO, FO371/108505/120: Dixon to Foreign Office, 29 Sept. 1954 and ISA, 164/8: Bendor to Foreign Ministry, 24 Nov. 1954; 2382/12: Tsur to Najjar, 1 Oct. 1954.

40. USNA, 784.53/11–2954: Dulles Conversation with Caffery. PRO, FO371/108506/191: Dixon to Foreign Office, 2 Dec. 1954; 108314/49: Egyptian Ambassador to Foreign Office, 29 Nov. 1954. ISA, 2403/12: Gazit Conversation with Tripp, 22 Dec. 1954; 164/8: Elath to Sharett, 21 Dec. 1954; 2452/3: Sharett Conversation with Nicholls, 9 Dec. 1954.

41. ISA, 2452/3: Tekoah to Foreign Ministry, 18 Jan. 1955; Eban to Eytan, 17 Jan. 1955. Sharett, op. cit., pp. 640, 681, 629, 650. Israel, though loathe to discuss the *Bat Galim* in any EIMAC forum, accepted Burns's proposal on the condition that the vessel be allowed to continue through the Canal under Egyptian guard and be returned to its original crew in Port Said; it also demanded a full review of the blockade issue. Egypt was quite willing to co-operate with Burns, but not under such conditions. See ISA, 2477/20A: Arel to U.S. Desk, 18 Feb. 1955. PRO, FO371/113713/10: New York to Foreign Office, 8 Jan. 1955. /11: Cairo to Foreign Office, 10 Jan. 1955; 113714/6: Skeet Minute, 13 Jan. 1955.

42. Sharett, op. cit., pp. 659, 664. Dayan, op. cit., p. 140. See also Aviezer Golan, *Operation Susannah* (New York, 1978), p. 38. Hagai Eshed, *Mi Natan et HaHora'ah?* (Jerusalem, 1979), pp. 65–7. Dan Horowitz and Eliahu Hasin, *HaParasha* (Tel Aviv, 1961), pp. 34–5.

43. ISA, 2387/7: Arabic Press Review, Clippings from *Akher Sa'ah*, *al-Akbar* and *al-Ahram*.

44. Ibid., Untitled, 24 Nov. 1954; Divon, Palmon to Sharett, 21 Nov. 1954.

45. Heikal, *Cutting the Lion's Tail*, p. 48. See also ISA, 2452/4: Text of Lutfi Speech in the UN, 4 Dec. 1954.

NOTES

46. The exchanges between Sharett and Nasser on the *Bat Galim* and sabotage affairs are discussed in greater detail in Chapter 5. These took place directly in Paris between the Egyptian Press Attaché, Abd al-Rahman Sadiq, and two Israeli diplomats, Shmuel Divon and Gideon Rafael. Indirect communications were conveyed by Maurice Orbach, a British MP and a leader of the World Jewish Congress. ISA, 2453/20: Rafael to Sharett, 18 Dec. 1954; Rafael to Sharett, 14 Dec. 1954; Divon to Sharett, 31 Dec. 1954; /21: Orbach Report, 4 Nov. 1954; Rafael to Sharett, 22 Dec. 1954; Rafael and Divon to Sharett, 2 Jan. 1955; 2460/4: Rafael to Sharett, 19 Jan. 1955. See also Rafael, op. cit., p. 39 and Sharett, op. cit., pp. 680–94. Communication of Israeli threat of retaliation in PRO, FO371/108458/23: Nicholls to Foreign Office, 17 Dec. 1954.
47. ISA, 2599/6: Middle East Desk to Chargé D'Affaires, Sidney, 4 Aug. 1955; 2427/5: Report on Blockade (Yaari), 23 March 1956; 2451/9: The Arab Economic War (Yaari), 4 Oct. 1956.
48. USNA, 976.72/1–2256: Tel Aviv to Department. ISA, 2446/3: Israel *Aide Mémoire* to the Tripartite Powers, Nov. 1955; 2419/5: Bartov to Sharett, 2 Sept. 1955; Sharett to Rafael, 23 Sept. 1955; 43/8: Eytan to Embassies, 12 Aug. 1956. Sharett, op. cit., p. 1185. Milstein, op. cit., pp. 341–2.
49. ISA, 2477/17: Summary of Reports from the Washington Embassy on the Possibilities for Change in U.S. Policy Toward Nasser, 23 July 1956. The file contains précis of Eban's conversations with Dulles on the Aswan issue. Eban, op. cit., p.205. On Dulles's reasons for withdrawing from the Aswan project see FRUS, XV, 793–7, 850–3, 867–73. JFD, Oral Histories of Allen Dulles (pp. 39–43), Dillion Anderson (p. 36), James R. Wiggins (p. 10), Herbert Prochnow (p. 36), and Robert Bowies (p. 39).
50. PRO, FO371/119150/2008: Shepherd Minute, 28 Oct. 1956. DDE, Diary Box 16: Entry for 28 July 1956. Selwyn Lloyd, *Suez 1956* (London, 1978), p. 103. Tsur, *Prélude à Suez*, 390. Anthony Eden, *Full Circle* (London, 1960), pp. 426, 436. Dulles's exclusion of Israel from SCUA did not, however, prevent him from considering the use of Israel's supposed connections with Jewish bankers to levy economic sanctions against Egypt. See Lloyd, op. cit., p. 145.
51. USNA, 976.7301/8–456: Allen Conversation with Shiloah. ISA, 48/3: Eytan to Foreign Ministry, Conversation with Lloyd, 3 Aug. 1956.
52. USNA, 976.7301/10–1056: Meir to Lawson;/8–656: Tel Aviv to the Secretary of State; /8–1656: Eban to Dulles; /9–1056: Dulles Conversation with Eban. ISA, 2409/6: Eytan to Alon, 13 Aug. 1956; Israel Aide Mémoire to the London Conference, 16 Aug. 1956; Efrat to Foreign Ministry, 20 Oct. 1956; /6: Eytan to New York, 13 Oct. 1956; 2427/6: Israel Protest on the *Panagia*; 2452/2: Press Campaign on the Arab Boycott, 11 Sept. 1956. Sharett, op. cit., pp. 1594, 1603. Eban, *An Autobiography*, p. 208. Dulles was reported by the Israelis to have taken a genuine interest in the test convoy idea. He rejected the Haifa–Eilat pipeline, however, as outdated; the US, he explained, preferred to invest its money in larger tankers.
53. USNA, 976.7301/8–2256: Dulles Conversation with Hussein; /8–456: Port Said to the Secretary of State. Urquhart, op. cit., p. 166. BBC, Daily Report 64, p. 2; 30, p. a4; 9, p. ii; 15, p. iii; 12, p. iv. ISA, 2477/8: Survey of Arabic News, 6 Aug. 1956. Throughout the summer, Radio Cairo in Hebrew praised Israel's attitude towards the crisis and its co-operation with Egypt in fighting imperialism. On 4 August the broadcasts featured a unique item: greetings from an Egyptian air force commander to his Israeli colleagues.
54. USNA, 976.7301/9–2556: Ludlow Conversation with Arab;/9–2756: New York to the Secretary of State; /9–2856: Dulles Conversation with Rifai.
55. ISA, 2460/4: Eliav to Foreign Ministry, 5 Oct. 1956; 2409/8: Untitled, 23 Sept. 1956. Eden, op. cit., p. 466. Anthony Nutting, *No End of a Lesson* (London, 1967), pp. 45–7.
56. Nasser rejected Hammarskjöld's proposals for a secret meeting on the blockade between the Egyptian and Israeli Foreign Ministers as well as Eisenhower's suggestion that the two countries send representatives for private talks on the subject, at the White House. See ISA, 2409/9: Foreign Ministry to London, 19 Oct. 1956. JFD, White House Files, Box 3: Eisenhower to Hoover, 8 Oct. 1956. Heikal, *Millafat al-Suways*, p. 519.
57. JFD, Dulles–Herter Files, Box 6: Opportunities for the Middle East, 16 Oct. 1956.

USNA, 976.7301/9–456: Dulles to Henderson. Eden, op. cit., p. 504. Harold MacMillan, *Riding the Storm* (London, 1971), p. 141. Christian Pineau, *1956 Suez* (Paris, 1976), p. 118.
58. Sharett, op cit., p. 947.
59. ISA, 2532/1: Israel Circular to Major Capitals, 29 Oct. 1956.

CHAPTER THREE

1. William Roger Louis, *The British Empire in the Middle East, 1945–1951* (Oxford, 1984), pp. 583–90, 720–1.
2. ISA, 2566/7: Egypt's Position on Regional Defence, 28 Oct. 1951. PRO, FO371/102780/4: Bowker to Stevenson, 27 March 1953; /3: British Middle East Office to Stevenson, 18 March 1953. USNA, 780.5/3–2153: Caffery Conversation with Ahmad Hussein.
3. Dean Acheson, *Present at the Creation* (New York, 1969), pp. 562–8. John C. Campbell, *Defense of the Middle East* (New York, 1958), pp. 29–38. See also James Decker, *U.S. Policy Regarding the Baghdad Pact* (unpublished doctoral dissertation, American University, 1975).
4. PRO, FO371/91731/3: Chadwick to Bevin, 24 Feb. 1951; /6: Shinwell to Morrison, 18 May 1951; 982891/15: Helm to Furlonge, 27 Feb. 1951. ISA, 2457/5: Yadin Conversation with Robertson, 20 Feb. 1951; 2475/5: Foreign Ministry Discussion on Regional Defence, 15 Nov. 1952. Diaries: 28 March 1953, 30 April 1953.
5. PRO, FO371/98820/1: Wardrop to Evans, 18 Sept. 1952; 96942/2: Foreign Office to Tel Aviv, 25 Feb 1952; CAB 128/25: 23 Oct. 1952. USNA, 780.5/11–652: Caffery to Acheson; 784A.13/6–1852: Byroade to Acheson; 680.84A/11–752: Byroade Conversation with Eban. ISA, 2566/17: Britain's Position on Middle East Defence. 28 Oct. 1951. 2460/5: Eban to Foreign Ministry Officers, 8 Aug. 1952.
6. On French policy towards Middle East defence, see ISA, 2551/11: Tsur Conversation with Maillard, 11 Jan. 1956; 25/1: Bendor to Avner, 15 Sept. 1955. Shimon Peres, *David's Sling: The Arming of Israel* (London, 1970), pp. 54–5. Tsur, *Prélude à Suez*, pp. 115–6. Sharett, *Yoman Ishi*, p. 498.
7. PRO, FO371/96986/6: Colbourn Conversation with Egyptian Leaders, 19 Sept. 1952. USNA, 780.5/7–2952: Alexandria to Acheson; 774.5/1–353: London to secretary of State; 774.5 MSP/9–252: Department to Caffery. DDQ, 1975 25E 75: Caffery to Naguib, 24 Nov. 1952. ISA, Eban to Foreign Ministry, 8 Aug. 1952. El-Barawy, *The Military Coup in Egypt*, pp. 208–11. Heikal, *Millafat al-Suways*, pp. 163–4.
8. USNA, 780.5/11–652: Caffery to Acheson; /3–2153: Caffery Conversation with Ahmad Hussein; /5–153: Dulles to Caffery; /2–1953: Notes for Dulles's Press Conference; 789.5/4–2853: London to Department, 28 April 1953; 680. 84A/11–752: Byroade Conversation with Eban. BG, Diary, 30 Dec. 1952. ISA, 2445/11: Foreign Ministry Report on Regional Defence, 20 June 1953; 458/13: Divon to Shiloah, 15 Feb. 1953; 2403/18: Elath to Sharett, 14 Nov. 1953.
9. PRO, FO371/102826/43: NEACC Report, 18 Feb. 1953; /37: Makins to Foreign Office, 20 Feb. 1953; 102897/7: Allen Minute, 9 Jan. 1953; 102780/1: Foreign Office Minute, 8 Jan. 1953; /2: Curle to Burrows, 29 Jan. 1953. JFD, International File, Box 1: Dulles to Naguib, 15 July 1953. DDE, White House Correspondence, Box 3: Eisenhower to Dulles, 16 June 1953. USNA, 774 5/5–653: Jernegan Conversation with General Ghalib; /7–1553: Cairo to Department; 774.5MSP/2–1453: Caffery to Byroade; 780.5/3–553: Caffery to Department; /2–1753: Dulles Note; 780.00/5–2953: Dulles to Representatives of U.S. Colleges and Businesses in the Middle East. See also Heikal, *Cutting the Lion's Tail*, p. 39.
10. The US also denied Israel's request for membership in NATO, but consented to grant $3 million to Israel for construction of a road to Eilat, ostensibly as part of the regional defence infrastructure. See ISA, 2460/5: Goitein Conversation with Hart, 26 Aug.

NOTES

1952; Shalit to Foreign Ministry, 2 Oct. 1953. 2403/18: Elath to Sharett, 14 Nov. 1953; /13: Eban to Sharett, 5 April 1953. 36/3: Eban to Ben Gurion, 2 March 1953 PRO, CAB 128/26: 10 Aug. 1953. Sharett, op. cit., pp. 152, 161.
11. USNA, 680.84A/11–752: Byroade Conversation with Eban.
12. PRO, FO371/102700/8: Summary of Events in Egypt, 28 Jan. – 10 Feb. 1953; 104196/ E1071/6: Amman to Salisbury, 15 Sept. 1953. ISA, 2593/17: Egyptian Press Release, 6 July 1953.
13. USNA, 684A.86/8–2153: Intelligence Advisory Committee to Dulles; 780.5/4–3053: Dulles to Caffery. JFD, Middle East File, Box 73: Important Points of Trip, June 1953. PRO, FO371/102780/3: British Middle East Office to Allen, 18 March 1953. ISA, 2403/13: Foreign Ministry Memorandum, 5 June 1953.
14. PRO, 110819/V1193/12: Foreign Office Blue Minute, 15 Jan. 1954; 110820/V1192/22: Eden to Foreign Office, 4 Feb. 1954.
15. ISA, 2445/12: Eban Conversation with Dulles, 15 Jan. 1954; Fisher to Eytan, 18 March 1954; Sasson to Sharett, 23 March 1954; 2475/3: Herzog Conversation with Eveland, 25 Aug. 1954; 2382/8: Avner to Lourie, 9 July 1954; 2403/8: Herzog to Intelligence Wing, 30 March 1954. PRO, FO371/110837/3: Powell-Jones Minute, 2 June 1954; 111118/1: Powell-Jones Minute, 9 July 1954. USNA, 784.5301/7–954: Assistant Secretary of Defence to Davis for Eban.
16. USNA, 786.00/6–2454: Beirut to State Department. PRO, FO371/110791/39: Damascus to Foreign Office, 26 May 1954; /24: Amman to Foreign Office, 8 May 1954. BBC, 437, pp. 28–9; 439, p. 31. Seale, *The Struggle For Syria*, p. 199.
17. USNA, 684A.86/12–3154: Ankara to Department; 774.00/12–1854: UK–US Talks, London. PRO, FO371/1Q8453/4: Makins to Foreign Office, 3 July 1954. ISA, 2457/3: Herzog Conversation with Eveland, 25 Aug. 1954.
18. ISA, 2593/18: Gazit to Eytan, 3 Sept. 1954; 413/2: Salah Press Conference, 30 July 1954. On Israel's attempts to clarify Britain's pledges for its security see PRO, FO371/108486/23: Eden to Elath, 23 Oct. 1954; 111075/238: Shuckburgh to Eden, 20 Oct. 1954. As one British diplomat wrote, 'Britain is not prepared to be led further down the road of clarification which undoubtedly ends in the Israeli mind in staff conversations'.
19. *Foreign Relations of the United States*, Vol. 9, Document 928, pp. 1707–10. USNA, 684A.86/10–2154: Conversation between Nixon and Hoover; /12–1154: Cairo to State Department. PRO, FO371/111095/10G: Shuckburgh Minute, Notes on the Arab–Israel Dispute, 15 Dec. 1954. RCC officials, on occasion, suggested to Western diplomats that their co-operation on regional defence could be gained through Israeli territorial concessions, specifically in the Negev. Such a move, the Egyptians explained, would facilitate the transfer of British troops from the Canal Zone to Jordan. See, for example, PRO, FO371/102835/2: Stevenson to Foreign Office, 11 Feb. 1953. USNA, 784.00/4–2954: Russell Conversation with Elath, 29 April 1954. ISA, 417/4: Elath Conversation with Russell, 17 March 1954; 2477/20: Shimoni to Jerusalem, 26 March 1955.
20. On Nasser's rejection of the American arms offer see USNA, 774.5MSP/8–2954: Caffery to Dulles; /8–3154: Jernegan Conversation with Hussein. Nuri's proposal for linking Egyptian involvement in the Northern Tier alliance with an Arab–Israel peace settlement was presented to Salah Salem, Nasser's emissary, at Sarsank in Iraq. Nuri convinced Salem of the wisdom of the plan, but on returning to Cairo, Salem was berated by Nasser for having fallen into Nuri's trap. PRO, FO371/110791/1: Baghdad to Foreign Office, 29 Aug. 1954. Seale, op. cit., pp. 201–4.
21. PRO, FO371/111092/3: Cairo to Foreign Office, 23 Dec. 1954. Seale, op. cit., p. 211. Heikal, *Millafat al-Suways*, pp. 319–20. Examples of Egyptian propaganda in BBC, 536, pp. 41, 46–7; 538, p. 36; 539, pp. 34–5; 542, p. 29.
22. FRUS, XIV, 149–151.
23. FRUS, XIV, 159. USNA, 684A.86/11–2254: Secretary of State to Certain Diplomatic and Consular Offices. PRO, FO371/115866/48: Macmillan to Shuckburgh, 24 March 1955. Sharett, op. cit., pp. 667, 712, 726, 732, 794, 797, 814.

24. FRUS, XIV, 80. ISA, 2454/5: Gaza Incident, Summary and Estimation, 22 March 1955. BBC, 540, p. 32; 548, p. 29; 549, p. 24. Heikal, op. cit., p. 340. Anwar Sadat, writing a quarter of a century after the event, still saw the Gaza raid as an act designed to weaken Egypt's resistance to the Baghdad Pact; see *In Search of Identity* (New York, 1977), p. 135.
25. Thanks to Nasser's efforts, the conference adopted a resolution calling for the realization of Palestinian rights and the implementation of the partition plan. See Ishmael Tareq, *The UAR in Africa* (Evanston, 1977), pp. 28–30. Heikal, op. cit., p. 343. See also *al-Ahram*, 21 March 1955; *Ruz al-Yusuf*, 28 March 1955; BBC, 567, pp. 19–20.
26. Heikal, op. cit., pp. 324, 441.
27. Ben Gurion, *Medinat Yisrael HaMehudeshet*, p. 476. Sharett, op. cit., pp. 808–9, 814. ISA, 2409/1: Eytan to Lourie, 19 Oct. 1955.
28. PRO, FO371/115871/82: Sharett to Macmillan, 5 May 1955; 115537/4: Record of Meeting, Secretary of State and Sharett, 26 Oct. 1955. Sharett, op. cit., pp. 836–7, 1018, 1021–4, 1266–7. Tsur, op. cit., p. 266. Eban, *An Autobiography*, p. 184.
29. Harold Macmillan, *Riding the Storm* (London, 1971), p. 656. Sharett, op. cit., p. 1305. ISA, 2450/7: Nasser's Decision to Purchase Eastern Bloc Arms, 1 Nov. 1955.
30. PRO, FO371/115657/103: Amman to Foreign Office, 13 Dec. 1955; 115910/442: Hadow Minute, 6 Dec. 1955. 'Abd al-Latif Baghdati, *Mudhakkirat* (Cairo, 1977), pp. 201, 207–9. *al-Gumhurriyah*, 24 Dec. 1955, editorial by Anwar Sadat. Burns, *Between Arab and Israeli*, p. 118.
31. FRUS, XIV, 146, 547, 722, 820–1; XV, 337–8. PRO, FO371/115867/57: U.S. Ambassador to Cairo to State Department (Telegram Copy), 6 April 1955; /58: Washington to Foreign Office, 6 April 1955; 115871/134: Shuckburgh to the Secretary of State, 15 July 1955; 115878/300: Washington to Foreign Office, 17 Sept. 1955; 113676/260: Record of Conversation, Dulles, Macmillan, Russell, Hare, 3 Oct. 1955; 115469/25: Shuckburgh to the Secretary of State, 9 Nov. 1955. JFD, Allen Dulles Papers, NCS Report, 7 Dec. 1955. DDQ, 1978 383A: U.S. Policy on Pact, 18 July 1955.
32. PRO, FO371/115469/20: Trevelyan to Foreign Office, 3 Nov. 1955.
33. PRO, FO371/115654/46: Duke to Macmillan, 22 Nov. 1955; PREM-11859: Cairo to Foreign Office, 2 Nov. 1955. FRUS, XV, 101–7, 121. Harold Macmillan, *Tides of Fortune* (New York, 1969), p. 93.
34. FRUS, XIV, 70, 78–9; XV, 39–40, 287–8, 293. Heikal, op. cit., pp. 325, 327.
35. On 18 December, for example, Israel Arabic Radio announced that 'Jordan is not compelled to submit to any foreign force, whether from the Middle East or outside it'. See BBC, 631, pp. 20–1. On Israel's border policy towards Jordan, see Copeland, *The Game of Nations*, p. 218.
36. PRO, FO371/115653/22: Duke to Shuckburgh, 10 Nov. 1955; /27: Memorandum on Jordan and the Baghdad Pact, 10 Nov. 1955. Aqil Hyder Hasan Abidi Abidi, *Jordan, A Political Study: 1948–1957* (New Delhi, 1965), p. 128. Naseer H. Aruri, *Jordan: A Study in Political Development* (The Hague, 1972), p. 122. Mohammad Ibrahim Faddah, *The Middle East in Transition: A Study of Jordan's Foreign Policy* (New York, 1974), pp. 201–10.
37. PRO, FO371/115880/331: Arthur Minute, 4 Nov. 1955; 115469/25: Shuckburgh Minute, 9 Nov. 1955.
38. PRO, FO371/115652/27: Memorandum on Jordan and the Baghdad Pact, 11 Nov. 1955; 115656/84: Foreign Office to Amman, 12 Dec. 1955; /84c: Amman to Foreign Office, 12 Dec. 1955; 115655/61: Shuckburgh Minute, 3 Dec. 1955; 115658/127: Report by Sir Gerald Templer on His Visit to Jordan, 22 Dec. 1955. See also Glubb, *A Soldier with the Arabs*, p.29.
39. PRO, FO371/115653/33: Glubb to Foreign Office, 15 Nov. 1955; 121476/3: Mason to Rose, 31 Dec. 1955; 121491/9: Wikeley to Rose, 28 Dec. 1955. FRUS, XIII, 1–19. Sadat, op. cit., p. 136. BBC, 620, pp. 20–1; 631, pp. 20–5. See also Hazza' al-Majali, *Mudhakkirati* (Amman, 1960), pp. 125–9; *Hadha Biyan al-Nass: Qissah Muhadathat Tamblar* (Amman, 1956). M. Mahdi, and S. Musa, *Tarikh al-Urdun fi al-Qarn al-'Ashrin* (Amman, 1959), pp. 202–32.

40. PRO, FO371/121491/26: Cairo to Foreign Office, 23 Jan. 1956; 115645/2: Trevelyan to Duke, 2 Nov. 1956.
41. PRO, FO371/118842/8: Trevelyan to Shuckburgh, 9 Feb. 1956; 121733/28: Rose Minute, 25 Jan. 1955. ISA, 2455/9: Foreign Ministry Report on the First Year of the Baghdad Pact, 17 Feb. 1956. DDE, Diary, Box 13: Memorandum of Conference with the President, 29 March 1956; Dulles–Eisenhower Conversation, 29 March 1956; Box 15: Dulles–Eisenhower Conversation, 6 April 1956. DDQ, 1978 354D: Joint Chiefs of Staff Report, 21 Dec. 1955; 283B: Dulles–Eden Talks, 7 Feb. 1956; 123E: Eisenhower Diary, 8 March 1956; 1984 1051: Dulles to MacMillan, 19 Aug. 1955; 1980 2670: U.S. Embassy London to Dulles, 7 March 1956. See also Anthony Eden, *Full Circle*, p. 333. Macmillan, *Riding the Storm*, pp. 632–3, 642.
42. On the Eisenhower Administration's deliberations over security guarantees for Israel see DDQ, 1978 123E: Eisenhower Diary, 8 March 1956. DDE, Diary, Box 15: Conversation with Dulles, 6 April 1956.

CHAPTER FOUR

1. On the concept of the NEACC and 'habitual source' see PRO, FO371/104191/11: Strang to Paris Embassy, 24 Sept. 1953; /10: Falla Minute, 22 Sept. 1953. DDQ, 1978 387C: NSC Report to the President, 17 May 1950.
2. USNA, 784.5 MSP/1–2852: Stabler to Byroade, 28 Jan. 1952. ISA, 2460/5: Eban to Foreign Ministry Officers, 8 Aug. 1952; 2445/11: U.S. Position on Regional Defence, 27 Oct. 1952.
3. Although Britain's position stemmed largely from economic considerations, the Foreign Office depicted the US–Egypt deal as presenting a threat to the security of British troops in the Canal Zone and as removing Egypt's incentive to join MEDO. PRO, CAB 128/25: 23 Oct. 1952; FO371/102826/34: Bowker Minute, 12 Feb. 1953; 102878/7: Foreign Office Minute, 8 Jan. 1953; 102825/7: Eden Conversation with Byroade, 6 Jan. 1953. On the renewal of America's offer to Egypt see USNA, 780.5/11–2552: Caffery to Acheson. Paul Jabber, *Not by War Alone* (Los Angeles, 1981), p. 133. Acheson, *Present at the Creation*, pp. 566–7.
4. Israel's arguments against arms sales to the Arab's lack of commitment to the West and their unreliability as soldiers. Israel, by contrast, supported the West in the Cold War and, alone among the Middle East states, could field a serious army. See ISA, 42/12: Israel Aides-Mémoire to London and Washington, 31 Oct. 1952; 42/13: London to Sharett, 8 Jan. 1953; 2430/12: Eytan to London, 10 Oct. 1952; 2403/8: Sharett Note, 22 Sept. 1952; 2475/9: Shiloah Conversation with Jernegan, 17 Dec. 1952; 2403/18: Bendor to Sharett, 26 Dec. 1952. USNA, 774.5 MSP/12–2952: Acheson to Harriman. PRO, FO371/102831/16: Foreign Office Minute, 14 Feb. 1953. Yitzhak Steigman, *Mivtzah Kadesh: Hayl HaAvir baShanim 1950–1956*, Hitatzmut vePeilut (Tel Aviv, 1986), pp. 41–2.
5. USNA, 774.5 MSP/12–1652: Caffery Conversation with Naguib. ISA, 2460/6: Shalit Conversation with Hart, 24 Dec. 1952. A report of a $100 million American arms offer to Egypt was allegedly made by the US Deputy Secretary of Defence, William Foster, during a visit to Cairo in November 1952. See Jabber, op. cit., pp. 133–4. Heikal, *Milaffat al-Suways*, pp. 178, 180.
6. In drafting the arms offer to Egypt, the State Department was influenced by the Pentagon's estimate that Egypt, if given arms, would grant base rights to the U.S. army. USNA, 774.5 MSP/1–453: Jernegan to Acheson; /1–2253: Martin to Mathews; /11–2852: Stabler to Byroade; /1–1852: NEA to Dulles; /11–152: U.S. Army Report. See also DDE, Dulles–Herter Files: Eisenhower to Dulles, 22 April 1953.
7. USNA, 774.5 MSP/12–1752: Report on the Visit of Sabri and Niklowi; /1–253: Pentagon List for Egypt. PRO, FO371/102843/2: U.S. Assistance to Egypt, 15 Jan. 1953; 102826/JE1193/34: Allen Minute, 7 Feb. 1953. Heikal, op. cit., pp. 180–3.

8. The Anglo-American crisis over US arms sales to Egypt reached a climax in May 1953, during Dulles's Middle East tour, when the British press carried reports of a $200 million American arms offer to Egypt. In a vituperative series of letters, Eisenhower explained that the deal was necessitated by domestic pressure to make amends for America's 'shabby' treatment of the Arabs, while Churchill threatened to reconsider the status of US bases in Britain and Britain's compliance with the boycott of Communist China if the offer were not retracted. JFD, Middle East File, Box 73: Important Points of Trip, 6 Jan. 1953. DDE, International File, Box 8: Churchill to Eisenhower, 15 June 1953. PRO, FO371/102843/9: Churchill to Eisenhower, 19 Dec. 1953; /10: Eisenhower to Churchill, 21 Dec. 1953. See also Wilbur Crane Eveland, *Ropes of Sand* (New York, 1980), pp. 148–9. Israel's protests to London and Washington are found in ISA, 2460/6: Eban Conversation with Byroade, 13 Nov. 1953; 2403/18: Gazit to Elath, 27 Aug. 1953; Goitein Conversation with Byroade, 4 Feb. 1953.
9. JFD, International File, Box 1: Dulles to Naguib, 15 July 1953. DDE, White House Correspondence, Box 3: Eisenhower to Dulles, 16 June 1953. USNA, 774.5/5–653: Jernegan Conversation with Brig. Gen. Abdel Hamid Ghalib.
10. Egyptian press reports on the impending arrival of American arms in *al-Misri*, 28 Aug. 1952; 17 Sept. 1953; *Akhbar al-Yawm*, 1 Nov. 1952; BBC, 430, p. 20. The arguments employed by Egyptian representatives in talks with American officials appear in USNA, 774.5/1–753: Caffery to Dulles; /2–1453: Caffery to Byroade; /7–1553: Cairo to Department; 780.5/3–553: Caffery to Department. Hussein's appeal for a symbolic delivery in 774.5 MSP/10–2053: Byroade Conversation with Hussein.
11. In addition to the Iraqi and Egyptian offers, the US in 1954 sold, or attempted to sell, arms to Pakistan, Saudi Arabia, Syria, Lebanon and Jordan. See PRO, FO371/110822/79: Chiefs of Staff to Foreign Office, 25 June 1954; 110823/90: Ministry of Defence Note, 3 Sept. 1954. On Washington's decision to renew arms talks with Cairo see USNA, 774.5/7–754: Draft U.S.–Egypt Military Assistance Agreement; 774.5 MSP/7–2254: Byroade Conversation with Hussein; /7–3054: Byroade Conversation with Hussein. ISA, 2403/8: Herzog Conversation with Eveland, 19 Aug. 1954.
12. USNA, 774.5 MSP/8–2954: Caffery to Dulles; /8–3154: Jernegan Conversation with Hussein; /9–2054: Allen to Department; 774.5/7–3054: Byroade to Dulles. PRO, FO371/110791/24: Duke to Foreign Office, 8 Sept. 1954. ISA, 2401/4: Egyptian Statement on American Arms; 2547/2: Gazit to Elath, 12 Oct. 1954.
13. USNA, 780.5/12–354: Dorsey Conversation with Fahmy; 774.5 MSP/12–2154: Dorsey to Byroade; 684A.86/11–854: Cairo to Department. ISA, 2450/7: U.S. Arms for Egypt, 8 Feb. 1955. See also Eveland, op. cit., p. 101 and Jabber, op. cit., p. 150. Eveland and Harrison Allen Gerhardt were the emissaries who met with Nasser in October. They reportedly offered to reduce the MAAG to 40 members, dressed in civilian clothes, who would return to the US immediately after supervising delivery of the arms. A similar mission was undertaken by Norman Paul, director of the Middle East section of the Foreign Operations Administration.
14. In his conversation with Dulles in Cairo in May 1953, for example, Nasser requested arms in order to enable Egypt to negotiate with Israel from a position of strength, not to meet an Israeli threat. By January 1954, however, Egypt had begun protesting about French and British arms sales to Israel. See PRO, FO371/115628/66: Kirkpatrick Minute, 4 March 1955. USNA, 680.84A/3–2454: Dulles with the Heads of Seven Arab Missions; 684A.85/1–1354: Caffery Conversation with Fawzi. Humphrey Trevelyan, *The Middle East in Revolution* (London, 1970), p. 27.
15. USNA, 784A.56/9–754: Paris to Dulles; /9–2854: Jernegan to Dulles; /11–1553: Grant Conversation with Dayan and Herzog. ISA, 2467/7: Eban to Sharett, 19 May 1954; 2403/8: Herzog to Foreign Ministry, 19 Aug. 1954;/18: Bowker to Elath, 23 Jan. 1953; 2384/3: Kalmon Report, 31 Dec. 1954. PRO, FO371/104227/75: Powell-Jones to Gautrey, 23 Oct. 1953; 104224/238: Evans to Bowker, 14 Aug. 1953; 104229/4: Scott to Foreign Office, 11 Dec. 1953.
16. DDQ, 1982 295: Memorandum for the President, 16 March 1953. PRO, FO371/102831/16: Foreign Office Minute, 23 Jan. 1953. NAC, RG 25, vol. 2180, File

50000-B-pt. 1: Arms for Israel, 14 Dec. 1950; pt. 4: Pearson to the Canadian Ambassador, Washington, 21 Nov. 1953.

17. Through private agents, Israel purchased tanks in the Philippines, frigates in Mexico, and artillery in France, Canada and Italy. Such acquisitions, however, could barely maintain IDF stocks. As late as October 1952, the IDF could not fully clothe and arm its fifteen brigades. See Peres, *David's Sling*, pp. 47–8. BG, Diary: 18 July 1952; 10 Oct. 1952. Steigman, op. cit., pp. 22–3, 38, 54.

18. On the Powers' reservations vis-à-vis the scope of the Tripartite Declaration see PRO, FO371/104223/196: NEACC Report, 24 July 1953; 110819/12: Foreign Office Blue Minute, 15 Jan. 1954; 110820/22: Eden to Foreign Office, 4 Feb. 1954; 115559/168: Arms Deliveries, 29 March 1955; 115654/39: Rose Minute, 15 Nov. 1955. ISA, 42/13: Avner to Foreign Ministry, 8 Sept. 1954; Foreign Ministry to Ankara, 12 Aug. 1954; 40/16: Tsur to Foreign Ministry, 24 July 1953; 2403/18 Bendor to Sharett, 26 Dec. 1952.

19. PRO, FO371/104191/5: Draft for Anglo-French Talks on the Middle East, June 1953; 104224/238: Evans to Bowker, 14 Aug. 1953;/234: NEACC Report, 7 Aug. 1953; CAB 129/62: 7 Aug. 1953. USNA, 784A.56/9–764: Paris to Dulles; 780.00/12–2154: Jernegan Conversation with François de Laboulage. ISA 40/16: Tsur to Foreign Ministry, 14 March 1954.

20. ISA, 42/13: Avner to Foreign Ministry, 8 Sept. 1954; Foreign Ministry to Ankara, 12 Aug. 1954; 40/16: Tsur to Foreign Ministry, 28 Oct. 1954. PRO, FO371/104223//196: NEACC Report, 24 July 1953. Sylvia Crosbie, *A Tacit Alliance* (Princeton, 1974), pp. 43–4, 58.

21. In 1953, for example, the Quai d'Orsay opposed Britain's jet sales to Israel, while Israel's negotiations for the purchase of French 155mm. guns fell through with the collapse of the Laniel government. See USNA, 784A.56/9–754: Paris to Dulles. Peres, op. cit., p. 48.

22. Among the key French figures involved in cementing the Franco-Israeli arms relationship was France's pro-Zionist ambassador to Tel Aviv, P. E. Gilbert. ISA, 2382/3: Tsur to Foreign Ministry, 14 March 1954; 2381/12: Tsur to Sharett, 28 April 1954 Tsur, *Prélude à Suez*, pp. 74–8, 96–7, 109–10, 115–16. Dayan, *Avnei Derech*, pp. 123–5. Peres, op. cit., pp. 50–5. Crosbie, op. cit., pp. 45–6.

23. USNA, 780.5/6–854: Byroade to Eban; 784A.5/8–754: Dulles to Israel Embassy. ISA, 2467/7: Eban Conversation with Byroade, 1 June 1954; 2587/15: Comay to Lourie, 17 June 1954; 468/1: Nevo to Comay, 19 May 1954.

24. NAC, RG 25, 2180, 50000-B-pt. 6: The Sale of Jet Aircraft to Israel, 28 April 1954; pt. 7: Pearson to the Canadian Ambassador, Washington, 28 June 1954. ISA, 2587/15: Ottawa to Foreign Ministry, 13 July 1954.

25. PRO, FO371/108451/96: Caffery to Foreign Office, 31 July 1954; 113699/8: Kirkpatrick Minute, 19 Jan. 1955;/35: Shuckburgh Minute, 14 March 1955; 113670/41: Paris to Foreign Office, 21 March 1955; 113672/105: Shuckburgh Minute, 20 June 1955; 115551/20: Macmillan to Eden, 4 Jan. 1955; 115662/367: Tanks for Egypt and Israel (Rose), 18 Aug. 1955. Trevelyan, op. cit., pp. 26–7.

26. For an example of Egyptian threats to turn to the East see USNA, 774.5/1–753: Caffery to Dulles. On Egypt's approaches to Moscow and Prague see PRO, FO371/102870/28: Chancery to Foreign Office, 23 Sept. 1953. 108468/34: Stevenson to Foreign Office, 17 July 1954. Ya'akov Roi, *From Encroachment to Involvement* (Tel Aviv, 1974); p. 115. Uri Raanan, *The USSR Arms the Third World: Case Studies in Soviet Foreign Policy* (Cambridge, 1967), p. 69. Sadat, *In Search of Identity*, p. 127. Jabber, op. cit., p. 165. See also *Ruz al-Yusuf*, 12 April 1977, article by Ahmad Hamrush.

27. FRUS, XIV, 396, 517. PRO, FO371/113699/25: Cairo to Foreign Office, 22 Feb. 1955. Raanan, op. cit., p. 84.

28. PRO, FO371/113675/203: Cairo to Foreign Office, 1 Oct. 1955; 113699/40: Cairo to Foreign Office, 21 March 1955; 113672/105: Shuckburgh Minute, 20 June 1955. FRUS, XIV, 395, 255–62. ISA, 2409/1: Tekoah to Harkabi, 14 Oct. 1955; 2450/7: Chain of Events Which Led to Nasser's Decision to Purchase Arms from the Soviet Bloc, 1 Nov. 1955. 'Ali Muhammad Labib, *al-Quwah al-Thalithah* (Cairo, 1977), pp. 92–3. Bagh-

dati, *Mudhakkirat*, pp. 197–8. Heikal, op. cit., p. 341. Eban, *An Autobiography*, p. 192.

29. PRO, FO371/113672/107: Cairo to Foreign Office, 28 June 1955; 113680/368: Trevelyan to Macmillan, 24 Oct. 1955. ISA, 2450/7: Chain of Events, 1 Nov. 1955. Ro'i, op. cit., p. 144. Baghdati, op. cit., p. 202. Heikal, op. cit., pp. 352–3.

30. PRO, FO371/113699/8: Kirkpatrick Minute, 19 Jan. 1955;/39: Shuckburgh Minute, 14 March 1955; 113670: Aide-Mémoire, Great Britain to France, 22 March 1955; 113671/74: Beith to Rose, 29 March 1956; 113674/159: Garvey to Bromely, 19 Sept. 1955; 113678/303: Arms Releases to Egypt, 10 Oct. 1955; /306: Cairo to Foreign Office, 13 Oct. 1955; 118966/112: Rose Minute, 2 Oct. 1956. FRUS, XIV, 8–9, 129. ISA, 2409/1: Ben Horin to U.S. Desk, 13 April 1956; 2450/7: Summary of Shipment of Valentine Tanks to Egypt, 20 Jan. 1956; 177/10: Najjar to Paris Embassy, 4 May 1955.

31. FRUS, XIV, 238–40, 274, 338–9, 353–4, 471, 491. PRO, FO371/113672/107: Cairo to Foreign Office, 28 June 1955;/105: Shuckburgh Minute, 20 June 1955; 113673/130: Trevelyan to Shuckburgh, 18 Aug. 1955; 113675/185: Hadow Minute, 23 Sept. 1955; 113674/159: Garvey to Bromely, 20 Sept. 1955. Dwight David Eisenhower, *The White House Years: Waging Peace, 1956–1961* (New York, 1965), p. 24. Trevelyan, op. cit., pp. 27–30.

32. Estimates of the actual dimensions of the Czech arms deal vary. The approximate figures cited are based on PRO, FO371/113674//151: Shuckburgh Minute, 26 Sept. 1955. ISA, 192/36: Assessment of Egyptian Armed Strength, 14 May 1956. FRUS, XIV, 507–8. Lloyd, *Suez 1956: A Personal Account*, p. 28. Heikal, *Nasser: The Cairo Documents* (New York, 1973), p. 63. Hofstadter, *Egypt and Nasser*, p. 77. Trevelyan, op. cit., p. 33.

33. Menahem Mansoor, *Political and Diplomatic History of the Arab World* (Washington, 1972), Vol. 3, 4 and 21 Sept. 1955. BBC, 600, p. 20; 607: pp. 14, 16–18. *Akhir Sa'ah*, 17 Aug. 1955, article by M. Heikal. PRO, FO371/113680/358: Trevelyan to Foreign Office, 1 Nov. 1955; 113681/384: Turton Minute, 20 Oct. 1955; 113677/262: Trevelyan to Foreign Office, 6 Oct. 1955; 113674/161: Trevelyan to Foreign Office, 26 Sept. 1955. ISA, 2474/16: Memorandum of Conversation, Pearson and Nasser, 11 Nov. 1955; 2456/3: Notes on Conversation, Crossman and Nasser, 27 Dec. 1955. Hofstadter, op. cit., p. 79.

34. FRUS, XIV, 524–6, 537–40, 551–2, 604–7, PRO, FO371/115480/5: Shuckburgh Minute, Policy in the Middle East, 14 Oct. 1955; 115653/27: Duke to Shuckburgh, 10 Nov. 1955; 113676/258: Nicholls to Macmillan, 3 Oct. 1955. DDQ, 1982 2568: Memorandum for the Secretary, 5 Nov. 1956. Eden, *Full Circle*, p. 30. Seale, *The Struggle For Syria*, pp. 233–4, 256. Baghdati, op. cit., pp. 206–9. Heikal, op. cit., pp. 359–64.

35. FRUS, XIV, 528–9, 553–4, 558 561, 705–7. PRO, FO371/115560/211: Draft Minute of the Foreign Secretary and Minister of Defence, 29 April 1955; CAB 128/29: 14 June 1955; 128/266, 4 Oct. 1955. ISA, 2450/7: Elath to Foreign Ministry, 10 Jan. 1955; Eban to Foreign Ministry, 8 Nov 1955. PRO, FO371/121499/216: Ministry of Defence, The Strategic Importance of Jordan, 25 Oct. 1956. Heikal, *Cutting the Lion's Tail*, pp. 80–5.

36. FRUS, XIV, 658, 629, 892; XV, 399–400. PRO, FO371/115537/4: Record of Meeting, Sharett and the Secretary of State, 26 Oct. 1955. ISA, 2409/1: Tsur to Sharett, 4 Oct. 1955; Israel Aide-Mémoire to the Soviet Union, 21 Oct. 1955; 2409/3: Geneva Embassy to Foreign Ministry, 31 Oct. 1955; 2456/3: Eban to Dulles, 16 Nov. 1955; Eban to Foreign Ministry, 26 Oct. 1955. JFO, Box 100: Press Conference, 24 Feb. 1956. Sharett, *Yoman Ishi*, pp. 1180, 1214–5, 1337, 1348. Eban, op. cit., p. 185.

37. PRO, FO371/113678/309: Cairo to Foreign Office, 20 Sept. 1955; 113676/260: Record of Conversation, Dulles and Macmillan, 3 Oct. 1955; 113675/210: Washington to Foreign Office, 1 Oct. 1955; 113677/274: Record of Conversation, Dulles and the Secretary of State, 6 Oct. 1955; 113678/317: Trevelyan to Foreign Office, 17 Oct. 1955; 115469/23: Kirkpatrick to Shuckburgh, 10 Nov. 1955.

38. Nasser's figures on the supply of tanks to Israel were, however, generally accurate: 100 AMX-13s and 100 surplus Shermans in 1955. British diplomats were apparently ill-

informed of these acquisitions, and believed Israel had obtained far fewer tanks. In their judgement, Nasser's statistics, based on alleged secret British and French documents leaked to Egypt, were no more than 'journalistic forgeries'. PRO, FO371/113678/287: French Document on Arms Supplies to Israel, 2 Oct. 1955;/298: Garvey to Bromely, 6 Oct. 1955. 113675/JE1194/224: Cairo to Foreign Office, 2 Oct. 1955; 115463/V1192/197: Beith to Rose, 26 April 1955. On Israel's arms acquisitions in 1955, see BG, Diary, 7 Aug. 1954; 27 Dec. 1955. Steigman, op. cit., 63–4.

39. FRUS, XIV, 673, 803. DDQ, 1982 2563: Adams to Goodpaster, 31 Oct. 1955. Tsur, op. cit., pp. 249, 252, 258–61, 267, 271–2. Crosbie, op. cit., p. 60. Dayan, op. cit., pp. 148–9, 153. Sharett, op. cit., pp. 1249, 1251–3. Steigman, op. cit., p. 64.

40. Tsur, op. cit., pp. 271–2, 275–81. PRO, CAB 128/129, 5 Sept. 1955. FRUS, XIV, 705–7, 740–2, 748–9; XV, 3–6. ISA, 2450/7: French Equipment for Egypt, 20 Nov. 1955.

41. FRUS, XIV, 629, 717–9. PRO, FO371/113682/434: Kirkpatrick Minute, 22 Dec. 1955. ISA, 2456/3: Eban to Foreign Ministry, 26 Oct. 1955; 2460/4: Raanan Conversation with Lawson, 1 Nov. 1955. DDQ, 1983 2238: Dulles–Eisenhower Conversation , 8 Dec. 1955. JFD, Subject File, Box 10: Dulles to Dean, 27 March 1956. Steigman, op. cit., pp. 64, 67. Tsur, op. cit., pp. 275, 279, 281.

42. FRUS, XIV, 874–5, 884–5, 890–2; XV, 473–6, 482–3, 569, 641. NAC, RG 25, 2180, 50000-B-pt.12: Export of Arms to the Middle East, 3 April 1956. DDE, Diaries, Box 13: Eisenhower Conversation with Dulles, 28 March 1956; International File, Box 9: Dulles to Hoover, 6 March 1956. JFD, White House File, Box 4: Hoover to Dulles, 16 March 1956; Subject File, Box 10: Dulles to Eisenhower, 1 March 1956; Dulles to Eisenhower, 2 March 1956; Dulles to Dean, 27 March 1956.

43. FRUS, XV, 3–6, 14, 367–70, 372–4. BG, Diary, 10 July 1956. Sharett, op. cit., pp. 1385–6.

44. FRUS, XV, 163–6, 243, 242, 260, 276–81. DDQ, 1982 2573: Conversation Between Eisenhower, Dulles, and Rabbi Silver, 26 April 1956; 2568: Hanes, Jr. to MacArthur, 11 May 1956. ISA, 2460/4: Conversation Between Eisenhower and Silver, 29 Feb. 1956; 2455/9: Herzog to Sharett 29 March 1956; Eban to Sharett, 10 Feb. 1956; Eytan to Washington, 9 March 1956; Sharett to Eban, 10 March 1956. Sharett, op. cit., pp. 1306–11. Eban, op. cit., pp. 197–8. Rafael, *Destination Peace*, p. 51. Tsur, op. cit., p. 351.

45. FRUS, XV, 497, 575–7, 630–2, 837. DDQ, 1982 2567: Hanes to MacArthur, 1 May 1956. DDE, White House Correspondence, File D: Dulles to Eisenhower, 28 Sept. 1956.

46. NAC, 2180, 50000-B-pt. 12: Washington to Ottawa, 24 May 1956; Cabinet Conclusions, RG 2, Box 16, Vol. 5775: 14 June 1956, 12, 27 and 31 July 1956; Pearson Papers, MG 26, N1, Vol. 37: Conversation with Dulles, 10 May 1956. USNA, 974.72/7–2756: Hoover to Ottawa; /7–2856: Paris to the Secretary of State. FRUS, XV, 601, 609, 692–3, 818–9 723–4. ISA, 2583/12: Foreign Ministry to Ottawa, 13 July 1956; 2587/12: Comay to Foreign Ministry, 3 Aug. 1956.

47. FRUS, XV, 615–8.

48. BG, Correspondence, 12 April 1956: Ben Gurion to Guy Mollet. Ben Gurion sent a similar appeal to Bourgès-Maunoury. DDQ, 1980 322C: For Information of President, 11 April 1956. JFD, Subject Box 10: Conversation with Eban, 11 July 1956. PRO, FO371/121494/115: Hadow to Duke, 5 May 1956. Crosbie, op. cit., p. 59, 64. Tsur, op. cit., pp. 345–6, 381–2. Sharett, op. cit., p. 1611.

49. PRO, FO371/118966/34: Trevelyan to Foreign Office, 16 Feb. 1956; 118842/JE1022/25: Bailey to Watson, 18 May 1956;/26: Cairo to Foreign Office, 25 May 1956; 113682/434: Kirkpatrick Minute, 22 Dec. 1955; ISA, 2450/7: Equipment for Egypt 20 Nov 1955; 192/36: Estimate of Egyptian Armed Strength, 14 May 1956; Bendor to Tsur, 7 Jan. 1956. BBC, 623, pp. 10–11. Tsur, op. cit., pp. 353–4.

50. FRUS, XV, 643, 669–70. BG, Diaries, 11 Sept. 1956. Roi, op. cit., p. 144. Heikal, *Millafat al-Suways*, pp. 442–3.

51. DDQ, 1982 2568: Dulles to Eisenhower, 11 May 1956. BG, Diary, 11 Sept. 1956. ISA,

2450/7: Ankara to Foreign Ministry, 10 Dec. 1955. Robert Murphy, *Diplomat Among Warriors* (New York, 1964), p. 377. Eden, op. cit., p. 420. Hofstadter, op. cit., p. 118.
52. BG, Diaries: 10 July 1956. Crosbie, op. cit., pp. 70–1.
53. The Dakotas were vital to the IDF's paratroop drop into the Mitla pass. ISA, 48/3: Tsur to Foreign Ministry, 9 July 1956. BG, Diaries, 30 July 1956; 4 Oct. 1956; 5 Oct. 1956.
54. USNA, 976.7301/10–2956: Dulles to Paris. ISA, 48/3: West European Desk to Embassies, 13 Aug. 1956; Elath to Foreign Ministry, 18 Aug. 1956. JFD, Subject File, Box 16: Dulles Conversation with Eban, 8 Oct. 1956; Oral History, Arthur W. Redford (Former Chairman, Joint Chiefs of Staff), p. 62. Nutting, *No End of Lesson*, p. 88. Crosbie, op. cit., pp. 70–1. Steigman, op. cit., p. 73. The Canadian F-86s in fact never reached Israel. Due for delivery on 31 October, the shipment was cancelled with the first word of Israel's invasion of Sinai. See NAC, RG 2, Box 16, Vol. 5775: Cabinet Conclusions, 30 Oct. 1956.
55. BG, Diary: 3 Sept. 1956; 29 Sept. 1956. ISA, 192/36: Estimate of Egyptian Arms Strength, 14 May 1956.
56. On Israel's difficulty in absorbing jets see BG, Diary: 25 Sept. 1956. Steigman, op. cit., pp. 68–9. Peres, op. cit., p. 125. Egypt's problems recorded in DDQ, 1982 2568: Dulles to Eisenhower, 11 May 1956. JFD, White House Files, Box 3: Dean to Dulles, 22 May 1956. ISA, 172/10: Col. Arieli to the Chief of Military Intelligence, 9 Oct. 1955. BG, Diaries: 15 July 1956; 4 Sept. 1956; 11 Sept. 1956. Steigman, op. cit., pp. 101–2. Sadat, *In Search of Identity*, p. 142. Israel returns French tanks in Moshe Dayan, *Diary of the Suez Campaign* (London, 1967), p. 29. Transfers of Egyptian tanks to Syria in BG, Diary: 11 Sept. 1956.
57. John Glassman, *Arms for the Arabs* (Baltimore, 1975), p. 14.

CHAPTER FIVE

1. Neil Caplan and Avraham Sela, 'Zionist Egyptian Negotiations and the Partition of Palestine, 1946, *Jerusalem Quarterly*, No. 41 (Winter 1987), pp. 19–30. Michael J. Cohen, *Palestine and the Great Powers* (Princeton, 1982), pp. 194–7. Yoav Gelber, MaGa'im Diplomati'im Terem Hitnagshut Tza'it – HaMasa uMatan ben HaShuchnut HaYehudit ReMitzrayim veYarden', *Katedra*, No. 35 (April 1985), pp. 125–62. Eliahu Sasson, *BaDerech el HaShalom* (Tel Aviv, 1978), pp. 352, 365, 377–85, 386.
2. *Documents on the Foreign Policy of Israel*, Vol. I, pp. 632–4; Vol. II, pp. 21–9, Vol. III, pp. xi–xviii. ISA, 2460/4: Rafael to Sharett, 19 Jan. 1956 USNA, 774.51/4–1350: Acheson Conversation with the Egyptian Ambassador; 684.84A//1–651: Caffery Conversation with Fawzi. PRO, FO371/98476/9: Stevenson to Foreign Ministry, 23 July 1952. Avi Shlaim, *Collusion Across the Jordan* (New York, 1988), pp. 315–17, 346–8. Louis, *The British Empire in the Middle East*, pp. 554–5.
3. FRUS, 1060, 1076, 1090, 110, 1180, 1124, 1171. *Documents on the Foreign Policy of Israel*, Vol. II, pp. 98–9. Forsythe, *United Nations Peace Making*, pp. 59, 74. Benny Morris, *The Birth of the Palestine Refugee Problem, 1947–1949* (New York, 1987), pp. 266–75.
4. Eban often met with Azmi to discuss bilateral matters. In July 1951 and again in March–April 1952, Eban, together with the American Jewish leader Jacob Blaustein, presented Azmi with Israeli peace plans. These, however, proved unacceptable to the Egyptians. Azmi nevertheless continued to maintain close relations with the Israelis. When his wife, who was Jewish, died, he received a personal letter of condolence from Sharett. ISA, 339/3: Eban to Sharett, 20 July 1951; 2453/12: Eban to Sharett, 9 April 1952; 2410/10 Sharett's Letter to Azmi, 5 Aug. 1952.
5. ISA, 339/3: Eban to Sharett, 20 July 1951; 2456/3: Leven Conversation with the Egyptian Delegate to Le Hague, 23 May 1951; 2953/22: Report on Rafael–Azmi Lunch, 23 June 1952.
6. To facilitate inter-Arab communications, Israel was prepared to create a corridor

leading to the West Bank. Israel would retain the right to inspect vehicles using the road, and would eventually build a road from Eilat to Beershevba, enabling it to cut off the Egypt–Jordan axis in time of emergency. See ISA/2451/1: Sharett to Eytan, 6 Dec. 1952.

7. ISA, 2565/19: Divon to Jerusalem, 30 Dec. 1951; 14 Nov. 1951; /17: Sasson to Eytan, 30 Jan. 1952; 2460/5: Paris to Sharett, 4 Aug. 1951; 2546/3: Sasson to Avner, 13 Dec. 1951; 2532.2: Tolkowsky (Bonn) to Jerusalem, 8 Jan. 1951; 388/22: Amir (Brussels) to Foreign Ministry, 19 Oct. 1951.

8. USNA, 683.84A/11–1452: Waller to Hart.

9. ISA, 2543/12: Eban to Sharett, 19 March 1952; 2403/12: Elath to Comay, 14 July 1952; 2565/17: Questions for Discussion (n.d., but circa Dec. 1951); 2565/18: Policy Toward Egypt, 19 July 1952. USNA, 684A.86/7–2352: Byroade Conversation with Eban.

10. ISA, 2477/10: Egyptian Statements, Feb. 1952; /15: Egypt's Struggle and Its Consequences, 22 April 1952; 2565/19: Press Review, 26 March 1952; 2543/12: Eban Conversation with Acheson, 5 March 1952. USNA, 684A.86/3–352: Davis to Department; /3–552: Department to Middle East Embassies, /3–752: Caffery to Department. PRO, FO371/98476/9: Stevenson to Foreign Office, 3 March 1952.

11. ISA, 2460/4: Rafael to Sharett, 19 Jan. 1956.

12. Israel viewed Egypt's treatment of Egyptian Jews as an indicator of its relations with the Jewish State. On the new regime's gestures to Israel see PRO, FO371/96898/39: Bowker to Stevenson, 30 July 1952; BBC, 283, p. 45. Copeland, *The Game of Nations*, pp. 74–5. Jean and Simmone Lacouture, *Egypt in Transition* (London, 1958), p. 220. *al-Misri*, 29 Sept. 1952. On Israel's decision to launch a peace initiative see USNA, 774.00/7–3152: Hart Conversation with Eban. ISA, 2477/10: Shimoni to Eban, 13 Aug. 1952. David Ben Gurion, *My Talks with Arab Leaders* (Jerusalem, 1972), pp. 258–9.

13. ISA, 2453/20: Israel Message to the Government of Egypt, 22 Aug. 1952; Divon to Foreign Ministry, 23 Aug. 1952. Muhammad Muhsin, 'al-Ittisalat bayn Misr wa-Isra'il lil-Salam', *al-Akhbar*, 9 Nov. 1985.

14. On the debate within the Free Officers' regime see BGA, Diary, 26 Oct. 1952. ISA, 2460/4: Rafael to Sharett, 19 Jan. 1956; 2453/20: Sharett Conversation with Davis, 24 Aug. 1952. USNA, 683.84A/9–452: Eban Conversation with Acheson; /8–152: Davis to Acheson; 680.84A/9–2252: Byroade Conversation with Eban; 674.84A/9–852: Caffery to Department. Press reports on the alleged peace process in *Haaretz*, 5 Oct. 1952; *al-Misri*, 12 Nov. 1952 (editorial by Ihsan 'Abd al-Qaddus); *al-Ahram*, 24 and 30 Aug. 1952; *Ruz al-Yusuf*, 28 Sept. 1952. BBC, 289, p. 31; 301, p. 33; 308, p. 25. The US State Department accused Israel of purposely leaking such information to the press as a means of pressurizing Egypt; ISA, 2406/6: Herlitz Conversation with Stevler, 10 Oct. 1952; 2403/18: Sharett to Levin, 4 Nov. 1952.

15. USNA, 674.84A/9–852: Caffery to Department. ISA, 2402/12: Egypt's Position, 19 Nov. 1952. Heikal, *Milaffat al-Suways*, p. 194.

16. USNA, 774.00/10–252: Naguib Letter to the State Department. ISA, 42/12: Gazit Conversation with Mahmud Lahluf, 6 Oct. 1952; 2477/15: Comay to Bendor, 14 Sept. 1952; /10: Bendor to Shimoni, 14 Sept. 1952. Former SS officers had been serving in the Egyptian army since 1950 and were often supplied by the CIA. Their main function was internal security – they proved instrumental in foiling an attempted coup by the artillery corps in January 1953 – though they also filled military posts. A former SS officer commanded the Egyptian batteries at Tiran. See PRO, FO371/102835/2: Stevenson to Foreign Office, 11 Feb. 1953. Eveland, *Ropes of Sand*, p. 103. Copeland, op. cit., pp. 103–4.

17. The sponsors of the Blueprint resolution were Norway, Denmark, Cuba, Uruguay, Holland, Ecuador, Panama and Canada. ISA, 2593/22: Eban to Rafael, 8 Dec. 1952; 2451/8: Eban to Sharett, 26 Nov. 1952; 2446/6: Ben Gurion with Ambassadors, 1 Oct. 1952; 2453/1: Sasson to Sharett, 2460.6: Herlitz Conversation with Waller, 3 Oct. 1952. On Azmi's relations with Nasser see Heikal, op. cit., p. 188.

18. USNA, 684A.86/10–2052: Record of Conversation with Eban. ISA, 2477/20: Record of Naguib Conversation with George F. Pierrot, 29 Oct 1952; 2593/22: Eban to Rafael,

3 Dec. 1952; 2439/1: Basil Herman Conversation with Goha, 31 Dec. 1952.
19. PRO, FO371/98479/93: Stevenson to Foreign Office, 14 Nov. 1952. ISA, Goldmann to Sharett, 18 Dec. 1952. With regard to Fawzi's function in 'testing the waters' see FRUS, XV, 61–2: 'Since Fawzi is powerless to make decisions,' Robert Anderson reported after a conversation with Nasser, 'having him conduct negotiations assures Nasser of an opportunity to study carefully any propositions that are put to him and to make sure he comprehends them.'
20. ISA, 2439/1: Analysis of the Situation in Egypt, 17 Dec. 1952; 2451/8: Rafael to Shiloah, 10 Nov. 1952; 39/22: Eban to Sharett, 7 Dec. 1952.
21. Hassan Nafi'ah, *Sulh wal-Sira' al-'Arabi al-Isra'ili min al-Sira' al-Mahtum ila al-Taswiyah* (Beirut, 1984), pp. 37–40. Ahmad Hamrush, *Qissah Thawrat 23 Yulyu* (Cairo, 1985), Vol. v, p. 21. Thawrat 'Ukashah, 'Shahadati lil-Tarikh', *Akhir Sa'ah*, no. 2791, 20 April 1988, p. 24. USNA, 674.84A/6–3053: Caffery to the Director of NEA (Hart). ISA, 164/9: Egypt's Demand for Territorial Contiguity, March 1953.
22. USA, 974.5301/4–853: Memorandum by the Officer in Charge of Palestine–Israel–Jordan Affairs (Waller); 684A.86/2–1153: Dulles to Lodge; 674.84A/9–1053: Memorandum of Conversation, Theodore Faye (NEA) with Fawzi. PRO, FO371/104477/3: Stevenson to Bowker, 16 Jan. 1953; /1: Bowker to Crosthwaite, 3 Feb. 1953; /6: Crosthwaite to Bowker, 27 Feb. 1953. ISA, 2460/4: Eban Conversation with Dulles, 27 Feb. 1953; Herlitz to Eban, 14 Jan. 1953; 2403/12: Report on Crossman Visit to Egypt, 16 Jan. 1953; 2382/8: Elath to Comay, 19 May 1953. Heikal, op. cit., pp. 190–1.
23. ISA, 2477/20: Herzog to Foreign Ministry, 4 Feb. 1953, 12 March 1953, 22 April 1953; 2453/12: Israel's Proposals to Nasser, 29 Jan. 1953; Nasser's Replies, 13 May 1953; 2532/2: Sasson to Shiloah, 24 Feb. 1954; 2453/20: Government of Israel to the Government of Egypt, 3 June 1953. USNA, 780.5/3–1353: Ankara to Dulles; 674.84A/2–1753: Paris to Department.
24. ISA, 164/9: Avner to Rafael, 5 Oct. 1953; 2460/4: Rafael to Sharett, 19 Jan. 1956.
25. ISA, 169/9: Egypt's Demand for Territorial Contiguity, March 1953.
26. Copeland, op. cit., p. 195. The rise in Egyptian anti-Zionism was evident in the appearance, for the first time since 1948, of Egyptian propaganda pamphlets on Palestine. Typical of these were Ahmad al-Sharbasi's *Min 'Ajli Filastin*, which gave a religious interpretation of the conflict, and the more secular *al-Sulh ma'a Isra'il* by 'Amid al-Imam. *Hadhahi hiya al-Sahyuniyyah*, written by the Jewish author Isra'il Kuhun, features a lengthy introduction by Nasser. Further references to anti-Israel propaganda in Israel in 1954 in Mandelstan, 'La Palestine dans la politique de Gamal Abdul Nasser (dissertation), pp. 216–7, 241. ISA, 2565/17: Sasson to Foreign Ministry, 22 July 1954.
27. USNA, 684A.85/3–254: Conversation between RCC Leaders and Crossman; /4–654: Lodge Conversation with Azmi. ISA, 2475/3: Shimoni Conversation with Roosevelt, 25 April 1954; 42/13: Eban Conversation with Dulles, 5 Aug. 1954. The freeze in contacts continued into August, after the signing of the Heads of Agreement. See USNA, 784A.5/8–2254: Jernegan to Russel, /8–3054: Russel Conversation with Eytan. Tsur, *Prélude à Suez*, p. 137.
28. ISA, 2387/7 and 24–3/12. USNA, 784.A5274/12–1354: Caffery to Department. *al-Ahram*, daily coverage of the trial, 12 Dec. 1954 to 1 Jan. 1956.
29. For examples of the RCC's accusations against the Muslim Brotherhood see BBC, 525, p. 31; 526, p. 27. Background to the direct contacts in ISA, 2387/7: Discussion on Public Committee, 20 Dec. 1954; Gibli to Sharett, 26 Oct. 1954.
30. PRO, FO371/108548/23: Nicholls to Foreign Office, 17 Dec. 1954; /13. Murray to Foreign Office, 20 Dec. 1954. ISA, 2387/7: Divon to Sharett, 21 Nov. 1954. Sharett, *Yoman Ishi*, p. 712.
31. ISA, 2453/20: Rafael to Sharett, 14 and 18 Dec. 1954; /21: Orbach Report, 22 Nov. 1954; 2460/4: Rafael to Sharett, 19 Jan. 1956. Rida Shahata, 'Amrika wa-Thawrat Yulyu', *al-Musawwar*, 28 Aug. 1987. Heikal, op. cit., p. 293. According to Hamrush (op. cit., p. 18), other contacts took place in Paris between Yusuf Hilmi and Dr Murad

Khalaf and Amos Kenan and Eli Loebel, leftists from Egypt and Israel, respectively, and between Hilmi and Israel's Minister of Health, Israel Barzilai.
32. FRUS, XV, 32–34. ISA, 2387/7: Draft Cable, 30 Dec. 1954; /8: Rafael to Ariel, 2 Jan. 1955. Sharett, op. cit., p. 688. Heikal, op. cit., pp. 304–6.
33. Sharett quote in BBC, 540, p. 32. On Egyptian counter-propaganda see ISA, 2387/7: 'The Story of Zionist Espionage in Egypt'; 2453/20: Divon to Sharett, 31 Dec. 1954. Sharett, op. cit., pp. 633, 694.
34. FRUS, XIV, 612–3. DDE, Box 9, Dulles to Hoover, 6 March 1956 JFD, White House File, Box 4: Dulles to Dean, 22 May 1956; Subject File, Box 10: Dulles to Eisenhower, 1 March 1956. USNA, 780.00/5–2953: Dulles and the Representatives of U.S. Businesses and Colleges in the Middle East; /6–153: Eisenhower Conversation with Ahmad Abboud Pasha. ISA, 2460/6: Shalit Conversation with Hart, 24 Dec. 1952; Herlitz Conversation with Byroade, 12 Nov. 1952.
35. USNA, 611.80/11–225: Byroade to Middle East Embassies; 684.86/11–1053: Byroade to Dulles.
36. PRO, FO371/111105/183: Jebb to Foreign Office, 31 Aug. 1954; 104190/4: Makins to Foreign Office, 5 March 1953; 104753/27: Foreign Office Minute, 12 March 1953. ISA, 40/17: Lourie to Avner, 22 Oct. 1954; Elath to Foreign Ministry, 6 Oct. 1954.
37. PRO, FO371/102835/2: Stevenson to Foreign Office, 11 Feb. 1953; 98479/90: Bowker to Rapp, 20 Nov. 1952. USNA, 774.00/12–1152: Caffery Conversation with Lt. Col. Amin. For background on Britain's support for territorial contiguity see Louis, op. cit., p. 376. PRO, FO371/111072/125: Duke to Foreign Office, 22 June 1954. ISA, 40/17: Gazit to Foreign Ministry, 14 Nov. 1952.
38. In their joint planning for peace, Whitehall and the State Department agreed on extensive Israeli territorial concessions, especially in the Negev and the Galilee. The Americans, however, opposed Britain's proposal for transferring Israel's Arab population to neighbouring countries. PRO, FO371.104754/45: Washington to Foreign Office, 20 April 1953. On the reordering of Washington's priorities after Dulles's trip, see JFD, Middle East File, Box 73: Important Points of Trip, June 1953. PRO, FO371/104257/14: Evans to Churchill, 19 May 1953. ISA, 2403/13: Eban to Sharett, 5 April 1953; 2460/4: Ben Hurin to Eban, 28 May 1953. Heikal, op. cit., pp. 261–2, 265–6.
39. JFD, 'Important Points of Trip'. USNA, 684A.86/8–2153: Intelligence Advisory Committee to Dulles; /13–454: Secretary of State to Department. ISA, 2403/13: Foreign Ministry Memorandum, 5 June 1953. See also Samir Nicholas Saliba, *The Jordan River Dispute* (The Hague, 1968), p. 106. Don Peretz, 'The Jordan River Partition', *Middle East Journal*, Vol. IX, No. 4 (Autumn 1955), p. 401.
40. Egypt's reaction to Dulles's speech in PRO, FO371/104753/86: Hankey to Foreign Office, 10 Sept. 1953. On Egypt's role in the Johnston mission see USNA, 611.84A/8–3054: Jernegan to Dulles; 684A.85/1–1354: Caffery Conversation with Fawzi; 683.84A322/11–2453: Caffery Conversation with Dr Muhammad Ahmad Salim; /2–1054: Caffery to Department. Heikal, op. cit., p. 267.
41. FRUS, XIV, 43–5, 52–3, 54–5, 108–9. JFD, Eban Oral History, p. 18. Teddy Kollek, Oral History (conducted by author), 14 March 1987. As Director-General of the Prime Minister's office, Kollek was involved with the Johnston mission.
42. The US urged Israel to cease its work on the Jordan diversion project – at one point the Administration severed all economic aid to Israel – and conducted a diplomatic boycott of the Foreign Ministry in Jerusalem. In the aftermath of the Qibyah raid, the US called for an even stronger condemnation of Israel than that sought by Egypt. USNA, 684A.85/10–1753: Caffery Conversation with Fawzi. ISA, 2460/5: Eban Conversation with Dulles and Byroade, 8 Oct. 1953;/6: Eban Conversation with McGhee, 8 Oct. 1953. Evelyn Shuckburgh, *Descent to Suez* (London, 1986), p. 247.
43. An Egyptian annex to the Arab plan stipulated Israeli territorial concessions north and south of the Sea of Galilee to serve as an international watershed; Israel would be permitted to proceed with its diversion project. Israel rejected the proposal, as it involved some of the most fertile lands in the state. USNA, 684A.85322/5–2454: Russell to Department; /4–954: Caffery to Department.

44. DDE, Diaries, Box 6: Stanley High to DDE, 29 April 1954. USNA, 684A.85322/3–2754: Caffery Conversation with Riad; 684A.86/3–352: Davis to Department. Nasser's rejection of Nuri's proposal in PRO, FO371/11–791/1: Baghdad to Foreign Office, 29 Aug. 1954; 115874/186: Wright to Foreign Office, 24 Aug. 1954; 111076/270: Nicholls to Foreign Office, 16 Nov. 1954. ISA, 40/17: Lourie to Avner, 22 Oct. 1954; Elath to Foreign Ministry, 6 Oct. 1954; 2593/22: Elath to Foreign Ministry, 21 Sept. 1954. Seale, *The Struggle for Syria*, pp. 201–4. On the Blaustein mission see USNA, 684A.85/10–2854: Dulles to Cairo; /11–654: Cairo to Department; /11–854: Cairo to Department. ISA, 2460/4: Rafael to Sharett, 19 Jan. 1956.
45. USNA, 684.A86/1–2154: Conversation Between Nixon and Hoover; /12–1154: Cairo to State Department; /12–2354: Alpha to Amman; /12–2154: London to State Department. ISA, 2403/12: Sharett Conversation with Shuckburgh, 26 Nov. 1954; Rafael Conversation with Shuckburgh, 25 Nov. 1954. FRUS, XIV, 11–19, 21–8, 45.
46. USNA, 684A.86/11–2254: Byroade to Dulles; Dulles to Certain Diplomatic and Consular Officers. PRO, FO371/111095/10: Shuckburgh Minute, Notes and the Arab–Israel Dispute, 15 Dec. 1954. FRUS, IX, 1707–10; XIV, 11–19, 21–32, 209.
47. PRO, PREM-11, 945: Foreign Office to Washington, 7 Sept. 1955; FO371/115878/292: Arthur Minute, 15 Sept. 1955. For strategy towards Egypt, PRO, FO371/115865/22: Brief for Secretary of State's Visit to Cairo (Shuckburgh), 16 Feb. 1955; 115825/8: Record of Meeting with the Secretary of State, 9 March 1955. FRUS, XIV, 90–2, 114–6, 129–33, 167. Shuckburgh, op. cit., p. 266.
48. FRUS, XIV, 123–5, 141, 263–6, 282–3. PRO, FO371/115866/37: Foreign Office to New York, 10 March 1955; /45: Stevenson to Shuckburgh, 16 March 1955; 115867/51: Stevenson to Shuckburgh, 1 April 1955; /6: Washington to Foreign Office, 6 April 1955; /76: Arthur to Bailey, 7 April 1955. Examples of various Egyptian proposals for the Negev in FO371/115867/51: Stevenson to Shuckburgh, 1 April 1955; /60: Cairo to Foreign Office, 14 April 1955; 109973/28: Rose Minute, 14 Jan. 1955.
49. PRO, FO371/11868/82: Foreign Office to Washington, 5 May 1955; /84: Record of Conversation, Dulles and Macmillan, 6 May 1955; 115867/74: Shuckburgh to Kirkpatrick, 4 May 1955; CAB, 129/75: 11 June 1955. FRUS, XIV, 25, 34–42, 156–7. Shuckburgh, op. cit., p. 256. John R. Beale, *John Foster Dulles: 1888–1959* (New York, 1959), pp. 251–2. Macmillan, *Tides of Fortune*, p. 361.
50. PRO, FO371/115867/60: Cairo to Foreign Office, 3 June 1955; /74: Shuckburgh to Kirkpatrick, 4 May 1955; 115870/115: Alpha (Shuckburgh), 13 June 1955; 115869/107: Cabinet: Palestine Settlement, 3 June 1955; CAB, 129/75: 11 June 1955. FRUS, XIV, 204–5.
51. ISA, 2475/3: Shimoni Conversation with Roosevelt, 18 Nov. 1954; 2477/21: Elath to Lourie, 11 Feb. 1955. FRUS, XIV, 150, 159. PRO, FO371/115868/82: Sharett to Macmillan, 5 May 1955; 115887/523: Arthur Minute, 16 Dec. 1955; 121708/14: Summary of Alpha, 3 Jan. 1956. Eliahu Elath, *Mibad HaArfel Hayamim* (Tel Aviv, 1989), pp. 64–75. Sharett, op. cit., p. 688. Quote from FRUS, XIV, 173.
52. FRUS, XIV, 230–3, 278–9, 282–3, 363–4, 368–9, 399.
53. JFD, Subject Series, Box 1: Dulles to Bernard Katzen, 25 Aug. 1955; Alpha File, Box 1: Reactions to August 26 Speech, 29 Aug. 1955; White House Correspondence, Box 3: Dulles to Eisenhower, 1 Sept. 1955. PRO, FO371/115876/218: Reactions to Mr. Dulles' Speech on Palestine, 30 Aug. 1955; /30: Cairo to Foreign Office, 31 Aug. 1955; 115878/298: Record of Conversation, Dulles and Eban, 16 Sept. 1955; /288: Cairo to Foreign Office, 16 Sept. 1955; PREM-11, 945: Cairo to Foreign Office, 14 Sept. 1955. ISA, 2455/10: Washington to Israel Government, 7 Sept. 1955. FRUS, XIV, 402–3, 422–3, 439, 451–3, 455–61, 468–9.
54. DDQ, 1984, 1051: Dulles to Macmillan, 19 Aug. 1955. PRO, FO371/115869/102: Makins to Foreign Office, 1 June 1955; 115871/125: Makins to Foreign Office, 6 July 1955; PREM-11, 945: Extract from the Revised Draft of the Possible Public Statement by Mr Dulles on Arab–Israel Settlement, 15 July 1955; Washington to Foreign Office, 19 Aug. 1955; CAB, 128/76: Memorandum for the Secretary of State for Foreign Affairs, 13 July 1955.

55. PRO, FO371/115864/10: Makins to Foreign Office, 2 Feb. 1955; 115866/41: The Costs to the U.S. of a Palestine Settlement, 15 March 1955; 115868/34: Alpha, 5 May 1955. Shuckburgh, op. cit., pp. 245, 257.
56. FRUS, XIV, 480; 587–90; XV, 226. PRO, FO371/113676/225: Damascus to Foreign Office, 3 Oct. 1955. ISA, 2450/7: Research Department to Sharett, 14 Oct. 1955. Saliba, op. cit., p. 106.
57. Missions of Hirshmann and Abud discussed in ISA, 2477/19: Herzog to Chief of Mission, 11 July 1955; 2460/4: Rafael to Sharett, 19 Jan. 1956. Ira Hirshmann, *Caution to the Winds* (New York, 1962), pp. 264–74. Among other prominent figures approached to undertake such mediation were Bedell Smith and Dean Rusk. See DDQ, 1982, 310: Dulles to NEA, 3 June 1955. JFD, Alpha File, Box 1: Dulles to Gen. Klein, 8 Oct. 1955. Sharett, op. cit., p. 1117.
58. ISA, 2410/10: Rafael to Sharett, 9 Aug. 1955. FRUS, XIV, 431–2, 435–7, 470. Jackson, *Middle East Mission*, pp. 29–135.
59. PRO, FO371/113674/151: Shuckburgh Minute, 26 Sept. 1955; 115469/25: Record of Meeting, Macmillan and Dulles, 9 Nov. 1955; 114880/331: Arthur Minute, 9 Nov. 1955; PREM-11, 859: Cairo to Foreign Office, 2 Nov. 1955. FRUS, XIV, 493.
60. PRO, FO371/113674/151: Shuckburgh Minute, 26 Sept. 1955; 113676/260: Record of Conversation, Dulles, Macmillan, 3 Oct. 1955; /20: Cairo to Foreign Office, 12 Nov 1955. ISA, 2450/7: Rafael to Sharett, 24 Sept. 1955; Research Department to Sharett, 14 Oct. 1955; U.S. Desk to Embassy, 10 Nov. 1955. FRUS, XIV, 744–5, 778–85. Baghdati *Mudhakkirat*, p. 211.
61. PRO, FO371/115469/25: Foreign Office to Washington, 25 Nov. 1954; 121708/7: Trevelyan to Foreign Office, 1 Jan. 1956; /14: Summary of Alpha (Shuckburgh), 3 Jan. 1956; 115884/446: Baghdad to Foreign Office, 25 Nov. 1955; 115911/408: Shuckburgh Minute, 16 Dec. 1955. For the Khayrat statement, see BBC, 626, p. 17.
62. PRO/FO371/115886/490: Washington to Foreign Office, 8 Dec. 1955. FRUS, XIV, 733f, 772–7, 791.
63. ISA, 2455/10: Washington to Foreign Ministry, 7 Sept. 1955; Rafael to Eytan, 17 Nov. 1955; 2456/3: State Department Aide Mémoire to Israel, 21 Nov. 1955; Meeting of the Foreign Minister with the Secretary of State, 6 Dec. 1955; Israel Response to Aide Mémoir, 6 Dec. 1955; 2474/16: Eban to Foreign Ministry, 8 Nov. 1955. PRO, FO371/115884/463: Memorandum of Conversation, Dulles and Sharett, 2 Nov. 1955. FRUS, XIV, 793–6, 802, 823–32, 844–8.
64. FRUS, XIV, 504–5, 520–1, 674–5, 778–83, 793–6, 802, 807–8, 833–4 XV, 285. PRO, FO371/115469/28: Dulles to Macmillan, 6 Dec. 1955. PRO, FO371/115469/28: Dulles to Macmillan, 6 Dec. 1955.
65. FRUS, XIV, 491–2, 516–21, 561–2, 643–7; XV, 36–7. DDQ, 315, 1982: Memorandum of Conversation, Eisenhower, Dulles, Anderson, 11 Jan. 1956. PRO, FO371/15886/ 491: Washington to Foreign Office, 8 Dec. 1955; 115469/23: Kirkpatrick to Shuckburgh, 10 Nov. 1955; 115887/504: Arthur Minute, 5 Dec. 1955. ISA, 2450/7: U.S. Desk to Washington Embassy, 10 Nov. 1955. Heikal, op. cit., p. 380. Sharett, op. cit, pp. 1300–6, 1318–20, 1327–30.
66. ISA, 2475/3: Shimoni Conversation with Roosevelt, 18 Nov. 1955. Muhammad Tawil, *La'bat al-Umam wa-'Abd al-Nasir* (Cairo, 1986), p. 399. Issar Harel, *Bita'hon Vedemokratia* (Tel Aviv, 1989), pp. 389–95. Eveland, op. cit., pp. 114, 155–6. Copeland, op. cit., p. 93. Sharett, op. cit., pp. 675, 683, 691, 712, 728, 837–40, 856, 892, 906–8, 934–5, 1056.
67. FRUS, XIV, 713; XV, 155–6. Anderson was Eisenhower's second choice. The first, former Undersecretary of State Dean Rusk, declined the offer, see ibid., p. 675ff.
68. FRUS, XV, 16, 82–3, 92–3. Records of indirect mediation in, PRO, FO371/115887/128: Nicholls to Shuckburgh, 19 Dec. 1955. FRUS, XIV, 871–3 (Straitbert). ISA, 48/2: The Activities of Col. Banks, 12 Jan. 1955; 2474/16: Orgal to Foreign Ministry, 25 Nov. 1955 (Pearson); 2456/3: Notes on Conversations between Crossman and Nasser, 27 Dec. 1955. Aaron Cohen, *Israel and the Arab World* (Boston, 1976), pp. 331–2.
69. FRUS, XV, 28–36, 39–40, 56–8, 138–40. Heikal, op. cit., pp. 386–393, 780–4.

70. FRUS, XV, 12–13, 51–6. 63–70. Israeli protocols of the Anderson talks are contained in Ben Gurion, op. cit., pp. 275–325.
71. FRUS, XV, 120–22, 133–4, 146–8.
72. FRUS, XV, 157–8, 169, 198–203, 202–7.
73. FRUS, XV, 295–9, 302–7, 314. The story of Nasser's rejection of the triangles scheme is a favourite of Heikal's, appearing in his *Cairo Documents* (New York, 1973), p. 56, as well as in *Cutting the Lion's Tail: Suez Through Egyptian Eyes* (London, 1986), pp. 92–3. In reference to Nasser's response, members of the RCC called the talks with Anderson 'the pee-pee discussions'.
74. Frus, XV, 310–19, 320 – 22. DDQ, Diary, Box 9: Eisenhower Conversation with Hoover and Anderson, 13 March 1956; Entry for 20 Feb. 1956.
75. Frus, XV, 383 – 7, 419 – 25, 453 – 6. JFD, Subject Series, Box 10: Dulles to Lodge, 28 March 1956. DDQ, 1977, 252A: Memorandum of Conversation, Eisenhower, Hoover and Anderson, 13 March 1956. ISA, 2477/17: Dulles to Eban, 29 March 1956. PRO, FO371/18842/11: Commonwealth Relations Circular, 8 March 1956; 11861/13; Secretary of State to Trevelyan, 3 April 1956; 11862/37: Shuckburgh to Middle East Embassies, 28 May 1956. ISA, 2477/17: Dulles Conversation with Eban, 23 April 1956. Sharett, op. cit.pp. 1316, 1335, 1345, 1370.
76. ISA, 192/36: Ariel to Western European Desk, 31 Jan. 1956. PRO, FO371/121726/126: Foreign Office Minute (Reading), 19 March 1956. Lloyd, *Suez 1956*, pp. 44–6. Sharett, op. cit.,p. 1362.
78. ISA, 48/3: Visit of Ibrahim Izzat to Israel, 20 May 1956; Avner to Foreign Ministry, 26 May 1956; Avner to Lourie, 1 June 1956. PRO, FO371/121727/181: Trevelyan to Foreign Office, 6 June 1956.
79. ISA, 2593/22: Elath to Ariel, 17 May 1956. See, for example, 'Izzat's series in *Ruz al-Yusuf*, 21 May – 6 June 1956, and his later books, *Ana Kuntu fi Isra'il* (Cairo, 1957) and *Ana 'A'id min Isra'il* (Cairo, 1958).
80. DDQ, 1980, 322C: State Department Middle East Summary, 11 Jan. 1956. DDE, International File, Box 8: Byroade to Dulles, 10 April 1956. PRO, FO371/121709/49: Laurence Minute, 4 April 1956; 121738/180: Shuckburgh to Kirkpatrick, 20 April 1956; 121710/86: Trevelyan to Rose, 10 July 1956; /79: Washington to Foreign Office, 11 July 1956. FRUS, XV, 549–53.
81. PRO, FO371/121738/180: Aldrich to Lloyd, 20 April 1956; /189: Dixon to Foreign Office, 28 April 1956; 121739/223: Brief for the Secretary of State, 1 May 1956. FRUS, XV, 307–9, 604–5.
82. PRO, FO371/121733/50: Karachi to Foreign Office, 2 Feb. 1956; 121732/39: Crosthwaite to Rose, 5 March 1956. FRUS, XV, 281–3.
83. FRUS, XV, 602, 608–9, 621–22, 651. PRO, FO371/121739/235: Rose Minute, 9 May 1956; 121734/24: Memorandum from the Secretary-General, 22 May 1956.
84. PRO, FO371/121743/350: New York to Foreign Office, 5 July 1956; /75: Foreign Office to Washington, 8 July 1956; /80: Cairo to Foreign Office, 12 July 1956; /91: Cairo to Foreign Office, 26 July 1956. FRUS, XV, 778–9, 790–2.
85. PRO, FO371/121743/362: Cairo to Foreign Office, 30 June 1956; 121710/76: Washington to Foreign Office, 10 July 1956; /79: Washington to Foreign Office, 11 July 1956; 121744/388: New York to Foreign Office, 12 Sept. 1956; /383: Hammarskjöld to Lloyd, 3 Aug. 1956. FRUS, XV, 800–8, 815–6, 835–9, 847, 891–4.
86. ISA, 2532/3: Western European Desk to Ariel, 5 Sept. 1956. BGA, Correspondence: Goldmann to Ben Gurion, 26 July 1956. 'Ukashah, op. cit. p. 25.

CHAPTER SIX

1. ISA, 2419/1: Israel Air Force Report on the Canal Base, 19 Nov. 1951. Yitzhak Steigman. *Mivtzah Kadesh – Hayl HaAvir Bashanim 1950 – 1956: HitAtzmut v'Peilut* (Tel Aviv, Israel Defence Forces, Air Force History Branch), p. 54. Copy of the

NOTES

evacuation treaty is contained in J.C. Hurewitz, *Diplomacy in the Near and Middle East: A Documentary Record* (Princeton, 1956), pp. 383–4. The British, perhaps in an effort to deter an Israeli attack on the Canal after the evacuation, refused to inform Jerusalem which of the Canal Zone's stores had actually been transferred to Egypt. This policy succeeded only in further provoking the Israelis who were thus led to believe that Egypt had received far more equipment than they had in reality. For example, three valuable radar installations, which the Israelis assumed had been passed to Egypt, were actually dismantled after Egypt refused to participate in a joint air defence system with Britain. See PRO, FO371/108486/23: Eden to Elath, 23 Oct. 1954; /4: Stevenson to Foreign Office, 21 Aug. 1954. ISA, 2460/3: Eban Conversation with Dulles, 15 Jan. 1954; 2593/17: Gazit to Elath, 12 Oct. 1953.

2. Sharett, *Yoman Ishi*, pp. 557, 626, 654.
3. Ben Gurion had rejected the Gaza invasion notion when it was first proposed by Defence Minister Lavon in February 1954, at the time when Egypt was preoccupied with the struggle between Nasser and Naguib. See BG, Diaries: 27 Feb. 1954. Sharett, op. cit., pp. 374, 378–9. For his support of the idea beginning in March 1955 see Dayan, *Avnei Derech*, p. 143. BG, Diaries: 25 March 1955.
4. USNA, 684.84A/7–1354: Caffery to Department; /7–1254: Caffery to Department. For Egypt's anticipation of receipt of the Canal base stores see USNA, 780.00/5–2953: Dulles Conversation with Fawzi.
5. Nasser's decision to reinforce his position at El Arish was no doubt influenced by his recollection that the IDF had briefly occupied the area in 1948 in an effort to cut off Gaza. ISA, 2477/20: Shimoni to Foreign Ministry, 14 March 1955; 2454/5: Israeli Military Intelligence: Gaza Incident, Summary and Estimation, 22 March 1955. PRO, FO371/113678/290: Extract for Military Intelligence, General Staff, May 1955. Sharett, op. cit., p. 896.
6. BG, Diaries, 25 March 1955. Sharett, op. cit., pp. 864–5, 872–3, 877, Dayan, op. cit., p. 144.
7. Dayan, op. cit., p. 145. Sharett, op. cit., pp. 1059–60, 1117. Like Omer, the planned strike at Tiran called for an earlier attack on the Canal Zone airfields to neutralize Egypt's jets. The threat of Egypt's jet power was illustrated in August 1955 when Egyptian jets succeeded in penetrating Israel's air space and reaching the Jerusalem area. The flights ceased however, after Israel downed two of the planes in a dogfight on 1 September. See Steigman, op. cit., p. 54.
8. PRO, FO371/115902/172: New York to Foreign Office, 17 June 1955. ISA, 2454/1: Conversation of the UN Secretary-General with the Egyptian Foreign Minister, 21 June 1955; 2477/9: Nasser Conversation with Ira Hirshmann, 11 July 1955.
9. Allusions to this dilemma appear in PRO, FO371/115903/245: Cairo to Foreign Office, 1 Sept. 1955.
10. In his speeches, Ben Gurion often threatened to break the blockade by force. See, for example, BBC, 558, p. 22. Egypt's reaction to this statement appears in BBC, 594, p. 7.
11. BG, Diaries: 31 July 1955. Sharett, op. cit., pp. 1059–60.
12. ISA, 2477/16: Washington Embassy to Foreign Ministry, 6 Oct. 1955; Eban to Foreign Ministry, 31 Oct. 1955; 2451/8: Israel Aide Mémoire to the Tripartite Powers, Nov. 1955; 2456/3: Eban to Foreign Ministry, 1 Nov. 1955; Department of State Aide Mémoire to Israel, 21 Nov. 1955; /4: Rafael to Eytan, 15 Nov. 1955; Sharett Conversation with Dulles, 6 Dec. 1955. Sharett, op. cit., pp. 1182–7, 1200–2, 1207. Eban, *An Autobiography*, pp. 196–7. Milstein, *Historia shel HaTzanhanim*, pp. 341–2. Dayan, op. cit., p. 153. Heikal, *Millafat al-Suways*, pp. 397, 404.
13. In Ben Gurion's version of Omer, Israel would retain control of Tiran until international guarantees were received for ending the blockade. According to Dayan's plan, however, Israel would permanently occupy the Straits. *ISA, 2456/3: Ben Gurion to Hammarskjöld, 10 Jan. 1956; 2456/3: Sharett to Dulles, 16 Jan. 1956. BG, Diaries, 15 Jan. 1956. Dayan, *Suez Diary*, pp. 11–12. Steigman, *Mivtzah Kadesh*, pp. 57, 62.
14. ISA, 2456/3: Rafael to Foreign Ministry, 7 Oct. 1955. Sharett, op. cit., pp. 1185, 1191–2, 1239, 1246. Dayan, op. cit., pp. 13–15. The delay of Omer did not prevent

177

Sharett in his discussions with the Tripartite Foreign Ministers from citing the possibility of a pre-emptive strike if Israel did not receive arms. See PRO, FO371/115537/4: Sharett to Macmillan, 26 Oct. 1955.

15. PRO, FO371/113674/161: Trevelyan to Foreign Office, 26 Sept. 1955. FRUS, XV, 62, 128.
16. Baghdati, *Mudhakkirat*, pp. 201, 207–9. FRUS, XV, 128. ISA, 2450/7: Eytan to Foreign Minister, 1 Oct. 1955; Eban to Foreign Ministry, 8 Nov. 1955. Heikal, op. cit., pp. 378, 466.
17. ISA, 2456/3: Israeli Policy After the Arms Deal, 10 Nov. 1955. BG, Diaries, 10 July 1956. Dayan, op. cit., pp. 13–15. Sharett, op. cit., pp. 1391–2.
18. See, for example, USNA, 784A. 5/9–2854: Jernegan to Dulles. DDQ, 1980 267A: Joint Chiefs of Staff to Dulles, 13 July 1955. The Israelis did little to refute this assessment. During his visit to Washington in November 1953, Gen. Dayan reportedly claimed that the IDF could 'occupy four out of five Arab capitals within two weeks of the commencement of hostilities'. Quoted in USNA, 784A. 56/11–1553: Conversation between Grant and Dayan.
19. PRO, FO371/11105/183: Jebb to Foreign Office, 31 Aug. 1954; 111070/43: Allen Minute, 12 April 1954.
20. PRO, FO371/11073/10: Fox to Falla, 26 May 1954; 111105/191: Tripp Minute, 7 Sept. 1954; 115899/108: Washington to Foreign Office, 7 April 1955; 115901/VR1092/105: War Office Communiqué, 9 June 1955; 1105902/172: New York to Foreign Office, 17 June 1955; 113677/264: Washington to Foreign Office, 7 Oct. 1955; CAB 128/29: 14 June 1955. DDQ, 1982 2563: Goodpaster to Adams, 7 Oct. 1955. FRUS, XIV, 242, 652, 753f; XV, 248–54. ISA, 2456/3: Rafael to Foreign Ministry, 5 Oct. 1955; 2477/16: Eban to Foreign Ministry, 31 Oct. 1955; 2456/4: Rafael to Eytan, 15 Nov. 1955. Heikal, op. cit., p. 400.
21. FRUS, XV, 90–2, 149–50, 159–60, 255–7, 347–8.
22. PRO, FO371/121724/63: Foreign Office Brief, 7 Jan. 1956; 121733/48: Rose Minute, 21 Jan. 1956; 121759/VR1076/11: Nairne to Rose, 6 Feb. 1956; 121761/54: Foreign Office Minute, 10 Feb. 1956; 121730/266: Ministry of Defence, Middle East Land Forces, 9 Aug. 1956; FRUS, XIV, 542–8, 593–603, 616–30, 661–8; XV, 108–112, 131.
23. Quote from Anwar G. Chejne, 'Egyptian Attitudes Toward Pan-Arabism', *Middle East Review*, Vol. 2, No. 3 (Summer 1957), p. 262. The battle orders, dated 15 February 1956, were confiscated, along with other Egyptian documents, by Israel during its occupation of Gaza and later published in a pamphlet, *Nasser's Pattern of Aggression*, issued by the Israel Information Office. Though a propaganda piece, the pamphlet contains clear photocopies of the orders, which appear to be authentic.
24. PRO, FO371/121726/118: Trevelyan to Shuckburgh, 8 March 1956; /127: Shuckburgh Minute, 26 March 1956; 121725/105: Record of Conversation, the Secretary of State, 13 March 1956. FRUS, XV, 350–1, 391–4, 458 494, 654. ISA, 2459/9: Foreign Ministry to Israeli Embassies, 16 March 1956; 2456/3: Ben Gurion to Hammarskjöld, 10 Jan. 1956. Yosef Ben Ze'ev, 'HaModi'in beMa'arachet Sinai', p. 19. Macmillan, *Riding the Storm*, p. 93. Lloyd, *Suez 1956*, p. 57.
25. IDF, Egyptian Air Force Intelligence Report, 1 March 1956; Protocol of the Joint Chiefs of Egyptian and Syrian Intelligence, May 1956. PRO, PREM-11 945: Cairo to Foreign Office, 5 Nov. 1955; FO371/121724/69: Cairo to Foreign Office, 22 Feb. 1956; 121729/22: Cairo Chancery to Foreign Office, 18 Feb. 1956.
26. ISA, 2408/14: Sharett to Embassies, 4 March 1956; 2456/3: Report on the Deliberations of the Arab Chiefs-of-Staff, 20 Oct. 1955. PRO, FO371/121710/86: Trevelyan to Ross, 10 July 1956. FRUS, XV, 379, 769–80, /83–4. Seale, *The Struggle for Syria*, p. 253. Quotes from BBC, 558, pp. 22–3.
27. Ya'ari, *Mitzrayim vehaFidayeen*, pp. 25–6. BG, Diaries: 10 July 1956. Heikal, op. cit., pp. 460, 530–1. Ben Ze'ev, op. cit., p. 19. According to Ben Ze'ev, Egypt's entire force in Sinai at the time of the Israeli invasion consisted of one infantry division, one infantry battalion, one light armoured battalion, and two Palestinian battalions. In the vulnerable Eastern front from Eilat to Sharm el-Sheikh, which had so preoccupied Egypt

NOTES

in previous years, only token forces remained.
28. BG, Diaries: 29 July and 13 and 22 Aug. 1956; PRO, FO371/121744/386: Rose to Crosthwaite, 31 Aug. 1956. USNA, 976.7301/8–1556: Hoover to the Secretary of State. Dayan, op. cit., p. 22.
29. ISA, 48/3: Tsur Convseration with Pineau, 3 Sept. 1956; 2532/1: Elath Conversation with Cheval, 4 Sept. 1956; Bendor to Tsur, 5 Sept. 1956; Tsur Conversation with Pineau, 29 Sept. 1956. BG, Diaries: 23 Aug. 1956, 25 Sept. 1956. USNA, 976.7301/9–1956: Pineau Conversation with Alrich; /10–656: Paris to the Secretary of State. Crosbie, A Tacit Alliance, pp. 65–9. Christian Pineau, 1956 Suez (Paris, 1967), p. 82.
30. PRO, FO371/113715/142: Garvey to Shepherd, 25 Aug. 1956; 121499/216: Ministry of Defence, The Strategic Importance of Jordan, 25 Aug. 1956. ISA, 48/3: Elath to Foreign Ministry, 3 Oct. 1956; 2532/1: Western European Desk to Paris Embassy, 4 Sept. 1956. Nutting, No End of a Lesson, pp. 84–6.
31. PRO, FO371/121780/29: Amman to Foreign Office, 11 Oct. 1956. CAB 128/130: 9 Oct. 1956. USNA, 976.7301/10–1556: Developments in the Near East and France. ISA, 2410/10: The New Anglo-Iraqi Campaign, 9 Oct. 1956; 2474/16: Eban to Shiloah, 2 Oct. 1956. Eden, Full Circle, p. 512. Pineau, op. cit., p. 116. Macmillan, op. cit., p. 147.
32. PRO, FO371/CAB 128/130: 24 Oct. 1956; 25 Oct. 1956. Eden, op. cit., p. 513. Macmillan, op. cit., pp. 111–12. DDQ, 1978 369B: Memorandum of the Joint Chiefs of Staff, 14 Aug. 1956; 1984 626: Dulles to Eisenhower, 7 Sept. 1956. Michel Bar Zohar, Suez Ultra-Secret (Paris, 1964), pp. 154–5. Tsur, Prélude à Suez, pp. 408–9. Nutting, op. cit., pp. 84–6.
33. PRO, CAB 128/130: 16 Oct. 1956; 18 Oct. 1956. DEFE 10472: Implications of Israeli Aggression in Connection with Operation Musketeer, 27 Sept. 1956.
34. ISA, 48/3: Elath to Foreign Ministry, 25 Sept. 1956. BG, Diaries: 10 Aug. 1956; 9 Sept. 1956; 2 and 6 Oct. 1956.
35. Several sources exist for the Sèvres accords, among them Pineau, op. cit., pp. 149–52 and Bar Zohar, op. cit., p. 163. See also BG, Diaries: 21 and 25 Oct. 1956.
36. Ben Gurion's Knesset speech appears in BBC, Daily Report 73, pp. 12–13. He presented similar arguments to Eisenhower in a message responding to the President's warning against Israeli military action against Jordan. See David Ben Gurion, Medinat Yisrael HaMehudeshet (Tel Aviv, 1969), p. 526. DDE, Diary, Box 8: Entry for 15 Oct. 1956. Battle orders for Operation Kadesh are cited in Dayan, op. cit., pp. 38–9, 61, 67; Steigman, op. cit., p. 85.
37. BG, Diaries: 6, 21 and 25 Oct. 1956. ISA, 48/3: Elath to Foreign Ministry, 15 Aug. 1956. JFD, Subject File, Box 9: Dean Conversation with Eban, 14 Sept. 1956. Ben Gurion's plan for dividing Jordan – Israel was to receive the West and Iraq the East bank – was predicated on the notion that Iraq would absorb the Palestinian refugees and make peace with Israel. Even before Sèvres, there were indications that the idea had at least some support in official French and British circles. See ISA, 2403/12: Avner to Elath, 19 Oct. 1956; 2593/11: Elath to Western European Desk, 30 May 1956. BG, Diaries: 17 Oct. 1956.
38. ISA, 2532/3: Ariel to Western European Desk, 5 Sept. 1956. Baghdati, op. cit., pp. 327–8. BG, Diaries: 4 Sept. 1956. Ze'ev, op. cit., pp. 19–20. Reports of the secret Anglo-French-Israeli talks even appeared in the Egyptian papers, see al-Gumhurriyah, 9 Sept. 1956.
39. ISA, 2460/4: Eliav to Foreign Ministry, 5 Oct. 1956; 2532/3: Ariel to Western European Desk, 5 Sept. 1956; 245/9: Foreign Ministry to Israeli Embassies, 16 March 1956. Glassman, Arms for the Arabs, p. 14. Nutting, op. cit., pp. 45–7. Eden, op. cit., p. 466. Heikal, op. cit., p. 401.
40. USNA, 774.5883/10–3056: Damascus to the Secretary of State.

APPENDICES

APPENDIX I*

EGYPTIAN–ISRAELI MIXED ARMISTICE COMMISSION

July 23, 1953

The following is herewith agreed by both parties:

In the event a non-military vessel of either Party, carrying non-military cargo, is forced by engine trouble, storm or any other reason beyond the control of the vessel and its crew, to seek refuge in the territorial waters of the other party, it shall be granted shelter therein and shall be allowed thereafter to proceed on its way freely and at the earliest possible time, together with its cargo, crew and passengers.

For Egypt   For Israel
(s) Gohar   (s) Gaon
Lt. Col. Gohar   Lt. Col. Gaon
Witnessed by Chairman EIMAC
(s) T. M. Hinkle, Col. USMC
T. M. Hinkle

APPENDIX II**

April, 1954

SECOND DRAFT

SECRET

The Government of Israel deems it necessary to draw the urgent attention of the Government of Egypt to the grave deterioration of border security, in particular in the Gaza area. Conditions along the border have never been satisfactory and have been marked by an uninterrupted sequence of incursions and clashes as a result of continuous

* ISA, 164/8
** ISA, 2453/20

violations by groups and individuals coming from territory under Egyptian control.

The Egyptian Government is responsible, under the General Armistice Agreement, for the inviolability of the border and is bound to take all necessary steps to prevent violations.

During the last two weeks, continual acts of violence, such as robberies, murders, assaults and raids, have created a state of perilous lawlessness. This mounting tension along the borders, seen against the background of an Egyptian policy of active hostility and belligerent practices, constitutes a matter of grave concern to the Government of Israel.

In the face of such a challenge the Government of Israel is in duty bound to consider all effective measures for the prevention of any further forays into its territory and for the protection of the life and property of its citizens.

The Government of Israel hopes that the Government of Egypt will share its considered view that any further deterioration of the present situation cannot serve the interest of either country.

The Government of Israel does not wish to find itself in a position where its only recourse were to devise its own remedies for a situation which can be brought under control by joint efforts of both Governments. It therefore invites the co-operation of the Government of Egypt, to discuss urgently together with Israel effective measures for the improvement of a situation fraught with such dangers.

Experience has shown that the present armistice machinery is not adequate to meet the needs of the hour. The Government of Israel therefore proposes, as an immediate measure, that the Government of Egypt designate duly empowered plenipotentiaries, to meet without delay similarly empowered Israel representatives at a place mutually to be agreed.

It trusts that in the meantime the Government of Egypt will do all in its power without delay to prevent actions liable to inflame the situation further. The Egyptian Government can be assured of Israel's co-operation in this endeavor.

APPENDIX III*

8 July 1955

DRAFT

EGYPTIAN–ISRAELI MIXED ARMISTICE COMMISSION ARRANGEMENT TO MAINTAIN SECURITY ALONG THE DEMARCATION LINE

1. The purpose of this Arrangement is to prevent, to the greatest extent possible, the crossing of the Demarcation Line, and, generally, breaches of the General Armistice Agreement. It does not affect the responsibilities of the Parties as set forth in the General Armistice Agreement.
2. The Parties agree:

(a) That only well trained and disciplined regular military or police personnel will be employed on security duties in a zone one kilometer wide on either side of the Demarcation Line.

Notes:

(1) The definition of 'regular military personnel' is personnel serving full-time on a regular, continuous engagement in the armed forces; who are not engaged in any other occupation.

(2) This clause does not affect the right of proprietors of agricultural holdings, fields, groves, etc. to employ armed watchmen for the protection of their crops and property.

(b) That they will enforce strict measures for preventing civilians from crossing the line of demarcation.

(c) That they will exchange information concerning civilians who illegally cross the line of demarcation, including any penal sentences that may have been imposed upon them; and that they undertake to investigate suspected violations of the ordinances and regulations against illegal crossings, and, when indicated, take action as provided in paragraph 2 (b).

(d) That when civilians who have crossed the demarcation line are handed back, this will be done at a representatives' meeting.

(e) That they will use their best endeavors to recover property and livestock stolen from the other party.

(f) That recovered stolen property and livestock, and animals which have strayed across the Demarcation Line shall be handed back to the Party in whose territory the property or animals are owned within forty-eight (48) hours, subject to the requirements of legal process.

(g) That they will endeavor to keep complaints to the Mixed Armistice Commission to a minimum by settling minor incidents in Representatives' meetings.

* ISA, 2439/3

182

(h) That for the purpose of quickly stopping any outbreak of firing or other military action contrary to the General Armistice Agreement, each Party will nominate a senior officer in command of troops in the area covered by this Arrangement. Facilities will be established for quick intercommunication between these officers in emergencies, as set forth in paragraph 2(k) below.

(i) Periodic meetings shall take place between the officers nominated in the above paragraph, or their representatives, at Kilo 95 or at any other mutually agreed point to co-ordinate action on any of the matters dealt with in this Arrangement, or to discuss other measures of co-operation in regard to security along the demarcation line. The representative shall also be vested with authority to ensure action by the police in respect of any of the matters covered by this Arrangement. If either Party requests it, a United Nations Military Observer shall attend these meetings.

(j) That the Party in whose territory the meeting is to take place will make proper arrangements to ensure that the representative of the other party will have access without delay to the point of meeting in urgent cases.

(k) The Senior officers nominated as in paragraph 2(h) shall each have direct telephonic communication to a United Nations exchange at or near Kilo 95, where a United Nations Military Observer will be stationed, so that in urgent cases the officers may speak directly to one another to arrange for the rapid suppression of firing or other incidents.

(l) That the requests by either Party for an urgent meeting shall be complied with immediately.

(m) That when a Representatives' meeting is scheduled, and one Representative cannot attend, he will make every effort to inform the other Party's Representative through the Mixed Armistice Commission twenty-four (24) hours prior to the scheduled time of the meeting.

3. This Arrangement, upon signature of the parties concerned, is valid for a period of one year from the date of signature, but either Party may withdraw on giving one month's notice. Discussions on the extension of this Arrangement will begin one month prior to its expiration.

4. Either Party may propose additions and amendments to this Arrangement which will be considered by the other Party, and which, if accepted by both Parties, will be put into effect by being incorporated in an official document signed in the same manner as the present Arrangement.

DONE at .... on the .... day of

Senior Egyptian Delegate   Senior Israeli Delegate
                      WITNESSED BY:
                      Chairman, EIMAC

APPENDIX IV*

Notice to Mariners No. 44
issued weekly
October 1, 1955

U.S. NAVY HYDROGRAPHIC OFFICE

(5046) RED SEA – Gulf of Aqaba – Strait of Tiran – Information –

1. Vessels calling at Port Said or Suez, bound for the Gulf of Aqaba, should contact the Customs Administration regarding their destinations.
2. Ships heading northward in the Red Sea, bound for the Gulf of Aqaba, should notify the Regional Boycotting Office for Israel, Bulkeley Ramleh, Alexandria (Telephone no. 62927) at least 72 hours prior to entry in the Gulf of Aqaba. The cable should contain the following information:

(a) Name of vessel
(b) Nationality
(c) Type (cargo or passenger)
(d) International code signal letters indicating vessel's name.
(e) Expected time of entering Gulf of Aqaba (state date and time)
(f) Port of destination in the Gulf of Aqaba.

3. Ships should hoist their signal letters and reduce speed when 3 miles off the Naval Signal Station (27059'57"N., 340625'54"E.). Vessels shall be permitted to proceed if the Signal Station has been previously notified or ordered to stop for inspection by the Customs Authorities.
4. The permit to proceed will be valid for 48 hours.
5. Should any vessel be unable to pass within the permitted time, the shipping companies, agents or masters should renew the application to pass, giving the new expected time of passage.

* ISA, 2427/5

APPENDIX V*

The Government of Israel proposes to the Government of Egypt that a meeting be held to discuss the establishment of peace between the two countries.

While being ready to negotiate an immediate peace, the Government of Israel would also be willing, should this be preferable to the Egyptian Government, to enter at this stage into preliminary parleys for the purpose of exploring the possibility of a peace settlement or of paving the way thereto.

It is desirable that the Government of Egypt should communicate its reaction to this proposal as soon as possible. If the response is affirmative, the Government of Israel would suggest that the meeting take place somewhere in Europe, leaving the choice of place to the Egyptian Government.

The Government of Israel is convinced that this initiative is in the common interest of both countries, of the region as a whole, and of the peace of the world.

22.8.52

* ISA, 2453/20

APPENDIX VI*

June 3, 1953

SECRET AND CONFIDENTIAL

1. The Government of Israel notes with satisfaction the intention of the Egyptian Government to bring about a normalization of relations between Egypt and Israel. This should be the common purpose of both countries.
2. The Israel Government is of the opinion that there are ways of achieving this purpose but it would desire to see practical steps taken by Egypt such as are hereinafter suggested.
3. The Israel Government would expect to see a lifting of all restrictions on the free passage of ships through the Suez Canal to and from Israel. An intimation to the Government of Israel when the first oil tanker carrying oil for Israel might pass the Suez Canal would be considered by the Israel Government as practical proof of a determination to normalize relations. Such action is well overdue since Israel's rights to free navigation through the Suez Canal are not open to question and were reaffirmed by the Security Council on September 1, 1951.
4. The Israel Government would expect to see a cessation of hostile propaganda on the part of the Egyptian Government not alone in Egypt but also in the United States, in the United Nations and wherever such propaganda has until now been used. Israel would fully respond to a tone of moderation and reticence which would enable the atmosphere to subside.
5. The Israel Government would strive, both on a public level and on a diplomatic level, to further the understanding of Egypt's problems and aspirations by the outside world and would support Egypt's efforts to receive international aid for the strengthening of its economy.

To discuss further outstanding matters representatives of the two governments could meet at a place and at a time to be agreed upon. This meeting, of course, would be a secret meeting and both parties would do everything possible to see to it that no publicity is given to it or to the acts of the Egyptian Government above referred to. At such a meeting the parties could consider the advisability of a more formal conference under the terms of Article XII of the General Armistice Agreement.

* ISA, 2453/20

186

APPENDIX VII*

21.12.54

To: MEMISRAEL PARIS
From: SHARETT HAMISRAD JERUSALEM

Rafael. Defintely prefer direct personal message on plain paper no form address no signature but state orally this from Roham to Roham begins:

I have received report of yours message transmitted through a special emissary now in Paris.

I have noted with deep satisfaction that it is your desire to bring about a peaceful solution of the problems outstanding between Egypt and Israel. I welcome particularly your readiness to consider measures for improving the present situation and reducing the prevailing tensions. We for our part are eager to co-operate in efforts directed toward this end.

Many of us admire your brave idealism and tenacity of purpose and wish you the fullest success in attaining the emancipation of the Land of the Nile from the last vestiges of foreign domination and the initiation for the masses of the Egyptian people of an era of social regeneration and economic welfare.

We feel sure that your aims are peace and progress and that you fully realize the interdependence of the two.

It is for this reason that we are keenly looking forward to more tangile evidence that you and your friends are preparing the ground for an eventual settlement with Israel by educating your public opinion to appreciate the vital importance of peace within the Middle East.

There are two matters in particular the handling of which may well have a decisive effect on the development of relations between our two countries.

In the first place, freedom for all shipping to and from Israel to pass through the Suez Canal would be in keeping with Egypt's international obligations and would be widely acclaimed by the international community.

Secondly, there is the urgent question of the trial now proceeding in Cairo. I cannot emphasize too strongly the gravity of the issue which is there in the balance. I fervently hope that no death sentences will be passed, as demanded by the prosecution. They would inevitably produce a violent crisis, kindle afresh the flames of bitterness and strife and defeat our efforts to curb passions and lead our people into ways of peace.

We look forward to counsels of farsighted statesmanship prevailing

---

* ISA, 2453/20. Published in Gideon Rafael, *Destination Peace* (London, 1981), pp. 44–5.

over considerations of the moment, for the sake of the goal which we pursue in common – a settlement between Egypt and Israel and a state of peace and contentment inside the region as a whole.

This message which I am addressing to you above the din of daily conflict in a spirit of sincere quest for peace and friendship will, I hope, evoke a corresponding reponse. Ends.

SHARETT

APPENDIX VIII*

(Heading in Hebrew) Response Message Gamal Abdul Nasser

I have received your letter of the 21st of December 1954. I have instructed my special emissary to transmit a verbal answer to the questions you have mentioned in your letter.

I am very glad, that you realize the efforts spent from our side to bring our relations to a peaceful solution. I hope that they will be met by similar efforts from your side, thus permitting us to achieve the results we are seeking, for the benefit of both countries.

* ISA, 2453/20. Published in Gideon Rafael, *Destination Peace* (London, 1981), p. 45.

Bibliography

Archives and Documentary Sources

Allen Dulles Papers, Princeton, N.J.
The Ben Gurion Archives, Sde Boker, Israel.
Declassified Documents Quarterly, Rutgers University.
The Documentation Center of the Shiloah Institute, Tel Aviv University.
Documents on the Foreign Policy of Israel, Vol. III, edited by Yemima Rosenthal. Jerusalem, 1983.
The Dwight D. Eisenhower Library, Abilene, Kansas.
Foreign Relations of the United States, edited by John P. Glennon.
The Israel Defense Forces Archives, Gevatayim.
The Israel National Archives, Jerusalem.
John Foster Dulles Papers, Princeton, N.J.
National Archives of the United States, Washington, D.C.
National Archives of Canada.
The Public Record Office, London.

Books

Abidi, Aqil Haydar Hasan Abidi, *Jordan, A Political Study: 1948–1957*. New Delhi, 1957.
Acheson, Dean, *Present at the Creation*. New York, 1969.
'Aluba, Muhammad Ali, *Filastin wa-Juratuha*. Cairo, 1954.
Amos, II, John, *Arab-Israeli Military/Political Relations*. New York, 1979.
Art, Robert J. and Waltz, Kenneth N., *The Use of Force: International Politics and Foreign Policy*. Boston, 1971.
Aruri, Naseer H., *Jordan: A Study in Political Development, 1921–1965*. The Hague, 1972.
Avineri, Aryeh, *Peshitot HaTagmul*. Tel Aviv, 1971.
al-Baghdati, 'Abd al-Latif, *Mudhakkirat*. Cairo, 1977.
Baker, Raymond William, *Egypt's Uncertain Revolution Under Nasser and Sadat*. Cambridge, 1978.
Bar-Siman-Tov, Yaakov, *Linkage Politics in the Middle East: Syria Between Domestic and External Conflict, 1961–1970*. Boulder, 1983.
Bar-Yaakov, N, *The Israel-Syria Armistice: Problems of Implementation, 1949–66*. Jerusalem, 1967.
Bar Zohar, Michel, *Ben Gurion: A Biography*. London, 1977.
—, *Hamemuneh*. Jerusalem, 1971.
—, *Suez Ultra-Secret*. Paris, 1964.
Beale, John R., *John Foster Dulles: 1888–1959*. New York, 1959.
Be'eri, Eliezer, *Army Officers in Arab Politics and Society*. Jerusalem, 1969.
Ben Gurion, David, *Israel: A Personal History*. New York, 1971.
—, *Medinat Yisrael HaMehudeshet*. Tel Aviv, 1969.
—, *My Talks with Arab Leaders*. Jerusalem, 1972.
—, *Rebirth and Destiny of Israel*. New York, 1954.

Bloomfield, L.M., *Egypt, Israel, and the Gulf of Aqaba in International Law.* Toronto, 1957.

Brecher, Michael, *The Foreign Policy System of Israel.* Oxford, 1972.

—, *Israel, the Korean War and China.* Jerusalem, 1974.

Brook, David, *Preface to Peace: The United Nations and the Arab-Israel Armistice System.* Washington, 1964.

Brown, L. Carl, *International Politics and the Middle East: Old Rules, Dangerous Game.* Princeton, 1984.

Burns, Lt. Gen. Eedson L.M., *Between Arab and Israeli.* Beirut, 1964.

Cambell, John C., *Defense of the Middle East: Problems of American Policy.* New York, 1958

Cohen, Aaron, *Israel and the Arab World.* Boston, 1976.

Cohen, Michael J., *Palestine and the Great Powers, 1945–1948.* Princeton, 1982.

Cohen, Yerucham, *LeOr HaYom uveMahshecha.* Tel Aviv, 1969.

Confino, Michael and Shamir, Simon (eds.), *The USSR and the Middle East.* Jerusalem, 1973.

Copeland, Miles, *The Game of Nations: The Amorality of Power Politics.* New York, 1969.

Crabb, Cecil V., *Nations in a Multipolar World.* New York, 1968.

Crosbie, Sylvia, *A Tacit Alliance: France and Israel from Suez to the Six Day War.* Princeton, 1974.

Dawisha, A.I., *Egypt in the Arab World.* London, 1976.

Dayan, Moshe, *Avnei Derech.* Tel Aviv, 1976.

—, *Diary of the Suez Campaign, 1956.* London, 1967.

Dekmejian, R. Hrair, *Egypt Under Nasir: A Study in Political Dynamics.* Albany, 1971.

Eban, Abba, *An Autobiography.* New York, 1980.

Eden, Anthony, *Full Circle: The Memoirs of Sir Anthony Eden.* London, 1960.

Eisenhower, Dwight D., *The White House Years: Waging Peace, 1956–1961.* New York, 1965.

Eisenstadt, S.N., *Israeli Society.* New York, 1967.

Elath, Eliahu, *Israel and Elath.* London, 1966.

—, *Mibad HaArfel Hayamim.* Tel Aviv, 1989.

El-Barawy, Rasheed, *The Military Coup in Egypt.* Cairo, 1952.

Eshed, Hagai, *Mi Natan et HaHora'ah?.* Jerusalem, 1979.

Eveland, Wilbur Crane, *Ropes of Sand: America's Failure in the Middle East.* New York, 1980.

Eytan, Rafael, *Raful: Sipur Shel Hayyal.* Tel Aviv, 1985.

Eytan, Walter, *The First Ten Years.* New York, 1958.

Faddah, Mohammed Ibrahim, *The Middle East in Transition: A Study of Jordan's Foreign Policy.* New York, 1974.

Finer, Herman, *Dulles Over Suez.* Chicago, 1964.

Forsythe, David P., *United Nations Peace Making: The Conciliation Committee for Palestine.* Baltimore, 1972.

Gallman, Waldermar J., *Iraq Under Gen. Nuri: My Recollections of Nuri al-Said, 1954–58.* (Baltimore, 1964).

Gershoni, Israel, *The Emergence of Pan-Arabism in Egypt.* Tel Aviv, 1981.

Glassman, John, *Arms for the Arabs.* Baltimore, 1975.

Glubb, Sir John Bagot, *A Soldier with the Arabs.* London, 1957.

Golan, Aviezer, *Operation Susannah.* New York, 1978.

190

Gur, Mordechai, *Plugah Dalet*. Tel Aviv, 1977.
Hamrush, Ahmah, *Qissah Thawrat 23 Yulyu*. Cairo, 1983.
Harel, Issar, *Bitachon vedemokratia*. Tel Aviv, 1989.
Harkabi, Yehoshafat, *Arab Attitudes Toward Israel*. Jerusalem, 1971.
Heikal, Mohamad Hassanein, *Cutting the Lion's Tail: Suez Through Egyptian Eyes*. London, 1986.
—, *Millafat al-Suways*. Cairo, 1986.
—, *Nasser: The Cairo Documents*. New York, 1973.
Henriques, Robert, *One Hundred Hours to Suez: An Account of Israel's Campaign in the Sinai Peninsula*. London, 1957.
Hirshmann, Ira, *Caution to the Winds*. New York, 1962.
Hofstadter, Dan, *Egypt and Nasser. Vol. I. Facts on File*. London, 1973.
Horowitz, Dan and Hasin, Eliahu, *HaParasha*. Tel Aviv, 1961.
Hurewitz, J.C., *Diplomacy in the Near and Middle East: A Documentary Record*. Princeton, 1956.
Hussein, King of Jordan, *Uneasy Lies the Head*. New York, 1962.
Hutchinson, Elmo A., *Violent Truce: A Military Observer Looks at the Arab–Israel Conflict, 1951–1955*. New York, 1958.
al-Imam, Amid, *Al-Sulh ma a Isra'il*. Cairo, 1954.
Ismael, Tareq Y., *The UAR in Africa: Egypt's Policy Under Nasser*. Evanston, 1971.
Israel Government Yearbook. 1952–6. 1959–60.
Israel Information Office, *Nasser's Pattern of Aggression*. Tel Aviv, 1957.
Issawi, Charles, *Egypt in Revolution: An Economic Analysis*. Oxford, 1973.
—, *Egypt at Mid-Century*. Oxford, 1954.
'Izzat, Ibrahim, *Ana Kuntu fi Isra'il*. Cairo, 1957.
—, *Ana 'A'id min Isra'il*. Cairo, 1958.
Jackson, Elmore, *Middle East Mission*. New York, 1983.
Kerr, Malcolm, *The Arab Cold War*. New York, 1971.
Kollek, Teddy, *For Jerusalem*. Tel Aviv, 1978.
Kuhun, Isra'il, *Hadhahi hiya al-Sihyuniyyah*. Cairo, 1954.
Kuniholm, Bruce R., *The Origins of the Cold War in the Near East: Great Power Conflict and Diplomacy in Iran, Turkey, and Greece*. Princeton, 1980.
Labib, 'Ali Muhammad, *al-Quwah al-Thalithah: Tarikh al-Quwat al-Jawwiyah al-Misriyyah*. Cairo, 1977.
Lacouture, Jean, *Nasser: A Biography* (translation by Daniel Hofstadter). New York, 1973.
Lacouture, Jean and Simonne, *Egypt in Transition*. London, 1958.
Laqueur, Walter, *The Soviet Union in the Middle East*. London, 1959.
Lenczowski, George, *The Middle East in World Affairs*. Ithaca, 1980.
Lloyd, Selwyn, *Suez 1956: A Personal Account*. London, 1978.
Louis, William Roger, *The British Empire in the Middle East, 1945–1951*. London, 1984.
Love, Kennett, *Suez: The Twice-Fought War*. New York, 1969.
Luttwak, Edward and Horowitz, Dan, *The Israeli Army*. New York, 1975.
Mabro, Robert, *The Egyptian Economy, 1952–1972*. Oxford, 1974.
Macmillan, Harold, *Tides of Fortune: 1945–1955*. New York, 1969.
—, *Riding the Storm: 1956–1969*. London, 1971.
Mahdi, Muhammad and Musa, Sulayman, *Tarikh al-Urdun fi al-Qarn al-'Ashrin*. Amman, 1959.

al-Majali, Hazza', *Hadha Biyan al-Nass: Qissah Muhadathat Tamblar.* Amman, 1956.
—, *Mudhakkirati.* Amman, 1960.
Mansfield, Peter, *Nasser's Egypt.* Baltimore, 1969.
Mansoor, Menahem, *Political and Diplomatic History of the Arab World. Vol. 2, 1942–1952, Vol. 3, 1953–1959.* Washington, 1972.
Marshall, S.L.A., *Sinai Victory: Command Decisions in History's Shortest War, Israel's Hundred-Hour Conquest of Egypt East of Suez, Autumn, 1956.* New York, 1958.
Milstein, Uri, *Historia shel HaTzanhanim.* Tel Aviv, 1985.
Monroe, Elizabeth. *Britain's Moment in the Middle East, 1914–1956.* London, 1963.
Moore, John Norton, *The Arab–Israel Conflict: Readings and Documents.* Princeton, 1977.
Morgenthau, Hans J., *Politics Among Nations: The Struggle for Power and Peace.* New York, 1966.
Morris, Benny, *The Birth of the Palestinian Refugee Problem, 1947–1949.* London, 1987.
Murphy, Robert, *Diplomat Among Warriors.* New York, 1964.
Nafi'ah, Hassan, *Sulh wal-Sira' al-'Arabi al-Isra'ili min al-Sira' al-Mahtum ila al-Taswiyah.* Beirut, 1984.
Naguib, Mohammad, *Egypt's Destiny: A Personal Statement.* London, 1955.
Nasser, Gamal Abdul. *The Philosophy of the Revolution.* Washington, 1955.
Nutting, Anthony, *No End of a Lesson: The Story of Suez.* London, 1967.
O'Ballance, Edgar, *The Sinai Campaign, 1956.* London, 1959.
O'Brien, Patrick, *The Revolution in Egypt's Economic System: From Private Enterprise to Socialism, 1952–1965.* Oxford, 1966.
Perlmutter, Amos, *Military and Politics in Israel: Nation Building and Role Expansion.* London, 1969.
Peres, Shimon, *David's Sling: The Arming of Israel.* London, 1970.
Pineau, Christian, *1956 Suez.* Paris, 1976.
Raanan, Uri, *The USSR Arms the Third World: Case Studies in Soviet Foreign Policy.* Cambridge, 1967.
Rafael, Gideon, *Destination Peace: Three Decades of Israeli Foreign Policy, A Personal Memoir.* London, 1981.
Roi, Ya'akov, *From Encroachment to Involvement: A Documentary Study of Soviet Policy in the Middle East, 1945–1973.* Tel Aviv, 1974.
Rothenberg, Gunther E. *The Anatomy of the Israeli Army.* New York, 1979.
Rouleau, Eric, *Sans Patrie.* Fayolle, 1978.
Rubin, Barry, *The Arab States and the Palestine Conflict.* Syracuse, 1981.
Sachar, Howard M., *Europe Leaves the Middle East.* New York, 1972.
Sadat, Anwar, *Revolt on the Nile.* New York, 1957.
—, *In Search of Identity: An Autobiography.* New York, 1977.
Safran, Nadav, *Egypt in Search of Political Community: An Analysis of the Intellectual and Political Evolution of Egypt, 1804–1952.* Cambridge, 1961.
—, *From War to War: The Arab–Israel Confrontation, 1948–1967.* New York, 1969.
Saliba, Samir Nicholas, *The Jordan River Dispute.* The Hague, 1968.
Sasson, Eliahu, *BaDerech el HaShalom.* Tel Aviv, 1978.
Seale, Patrick, *The Struggle for Syria: A Study of Post-War Arab Politics,*

1945–1958. Oxford, 1965.

Segev, Tom, *1949: The First Israelis.* New York, 1986.

Shamir, Shimon (ed.), *Self-Views in Historical Perspective in Egypt and Israel.* Tel Aviv, 1981.

Sharabani, Naim, *The Arab–Israel Conflict: A Bibliography of Arabic Books and Publications* (Hebrew). Jerusalem, 1973.

Sharett, Moshe, *Yoman Ishi* (Volumes I-VI). Tel Aviv, 1978.

al-Shirbasi, Ahmad, *Min Ajli Filastin.* Cairo, 1954.

Sheffer, Gabriel (ed.), *Dynamics of a Conflict: A Re-examination of the Arab–Israel Conflict.* Atlantic Highlands, 1975.

Shuckburgh, Evelyn, *Descent to Suez.* London, 1986.

Shwadran, Benjamin, *Jordan: A State of Tension.* New York, 1959.

St. John, Robert, *The Boss.* New York, 1962.

Statistical Abstract of Israel, 1952–56.

Steigman, Yitzhak, *Mivtzah Kadesh: Hayl HaAvir baShanim 1950–1956, Hitatzmut vePeilut.* Tel Aviv, 1986.

Stevens, Georgiana (ed.), *The United States and the Middle East.* Englewood, 1964.

—, *Jordan River Partition.* Hoover Institute Studies, 1965.

Stock, Ernest, *Israel's Road to Suez.* Ithaca, 1967.

Tawil, Muhammad, *La'bat al-Umam wa-'Abd al-Nasir.* Cairo, 1986.

Touval, Saadia, *The Peace Brokers.* Princeton, 1982.

Trevelyan, Humphrey, *The Middle East in Revolution.* London, 1970.

Tsur, Jacob, *Prélude à Suez.* Paris, 1968.

Urquhart, Brian, *Hammarskjöld.* New York, 1972.

Vatikiotis, P.J., *Egypt: From Muhammad Ali to Sadat.* Baltimore, 1980.

—, *The Egyptian Army in Politics: Patter for New Nations?* Bloomington, 1961.

—, *Nasser and His Generation.* New York, 1978.

Ya'ari, Ehud, *Mitzrayim vehaFedayeen, 1953–6.* Givat Haviva, 1975.

Articles

Aronson, Shlomo and Horowitz, Dan, 'HaIstrategia shel Tagmul Mugbal', *Medina uMemshal* (Vol. 1, No. 1, Summer 1971).

Baham, Yaakov, 'HaMishtar HaHadash baMitzrayim', *Mizrah HaHadash* (No. 13, Fall 1952).

Baster, James, 'Economic Problems of the Gaza Strip', *Middle East Journal* (Vol. IX, No. 3, Summer 1955).

Ben Ze'ev, Yosef, 'HaModi' in beMa'arechet Sinai', *Maarachot* (No. 306–7, December 1986).

Bialer, Uri, 'Sichsuch HaAravi-HaYisraeli beAynei Ben Gurion veSharett', *Memshal uMedina* (Vol. 1, No. 2, Fall 1971).

Caplan, Neil and Sela, Avraham, 'Zionist-Egyptian Negotiations and the Partition of Palestine, 1946', *Jerusalem Quarterly* (No. 41, Winter 1987).

Chejne, Anwar G., 'Egyptian Attitudes Toward Pan-Arabism,' *Middle East Review* (Vol. 11, No. 3, Summer 1957).

Crossman, Richard, 'Nasser's Plan for Peace', *New Statesman* (22 January 1955).

Dayan, Moshe, 'Israel's Border and Security Problems', *Foreign Affairs* (Vol. 33, No. 2, January 1955).

Dishon, Daniel, 'Mediniut Hutz shel Mishtar HaMahafecha beMitzrayim', *HaMizrah HaHadash* (Vol. 27, No. 3, 1956).

193

Gardner, Patterson, 'Israel's Economic Problems', *Foreign Affairs* (Vol. 32, No. 2, January 1954).

Gelber, Yoav, 'MaGa'im Diplomati'im Terem Hitnagshut Tzva'it – HaMasa uMatan ben HaShuchnut HaYehudit leMitzrayim veYarden, 1948–1946'. *Katedra* (No. 35, April 1985).

Ionides, M.G., 'Disputed Waters of the Jordan', *Middle East Journal* (Vol. VII, Spring 1953).

Khuri, Fred, 'The Policy of Retaliation in Arab–Israel Relations', *Middle East Journal* (Vol. 20, No. 4, 1966).

Milstein, Uri, 'Hetz Shahor al Aza', *Maarachot* (February 1977).

Nasser, Gamal Abdul, 'The Egyptian Revolution', *Foreign Affairs* (Vol. 33, No. 2, January 1955).

—, 'Memoirs of the First Palestine War', *Journal of Palestine Studies* (Vol. II., No. 1, Summer 1973).

'Mivtza Yagev', *Maarachot Shiryon* (No. 27, October 1972).

Peretz, Don, 'The Jordan River Partition', *Middle East Journal* (Vol. IX, No. 4, Autumn 1955).

Shlonim, Shlomo, 'Origins of the 1950 Tripartite Declaration on the Middle East', *Middle Eastern Studies* (Vol. 23, No. 1, July 1987).

Newspapers, Journals

Akhir Sa'ah

al-Ahram

Akhbar al-Yawm

British Broadcasting Corporation Monitoring Service, Summary of World Broadcasts, Part IV, The Arab World, Israel, Greece, Turkey, Persia.

al-Gumhurriyah

Haaretz

al-Misri

al-Musawwar

Ruz al-Yusuf

Doctoral Dissertations

Akhavi, Shahrough, 'The Egyptian Image of the Soviet Union, 1954–1968'. Columbia University, 1969.

Decker, Donald James, 'U.S. Policy Regarding the Baghdad Pact'. American University, 1975.

Mandelstam, Jean, 'La Palestine dans la Politique de Gamal Abdel Nasser, Juillet 1952–Février 1955'. Foundation de Science politique, Paris, 1970.

Shimoni, Jonathan, 'Conventional Deterrence: Lessons from the Middle East'. Princeton University, 1986.

Index

INDEX

197